OXFORD READINGS IN PHILOSOPHY

THE PHILOSOPHY OF LAW

THE PHILOSOPHY
OF LAW

Edited by
R. M. DWORKIN

OXFORD UNIVERSITY PRESS

Oxford University Press, Walton Street, Oxford OX2 6DP

Oxford New York Toronto
Delhi Bombay Calcutta Madras Karachi
Kuala Lumpur Singapore Hong Kong Tokyo
Nairobi Dar es Salaam Cape Town
Melbourne Auckland Madrid

and associated companies in
Berlin Ibadan

Oxford is a trade mark of Oxford University Press

Published in the United States by
Oxford University Press Inc., New York

British Library Cataloguing in Publication Data
Data available
ISBN 0-19-875022-6

7 9 10 8

Printed in Hong Kong

CONTENTS

INTRODUCTION

THE philosophy of law studies philosophical problems raised by the existence and practice of law. It therefore has no central core of philosophical
problems distinct to itself, as other branches of philosophy do, but overlaps
most of these other branches. Since the ideas of guilt, fault, intention, and
responsibility are central to law, legal philosophy is parasitic upon the philosophy of ethics, mind, and action. Since lawyers worry about what law
should be, and how it should be made and administered, legal philosophy
is also parasitic on political philosophy. Even the debate about the nature
of law, which has dominated legal philosophy for some decades, is, at
bottom, a debate within the philosophy of language and metaphysics.

It follows that no limited selection of articles can represent the full range
of legal philosophy. This collection includes essays about the concept of law,
and essays that fall in the overlap between legal and political philosophy.
It includes no essays drawn from the philosophy of mind and action and
none about the important institution of punishment, because many of the
most influential essays on these topics, written by H. L. A. Hart, have recently
been published in a separate collection.[1] Whenever possible, essays have
been chosen that have provoked direct responses from other legal philosophers. In two cases these responses are included, and in other cases they
are noticed in a footnote at the beginning of the essay. Essays have also
been chosen to cast doubt upon the familiar assumption that the philosophy
of law is a discipline separate from the practice of law. The essays in this
collection suggest that legal philosophy is not a second-order study that
takes ordinary legal reasoning as its subject but is, on the contrary, itself
the nerve of legal reasoning.

I

The long debate about the concept of law has different facets. Law exists
in at least three different senses, each of which is problematical. (a) There
is *law* as a distinct and complex type of social institution. We say that 'law'

[1] Hart, *Punishment and Responsibility* (Oxford, 1968).

is one of the proudest achievements of man, or that 'law' is an instrument through which the powerful oppress the weak, or that 'law' is more primitive in some societies than in others. (b) There are *laws*, or *rules of law*, as distinct types of rules or other standards having a particular type of pedigree. We say that Parliament passed 'a law' taxing capital gains, or that Congress has enacted a series of 'laws' providing remedies against pollution, or that the courts have developed 'rules of law' about how offers of contract are made and accepted. (c) There is *the law* as a particular source of certain rights, duties, powers, and other relations among people. We say that 'the law is' that a doctor is responsible for damages caused by his negligence, or that 'the law provides' that a person has a right to leave his property to whomever he pleases, or that 'it is a principle of the law' that no man may profit from his own wrong. I shall call propositions of this last sort 'propositions of law' to distinguish them from propositions about law as a social institution and propositions about laws or legal rules.

These three ideas of law are plainly connected, so that a philosophical problem or theory about one idea will match a problem or theory about the others. It is nevertheless useful to distinguish these different ideas, and the problems they generate.

(a) *Law as a type of social institution.* We understand the idea of law as an institution well enough to know that Great Britain and Massachussetts and Uganda all have law, and why it might be doubtful whether a primitive society, with much less complex institutions, has law or not. Lawyers and philosophers dispute, not over such borderline cases, but about whether certain features present in standard cases of law are necessary, as some philosophers claim, or simply accidental, as others insist. It is debated, for example, whether law can exist only when the population has a certain attitude towards those who govern them, and, if so, what that attitude must be. Bentham, Austin, and their followers said that law exists whenever a population has developed the habit of obedience to the commands of a person or group not similarly in the habit of obeying the commands of others. According to this view, it is the habit of obedience to those who in fact have power, not the different motives or attitudes that may have nurtured that habit, that is decisive.

Hart has been a powerful critic of this command theory. Essay I gives some of his objections, and a later book provided many more.[2] He and his supporters argue that law does not exist unless the population, or at least that part of the population that administers the law, accepts a rule that gives those who exercise power the authority to do so. They must, that is, have developed not simply a habit of deferring to power but a sense that the power

[2] Hart, *The Concept of Law* (Oxford, 1961).

is legitimate because exercised in accordance with some constitutional rule they accept. Hart and others who hold this view have not yet made sufficiently clear, however, what attitudes distinguish a habit of obedience from the acceptance of constitutional rules by a people or by subordinate officials. Is it necessary, in order to say that someone accepts the rules of a constitutional system, that he believes that that system is just, or that he would consent to the system if given any genuine choice? If this is necessary, then there is great doubt, at least, whether there was law in Nazi Germany, or whether there is now law in South Africa. If not, then it remains unclear why an official, who has developed a disposition to obey the commands of a particular group out of fear, has not in the required sense accepted the constitutional rule that that group has authority to govern; but if that is so, then the difference between the rule theory and the command theory is much narrowed.

A second and related dispute has been even more prominent in recent argument. Is it necessary, in order for a particular system of government to count as law, that the regime obey certain procedural standards of morality, or that the rules they enforce themselves have a certain moral content? Hart shows, in Essay I, how much care is necessary to disentangle this issue from others often thrown together under the title 'law and morals'. He argues that the claim that law must have a minimal moral content is true only in a much less interesting way than many legal philosophies suppose.

It might be tempting to think that these disputes about the idea of law as a type of social organization are merely linguistic; but that would be a mistake. This sense of the concept of law is in many ways built into legal principles and political attitudes, and it is important to understand how far that concept presupposes further principles of legitimacy and morality. The Nazi informer cases discussed in Essay I provide one example. The Fifth and Fourteenth Amendments to the United States Constitution, which require that state and federal governments must observe 'due process of law', provide another. Similar questions may be raised in other ways and in other institutions: for example, in courts called upon to decide whether, when a new government replaces an old one by revolution, courts are obliged to enforce the decrees of the new government as decrees of law.

(b) *Laws*. The idea of a law or a rule of law as a particular kind of rule presupposes the idea of law as a social institution, because only rules enacted or developed within such an institution can be laws. Any theory of law as an institution is likely to include or suggest a theory of what laws are. Since Austin, for example, thought that law exists when a population habitually obeys the general commands of one person or a group, he also thought that laws are those commands. A theory about propositions of law will also include or suggest a theory about laws, because it will maintain some views about the way in which laws figure in the truth conditions of propositions of law. Recently, however, laws have become the object of a study distinct from these more general issues about law and propositions of law—the study of their logical character and structure.

Hart, among others, argues that rules of law fall into different logical categories that have distinct legal and social functions. He distinguishes primary rules, which are rules meant to guide the conduct of individuals and other legal persons, from secondary rules, which are rules about how primary rules are to be created or recognized. He also distinguishes duty-imposing rules, like the rule that taxes must be paid on capital gains, from power-conferring rules which, like the rules that allow people to make contracts, impose no duties but simply grant facilities that individuals may use or ignore.[3] In Essay I he shows how the latter distinction may be used to criticize theories about law as an institution and theories about propositions of law which provide no place for power-conferring rules. Dr. Raz, in a recent book, offers a more complex analysis.[4]

Lawyers traditionally assume that laws exist in systems of laws, which they call legal systems, and that each separate social organization that has law has a separate system of laws. There is, however, much that is unclear in that idea. Raz, among others, has called our attention to a variety of problems.[5] Can principles be laws, and members of a legal system? How do we decide where one legal system ends and another begins? How do we know that France and Britain have different legal systems, rather than sharing one legal system which has laws of different territorial application? How do we distinguish one law from another? How do we know that a particular law belongs to one legal system rather than to another? How do we know how many laws a complex statute, like the Internal Revenue Code or the Finance Act, adds to the legal system, or how many laws a system contains at any moment?

Questions like these force us to think more carefully about what laws are. Is a law constituted by a canonical verbal formulation, like the statutory words in which it is enacted, or which a court uses to formulate a new common-law rule, or which custom stipulates as the traditional form of a customary rule? Or is a law defined by the legal relations among persons that it creates, that is, the propositions of law that are true by virtue of the existence of that law? The answer we give to such problems will be different

[3] Ibid.
[4] Raz, *Practical Reason and Norms* (Hutchinson, 1975), particularly Chapter 3.
[5] Raz, *The Concept of a Legal System* (Oxford, 1970).

depending which of these two characterizations we accept. If a law is defined by its canonical verbal form, then the number of laws in a particular statute, or in the legal system as a whole, will depend upon some linguistic theory about basic sentences. If a law is defined by the propositions of law it makes true, then, since the same information about legal rights and duties can be conveyed by any number of different propositions of law of different levels of generality, the question of how many laws are contained in a particular statute, or in a legal system, will appear to be a question without an answer.

(c) *Propositions of law.* Lawyers use propositions of law to describe or declare certain relationships, particularly relationships of rights and duties, within the institution of law, and when they disagree about these relationships they argue about the truth of such propositions. They argue, for example, about whether the law, properly understood, provides that someone has a right to be compensated for economic damage he suffers because of an injury to someone else. Lawyers find difficulty, however, in setting out in any general way what such propositions mean, or, what comes to the same thing, the conditions under which they are true or false. There is a variety of theories in the field.

A group of academic lawyers who called themselves Legal Realists argued that the meaning of such propositions depends upon the context in which they are found. If a lawyer or a textbook writer asserts a proposition of law, he is simply predicting what legal officials, particularly courts, will do in particular cases. If he says, for example, that the law provides a remedy for pollution, then he is predicting that courts will hold a polluter in damages, or issue an injunction against him, if someone who is damaged so requests. If his prediction is right, then what he said was true; otherwise it was false. Of course, if a judge or some other legal official urges a proposition of law, in justification of his own decision, then he cannot be understood simply as predicting his own decision. He must be understood, instead, as expressing his approval of the state of affairs in which officials decide in the way he does. In that context, a proposition of law is neither true nor false, since it is only the expression of a political or moral opinion.

This answer to the question of what propositions of law mean is agreeably simple. But it cannot be accepted as a useful explanation of how lawyers and judges use such propositions. When a lawyer advises his client that the law taxes capital gains, he is not, or in any case not simply, predicting what the Tax Court will decide, but expressing his view that it would be right for the Court to reach that decision. When a judge says that the law allows recovery for economic damage, as he is about to order such damages paid, he means to offer a justification for his decision, not merely to say, redundantly, that he approves of it. The Legal Realist position is not now widely defended.

In Essay II I describe and criticize a different and more persuasive answer, which I call the positivist theory, and which Hart shares with Austin and with another influential contemporary philosopher, Hans Kelsen. According to this theory propositions of law are true when they correctly describe the content of laws or rules of law; otherwise they are false. That theory presupposes, of course, a theory of what laws are, and of when they exist. Austin, Hart, and Kelsen provided different theories about laws, but their disputes, located in more general disputes about the nature of law as a social institution, are independent of the theory they share, that propositions of law are propositions about laws.

Essay II describes an objection to that theory. It argues that in novel cases lawyers and judges assert propositions of law that are controversial because they appeal not to rules of law, whose existence is a matter of institutional enactment, but to principles whose content and weight are often a matter of controversy. Controversial propositions of law can never be true by virtue of the existence of laws that they describe. If a proposition of law is seriously contested among reasonable lawyers after all the facts about what courts and legislatures have done in the past are known, then it is safe to conclude that no law has been enacted or adopted in virtue of which alone that proposition of law can be true. Controversial propositions of law are therefore an embarrassment to the positivist. He must argue either that all such propositions are simply false, even though lawyers constantly assert them, which seems perverse, or that they are not genuine propositions of law after all, and so need not be explained by his theory.

The second of these options seems more attractive. If he takes that option however, he must provide an alternative theory of the function of controversial propositions of law, a theory that shows why these are not simply propositions of law that are controversial, but are propositions of a very different kind. He relies for this purpose on the doctrine of judicial discretion. He argues that in common law countries judges have two relevant powers in addition to the power to decide what propositions of law are true. They have what he calls a discretion to decide for one or another of the parties to a lawsuit, if they think that justice or policy so requires, in spite of the fact that that party has no legal right to win. They also have power, in reaching such a decision, to enact a law for the future that creates that right. The positivist therefore maintains that controversial propositions are different from ordinary propositions of law, because the former are not descriptions but, in the mouths of judges, enactments.

In Essay II I criticize this doctrine of discretion. It is important to notice a point not sufficiently brought out in my discussion. The positivist's theory of discretion is a *consequence* of his more general theory of propositions of law, not an *argument* for that theory. The theory assumes rather than supports the more general theory that controversial propositions of law cannot be true in a straightforward way. Suppose that a lawyer argues that his client, the plaintiff, has a right to recover for economic damage in tort, and counsel for the defendant disagrees. If no legal rule settles that question, then, according to the doctrine of discretion, the judge must decide whether to legislate a new rule providing for that right, and then settle the present case as if that right had already existed. But that view of the matter assumes the positivist's theory that, if no such rule already exists, then the plaintiff's proposition, that he already has the right, cannot be true. If the plaintiff's proposition *is* true, of course, then the judge has a duty to find in his favour, and no question of discretion, or of new and retroactive legislation, will arise. The theory of discretion therefore presupposes the positivist's more general theory about propositions of law, and it cannot be used to show why apparent counterexamples to that general theory may be disregarded.

The positivist therefore needs another argument to show why controversial propositions of law are not genuine propositions of law, and so may be disregarded. He may seek to find that argument in a certain philosophical theory about the concept of rights and duties. According to this theory, rights and duties exist only by virtue of commonly accepted rules of some form, either social rules, in the case of moral rights and duties, or legal rules, in the case of legal rights and duties. If this theory holds, of course, then all controversial propositions of law would be false if we took them at face value, that is, as asserting the legal rights and duties they seem to describe, and that would provide sufficient motivation for not taking them at face value.

This theory of rights and duties is important in moral and political as well as in legal philosophy, and it has been defended, not only by legal positivists, but by other philosophers whose principal interest is not law. But the grounds for the theory are nevertheless obscure.[6] It cannot be said simply to report the behaviour of those people who argue about rights and duties in morals and politics. The abolitionists argued that slaves had a right to be free, and that slave-owners had a duty to free them, when no social or legal rule existed to that effect. Civil rights groups, pacifists, vegetarians, and women's liberation groups make parallel arguments today. The rule theory of rights and duties supposes that these groups have made a philosophical mistake. But what mistake, and why is it a mistake?

The positivist cannot say that it is the mistake of supposing that non-

[6] See Dworkin, 'Social Rules and Legal Theory', 81 *Yale Law Journal* 855 (1972).

physical entities, like rights, can exist. Certain Legal Realists seemed to think that nothing can exist except physical things, and they relied upon that article of metaphysics to deny the possibility of such things as legal rights and duties and rules of law. But since the positivist believes in rules, and in rights and duties when provided by rules, he cannot rely upon crude physicalism for his view that rights and duties cannot otherwise exist.

I think that many positivists rely, more or less consciously, on an anti-realist[7] theory of meaning. They think that no sense can be assigned to a proposition unless those who use that proposition are all agreed about how the proposition could, at least in theory, be proved conclusively. Lawyers are agreed, according to positivism about how the existence of a law or a legal rule can be proved or disproved, and they are therefore agreed about the truth conditions of ordinary propositions of law that assert rights and duties created by rules. But controversial propositions of law, which assert rights that do not purport to depend upon rules, are another matter. Since there is no agreement about the conditions which, if true, establish the truth of such propositions, they cannot be assigned any straightforward sense, and must therefore be understood in some special way, if at all.

In this way a central and critical issue in the philosophy of law is also a central and critical issue in the philosophy of meaning. The anti-realist position has been defended in particular disciplines, particularly mathematics, and also as a general position. There are many enterprises, however, in which practice seems to challenge that general position. Scientists suppose that theories may be true even when they cannot be demonstrated to those who do not accept the general scheme of concepts in which the theory is drafted. Historians suppose that one explanation of events may be superior to others even though no method of demonstrating the superiority of historical positions has been agreed. Literary critics make the same assumption about competing interpretations of a novel or a play, and academics, including philosophers, make it when they mark essays or award prizes. Since the positivist offers no reason why the anti-realist position has special force in law, he seems to assume that that position must be right, and practice misconceived, in each of these enterprises.

There can be no effective reply to the positivist's anti-realist theory of meaning in law, however, unless an alternate theory of propositions of law is produced. That theory must assign a sense to controversial propositions of law comparable to the sense that controversial propositions in science, history, literature, and academic awards are supposed, by those who use

---

[7] I use 'anti-realist' as the term is used in the philosophy of language, not to describe a position contrary to Legal Realism. For a recent discussion of anti-realism, see Dummett, *Frege: Philosophy of Language* (London, 1973).

them, to have. It must at least show how disagreement about such propositions may seem genuine to lawyers and not, as the anti-realist position would insist, illusory. A recent article, which has not yet been tested by critical reaction, described a theory of adjudication that would have that consequence.[8] According to that theory, roughly summarized, controversial propositions of law are true just in case the political theory that supplies the best justification for non-controversial propositions of law provides for the rights or duties which the controversial proposition describes. Reasonable lawyers will differ as to which of two competing political theories provide a better justification for uncontroversial propositions of law, and no agreed test can be found to settle such disagreements. That fact accounts for the controversiality of the controversial propositions. But it also begins to explain how disagreements about such propositions can be genuine disagreements; certainly it shows how they can be as genuine as the disagreements in science, or history, or literary criticism just mentioned. This theory of propositions of law is therefore vulnerable only to anti-realist critiques so general as to include these enterprises as well as law. It remains to be seen whether any such general critique can be either made or refuted.

II

(a) *The enforcement of morals.* Legal philosophers worry not only about law as it is but also about law as it should be. This concern will, of course, have a different content at different times, because it will be aroused when the actual law, or some proposed law, seems to them unjust. One of the liveliest debates in modern legal philosophy, for example, was provoked by a recommendation of a law reform commission that the law against homosexuality should be made more lenient. In Essay III Sir Patrick Devlin, a prominent judge who later became Lord Devlin, objects to the reasoning, though not necessarily to the substance, of that recommendation. The commission argued that the criminal law should, as a matter of principle, respect John Stuart Mill's liberal theory that the only proper reason for limiting a person's liberty is that his act is likely to cause harm to others. It is never sufficient, according to Mill, that the act will harm the actor, or that it is immoral. Devlin objected that the law does not, nor should it, respect that limitation on its own authority. In Essay IV Hart replied. He conceded that the law might sometimes properly protect a man from himself, and thus far he conceded that Mill's principle was too strong. But he denied that it is ever proper to forbid an act which causes no harm either to others or to the actor, simply because the community considers the act immoral.

Liberals find Mill's doctrine attractive because it supports their view that

[8] See Dworkin, 'Hard Cases', 88 *Harv. L. Rev.* 1057 (1975).

it is wrong for the law to punish deviant sexual conduct, or to prohibit obscene books or plays, or to require religious observances. But it supports their view only on the assumption that no 'harm' to others follows if people are allowed to do what they like about sex or literature or religion. That assumption is, of course, controversial. Devlin's argument that society will fall apart without conformity in these matters is surely wrong, but the novel sexual or religious practices of any large group will have general social consequences that will change the social environment in which everyone must live, and those who regret that change will certainly suppose that they have been harmed.

It is not easy, however, to provide a definition of harm that will exclude these general social consequences and yet not prohibit, on Mill's principle, much social legislation that liberals find desirable. Many liberals argue, for example, that private schools should be abolished because the social divisions they foster are harmful to society as a whole. Is that justification consistent with Mill's principle? If we say that harm, within the meaning of that principle, is restricted to uncontroversial harm to particular people, then Mill's principle would not permit abolishing private schools. If we adopt a more generous definition of harm, such that the social consequences of permitting élitist education may count as harm within that definition, then the social consequences of permitting sexual licence may also count as harm. Mill's principle would then become, not a constitutional principle forbidding the government to decide whether a particular constraint on liberty would produce desirable consequences, but rather an invitation to government to consider just that question.

It is not only extreme egalitarian legislation, like laws forbidding private education, which raise this difficulty for Mill's principle. Much economic legislation is defended, not on the ground that it prevents direct harm to particular people, but because it creates an economic environment in which the community as a whole is able to prosper. Anti-trust laws, for example, and laws limiting production or development of scarce resources, are often defended in this way. Various forms of social legislation, including laws to improve race relations, are often justified along similar lines, and aesthetic regulations, like laws prohibiting the owners of buildings of historical interest from destroying or changing these buildings, are justified because they protect the environment or culture of the community as a whole, not because they prevent direct harm to particular individuals.

It remains for those who would support Hart's position against Devlin, therefore, to show why Mill's doctrine, or some comparable doctrine of liberty, condemns legislation against immorality but does not also condemn all legislation of this sort. Perhaps the attempt to distinguish between acts that cause harm and those that do not should be abandoned, in favour of a different distinction between basic liberties, which should never be curtailed except to prevent direct and serious harm to particular people, and liberty in general, which may be constrained, as it often is, simply to secure what is thought to be some over-all gain in welfare. There is some support, in Mill's text, for the argument that he had some such view in mind, and the idea of basic liberties has since been defended, most notably by John Rawls.[9] If such an approach is to succeed, however, then it must be shown why a person's liberty to choose sexual partners, and to read what he likes, is a basic liberty, while the liberty to conduct his business or use his property as he wishes is not.

(b) *Civil disobedience.*   Legal philosophers have also been provoked by another and much more intense political controversy. Under what circumstances is a person morally entitled to break the law of his country, and how should legal officials reply if he does? Much of the literature has been concerned to study the following distinctions. In some cases individuals break the law because they believe it would be immoral to do what the law commands, or immoral not to do what the law forbids. Pacifists, as well as those who believe that a particular war is immoral, refuse to obey the draft laws, and abolitionists refused to obey the fugitive Slave Laws, on that ground.

In other cases individuals break a law, not because what that law commands is immoral, but in order to protest against some other law, or against some policy of the government, which they believe to be unjust. Anti-war groups and civil rights demonstrators often violated laws against trespass, which they did not believe objectionable in themselves, in order to protest against war or segregation. In still other cases individuals break laws that they feel unfairly injure their own fundamental interests, not so much in order to call attention to the injustice they feel, but in order to exert political pressure for new legislation. Illegal strikes by municipal authorities and sit-ins by residents of a town to block a new airport are cases of that character. In some of these different sorts of cases the dissenters aim at a narrow reform in a structure of laws they generally approve. In others their purposes are more general, and sometimes embrace the destruction of the government, or even the form of government, that produced the law. In some of these cases those who break the law are ready, or even anxious, to be punished for their offences; in others they are unwilling to accept punishment, and attempt to evade it.

Philosophers have developed theories about how these different features of different cases affect the underlying question of when deliberate violation

[9] See Rawls, *A Theory of Justice* (Oxford, 1972).

of the law is justified, or even required. It is important to see that that underlying question may be put from two different standpoints: that of the prospective lawbreaker, who believes that the law or policy he is protesting against is unjust, and that of the legal official who generally believes that it is just. Both must take into account the fact that their views about the justice or injustice of the law or policy are controversial and disputed by others. Their answers might therefore depend, among other things, upon whether they hold an objectivist or subjectivist view about political morality. If they think that morality is simply a matter of taste, with no basis in any objective reality, then the dissenter must ask whether he is entitled to break the law, and the official whether he is entitled to prosecute, over a difference in taste. If they think that political morality is objective, then the consequences are more complex. They will no doubt think that their own views about justice are more imperative and demanding if objective, but they must also admit that if morality is objective, then anyone's views of what morality requires, including their own, may be wrong.

In Essay V John Rawls discusses the problems of civil disobedience from the standpoint of the prospective dissenter who believes that his society is on the whole (or, in Rawls's phrase 'nearly') just, but who believes that some particular act or decision is very unjust. Since Rawls discusses the general value to the community of tolerating disobedience under these circumstances, he also speaks from the standpoint of the officials who must be concerned to achieve these benefits. Rawls argues that each member of a just society has a responsibility himself to decide whether particular decisions offend the fundamental conception of justice the community shares, and therefore that each has a responsibility of disobedience, under certain circumstances, when he believes that those principles have been violated. The government's response must therefore recognize that the man or woman who disobeys the law, in the circumstances and for the reasons Rawls describes, is playing the role he or she must play as a full citizen of a well-ordered society.

In countries with a legal structure like that of Britain and the United States, the government's response lies in the hands of prosecutors, who have some discretion whether to prosecute those who have broken the law, and judges who have some discretion to vary the punishment for those found guilty. How should that discretion be exercised? If Rawls is right, prosecutors and judges should take the motives of political offenders into account, if these motives show that the offenders are playing the role in society which their fellow citizens should expect them to play. But prosecutors and judges must also take into account the competing rights of others whose rights the dissenter might deny. Their response to anti-war dissenters, who refuse to be drafted, should be different from their response to anti-civil rights dissenters, who block the school house door to blacks, if the government believes that the second group, but not the first, is frustrating important rights of those who have a prior claim on the government's sympathy.[10]

(c) *Abortion and free speech.* The final group of essays discuss issues of political philosophy that the United States Supreme Court has recently had to consider, though these essays discuss general principles and not particular law suits. In Essay VI Judith Thomson identifies three questions. Is an unborn child a person? If so, does an unborn child have the same right to life as people already born? If so, is it always wrong for the mother of an unborn child to terminate its life in order to improve the mother's welfare? Much of the earlier debate about abortion argued over the first two of these questions. Thomson offers an ingenious (and now famous) argument designed to show that even if the first two questions are answered affirmatively, it does not follow that the third question should be answered the same way. She argues that the right to live generally conceded to those already born does not include a right that other people, who have no special responsibility for that life, provide the necessary means at the cost of great inconvenience to themselves.

John Finnis's reply is valuable, not simply because it defends the opposite view about abortion, but because it argues that it is wrong and pointless to conduct the debate about abortion as a debate about competing rights. Finnis believes that abortion is wrong, not because the balance of rights cuts against it, but because acts that take life in any circumstances, including suicide, deny the fundamental value of life, and so are wrong quite independently of any theory of rights. The issue he thus raises is of great importance, because it questions certain widespread assumptions about the justification that is needed for any constraint on liberty.

A coherent political theory, such as might be used to justify the law of a community as a whole, must be grounded at bottom either in some idea of the collective welfare of citizens, or in some conception of their political and social rights, or in some theory of their moral duties.[11] Any political theory will, of course, make use of all these ideas, but it may arrange the collective goals, individual rights, and individual duties in such a way as to make one set of these fundamental and the others derivative. It will, for example, argue that citizens must have certain duties because these are necessary to protect the rights of others or to secure a collective goal, or it may

---

[10] See Dworkin, On Not Prosecuting Civil Disobedience', *New York Review of Books*, 6 June 1968.
[11] For an elaboration of these distinctions, see Dworkin, 'The Original Position', 40 *U. Chi. L.R.* 500 (1973).

argue that they must have certain rights, or pursue certain collective goals, because this is necessary in order to enforce their fundamental duties. Most legal philosophers who consider themselves liberals assume that either individual rights or collective goals or perhaps some mix of the two must be fundamental in any justification of the criminal law. They reject as illiberal the idea that duties may be taken as fundamental. Even Devlin, who might have put his argument about the enforcement of morals on grounds of fundamental duty, did not, but argued instead that the goals associated with social coherence required that morals be enforced. Finnis's duty-based theory, which has its roots in a certain conception of natural law, is therefore exceptional.

In the final essay Thomas Scanlon examines the philosophical basis of the right to freedom of expression which is thought, in democracies, to be of fundamental importance. His essay illustrates the importance of that philosophical issue to legal practice. The First Amendment to the United States Constitution protects freedom of expression, but it does not stipulate any particular conception of what that freedom requires in particular cases, or of when it must yield in the face of other rights or interests. These questions must be answered from time to time in constitutional litigation, however, and for two reasons they cannot be answered except by supplying a principled justification for the constitutional protection of speech. First, as Scanlon makes plain, the justification a lawyer supplies for the right will determine the precise statement of the right he accepts. Second, the justification he supplies will determine whether in his view the right survives conflicts with other rights or interests. Does a law limiting the money that a citizen may spend for a candidate in an election compromise that citizen's freedom of expression? If so, is the compromise justified by competing considerations of fairness in elections? Are dirty books a medium of expression? If so, is censorship justified by competing interests of good taste or public morality? Does slanderous speech fall within the protection of the right?

No one can answer these questions without a theory of free speech, and his answers will be different if he accepts a goal-based theory, like the theory that the right of free speech exists to make democracy work better overall, or a theory based on the right of citizens to hear what anyone wishes to say, or the different right of citizens to say whatever they want someone to hear. Scanlon's own theory of free speech is both original and important. He thinks that freedom of expression has different aspects, and that both goal-based and other sorts of considerations must figure in the justification of some of the different rights the First Amendment is thought to protect. But he takes the central element in this total range of rights to be what he calls the Millian principle, which prohibits government from restricting speech on the ground that people are harmed, or persuaded to harmful acts, by coming to believe what is said. He rejects any goal-based, or consequentialist, justification of this central principle. He does not argue for it, however, by supposing that citizens have any general right to the information they need to play their role in the democratic process. That supposed right would justify a principle much broader than the Millian principle, which does not require the government to furnish information, but only forbids it from relying on certain grounds for preventing others from doing so. Instead, he justifies the Millian principle by supposing that the autonomy of a citizen would be compromised if the government prevented him from making up his own mind about what to believe and what to do.

But this conception of autonomy, like the supposed right to information, looks for the justification of free speech in the rights of those who wish to hear what the speaker, if he is not prevented, will say. That may trouble readers who feel that the right of free expression belongs, in the end, to the speaker not to the audience. Scanlon confirms their disquiet when he suggests that the audience might consent, unanimously and temporarily, not to hear opinions it detests, and so warrant exceptions to the principle. His argument suggests, moreover, that the government might be justified, even without this unlikely consent, in limiting speech that adds no new reasons for belief or conduct to those already available. Suppose a speaker wishes not to advance any new arguments or grounds for his opinion, but simply to bear witness that he, like many others, holds it. That is, in fact, the motive of many protesters. Scanlon's argument suggests that his case does not fall within the centrally important Millian principle.

Can that principle, or something like it, be justified by supposing some fundamental right of the speaker, rather than the audience? We noticed, in discussing the Hart–Devlin debate, the idea of liberties so basic that the government has no right to compromise these liberties simply on a showing that indirect or general or controversial harm will follow from their exercise. It seems reasonable to suppose that if any such basic liberties exist, then the right to express political or moral or religious convictions is among them, and that any harm that follows from others accepting these convictions must ordinarily be indirect, general and controversial.

If such a justification could be provided, then it would offer a direct explanation for certain exceptions to the Millian principle that Scanlon must labour to explain. He is troubled, for example, by the fact that it seems right to forbid both defamation, when someone is harmed because others come to believe they have reason not to trade with him, and falsely pulling an alarm bell in a train, when the conductor, perhaps suffering from what Scanlon calls a diminished capacity for deliberation, comes to believe he has reason to stop the train. These are both cases of direct and uncontested harm, and would so fall outside a Millian principle drafted to protect a basic liberty from constraint justified by appeal to indirect or controversial harm. But Scanlon's defence of the principle does have the merit of avoiding arguments about what counts as a basic liberty and why.

I

POSITIVISM AND THE SEPARATION OF LAW AND MORALS

H. L. A. HART

I

UNDOUBTEDLY, when Bentham and Austin insisted on the distinction between law as it is and as it ought to be, they had in mind *particular* laws the meanings of which were clear and so not in dispute, and they were concerned to argue that such laws, even if morally outrageous, were still laws. It is, however, necessary, in considering the criticisms which later developed, to consider more than those criticisms which were directed to this particular point if we are to get at the root of the dissatisfaction felt; we must also take account of the objection that, even if what the Utilitarians said on this particular point were true, their insistence on it, in a terminology suggesting a general cleavage between what is and ought to be law, obscured the fact that at other points there is an essential point of contact between the two. So in what follows I shall consider not only criticisms of the particular point which the Utilitarians had in mind, but also the claim that an essential connection between law and morals emerges if we examine how laws, the meanings of which are in dispute, are interpreted and applied in concrete cases; and that this connection emerges again if we widen our point of view and ask, not whether every particular rule of law must satisfy a moral minimum in order to be a law, but whether a system of rules which altogether failed to do this could be a legal system.

There is, however, one major initial complexity by which criticism has been much confused. We must remember that the Utilitarians combined with their insistence on the separation of law and morals two other equally famous but distinct doctrines. One was the important truth that a purely analytical study of legal concepts, a study of the meaning of the distinctive vocabulary of the law, was as vital to our understanding of the nature of law as historical or sociological studies, though of course it could not supplant them. The other doctrine was the famous imperative theory of law —that law is essentially a command.

From 71 *Harv. L. Rev.* 593 (1958). Copyright 1958 by the Harvard Law Review Association. Professor Lon. L. Fuller replied to this essay in 'Positivism and Fidelity to Law—A Reply to Professor Hart', 71 *Harv. L. Rev.* 630, (1958).

These three doctrines constitute the utilitarian tradition in jurisprudence; yet they are distinct doctrines. It is possible to endorse the separation between law and morals and to value analytical inquiries into the meaning of legal concepts and yet think it wrong to conceive of law as essentially a command. One source of great confusion in the criticism of the separation of law and morals was the belief that the falsity of any one of these three doctrines in the utilitarian tradition showed the other two to be false; what was worse was the failure to see that there were three quite separate doctrines in this tradition. The indiscriminate use of the label 'positivism' to designate ambiguously each one of these three separate doctrines (together with some others which the Utilitarians never professed) has perhaps confused the issue more than any other single factor.[1] Some of the early American critics of the Austinian doctrine were, however, admirably clear on just this matter. Gray, for example, added at the end of the tribute to Austin, which I have already quoted, the words, 'He may have been wrong in treating the Law of the State as being the command of the sovereign'[2] and he touched shrewdly on many points where the command theory is defective. But other critics have been less clearheaded and have thought that the inadequacies of the command theory which gradually came to light were sufficient to demonstrate the falsity of the separation of law and morals.

This was a mistake, but a natural one. To see how natural it was we must look a little more closely at the command idea. The famous theory that law is a command was a part of a wider and more ambitious claim. Austin said that the notion of a command was 'the *key* to the sciences of jurisprudence and morals',[3] and contemporary attempts to elucidate moral judgments in terms of 'imperative' or 'prescriptive' utterances echo this ambitious claim. But the command theory, viewed as an effort to identify even the quintessence of law, let alone the quintessence of morals, seems breathtaking in

---

[1] It may help to identify five (there may be more) meanings of 'positivism' bandied about in contemporary jurisprudence:

(1) the contention that laws are commands of human beings.

(2) the contention that there is no necessary connection between law and morals, or law as it is and ought to be.

(3) the contention that the analysis (or study of the meaning) of legal concepts is (a) worth pursuing and (b) to be distinguished from historical inquiries into the causes or origins of laws, from sociological inquiries into the relation of law and other social phenomena, and from the criticism or appraisal of law whether in terms of morals, social aims, 'functions', or otherwise.

(4) the contention that a legal system is a 'closed logical system' in which correct legal decisions can be deduced by logical means from predetermined legal rules without reference to social aims, policies, moral standards, and

(5) the contention that moral judgments cannot be established or defended, as statements of facts can, by rational argument, evidence, or proof ('noncognitivism' in ethics).

Bentham and Austin held the views described in (1), (2), and (3) but not those in (4) and (5). Opinion (4) is often ascribed to analytical jurists, but I know of no 'analyst' who held this view.

[2] Gray, *The Nature and Source of the Law* (2nd edn., 1921), pp. 94–5.

[3] Austin, *The Province of Jurisprudence Determined* (Library of Ideas edn., 1954), p. 13.

its simplicity and quite inadequate. There is much, even in the simplest legal system, that is distorted if presented as a command. Yet the Utilitarians thought that the essence of a legal system could be conveyed if the notion of a command were supplemented by that of a habit of obedience. The simple scheme was this: What is a command? It is simply an expression by one person of the desire that another person should do or abstain from some action, accompanied by a threat of punishment which is likely to follow disobedience. Commands are laws if two conditions are satisfied: first, they must be general; second, they must be commanded by what (as both Bentham and Austin claimed) exists in every political society whatever its constitutional form, namely, a person or a group of persons who are in receipt of habitual obedience from most of the society but pay no such obedience to others. These persons are its sovereign. Thus law is the command of the uncommanded commanders of society—the creation of the legally untrammelled will of the sovereign who is by definition outside the law.

It is easy to see that this account of a legal system is threadbare. One can also see why it might seem that its inadequacy is due to the omission of some essential connection with morality. The situation which the simple trilogy of command, sanction, and sovereign avails to describe, if you take these notions at all precisely, is like that of a gunman saying to his victim, 'Give me your money or your life.' The only difference is that in the case of a legal system the gunman says it to a large number of people who are accustomed to the racket and habitually surrender to it. Law surely is not the gunman situation writ large, and legal order is surely not to be thus simply identified with compulsion.

This scheme, despite the points of obvious analogy between a statute and a command, omits some of the most characteristic elements of law. Let me cite a few. It is wrong to think of a legislature (and *a fortiori* an electorate) with a changing membership, as a group of persons habitually obeyed: this simple idea is suited only to a monarch sufficiently long-lived for a 'habit' to grow up. Even if we waive this point, nothing which legislators do makes law unless they comply with fundamental accepted rules specifying the essential lawmaking procedures. This is true even in a system having a simple unitary constitution like the British. These fundamental accepted rules specifying what the legislature must do to legislate are not commands habitually obeyed, nor can they be expressed as habits of obedience to persons. They lie at the root of a legal system, and what is most missing in the utilitarian scheme is an analysis of what it is for a social group and its officials to accept such rules. This notion, not that of a command as Austin claimed, is the 'key to the science of jurisprudence', or at least one of the keys.

Again, Austin, in the case of a democracy, looked past the legislators to the electorate as 'the sovereign' (or in England as part of it). He thought that in the United States the mass of the electors to the state and federal legislatures were the sovereign whose commands, given by their 'agents' in the legislatures, were law. But on this footing the whole notion of the sovereign outside the law being 'habitually obeyed' by the 'bulk' of the population must go: for in this case the 'bulk' obeys the bulk, that is, it obeys itself. Plainly the general acceptance of the authority of a lawmaking procedure, irrespective of the changing individuals who operate it from time to time, can be only distorted by an analysis in terms of mass habitual obedience to certain persons who are by definition outside the law, just as the cognate but much simpler phenomenon of the general social acceptance of a rule, say of taking off the hat when entering a church, would be distorted if represented as habitual obedience by the mass to specific persons.

Other critics dimly sensed a further and more important defect in the command theory, yet blurred the edge of an important criticism by assuming that the defect was due to the failure to insist upon some important connection between law and morals. This more radical defect is as follows. The picture that the command theory draws of life under law is essentially a simple relationship of the commander to the commanded, of superior to inferior, of top to bottom; the relationship is vertical between the commanders or authors of the law conceived of as essentially outside the law and those who are commanded and subject to the law. In this picture no place, or only an accidental or subordinate place is afforded for a distinction between types of legal rules which are in fact radically different. Some laws require men to act in certain ways or to abstain from acting whether they wish to or not. The criminal law consists largely of rules of this sort: like commands they are simply 'obeyed' or 'disobeyed'. But other legal rules are presented to society in quite different ways and have quite different functions. They provide facilities more or less elaborate for individuals to create structures of rights and duties for the conduct of life within the coercive framework of the law. Such are the rules enabling individuals to make contracts, wills, and trusts, and generally to mould their legal relations with others. Such rules, unlike the criminal law, are not factors designed to obstruct wishes and choices of an antisocial sort. On the contrary, these rules provide facilities for the realization of wishes and choices. They do not say (like commands) 'do this whether you wish it or not', but rather 'if you wish to do this, here is the way to do it'. Under these rules we exercise powers, make claims, and assert rights. These phrases mark off characteristic features of laws that confer rights and powers; they are laws which are, so to speak, put at the disposition of individuals in a way in which the criminal law is not. Much ingenuity has gone into the task of 'reducing' laws of this second sort to some complex variant of laws of the first sort. The effort to show that laws conferring rights are 'really' only conditional stipulations of sanctions to be exacted from the person ultimately under a legal duty characterizes much of Kelsen's work.[4] Yet to urge this is really just to exhibit dogmatic determination to suppress one aspect of the legal system in order to maintain the theory that the stipulation of a sanction, like Austin's command, represents the quintessence of law. One might as well urge that the rules of baseball were 'really' only complex conditional directions to the scorer and that this showed their real or 'essential' nature.

One of the first jurists in England to break with the Austinian tradition, Salmond, complained that the analysis in terms of commands left the notion of a right unprovided with a place.[5] But he confused the point. He argued first, and correctly, that if laws are merely commands it is inexplicable that we should have come to speak of legal rights and powers as conferred or arising under them, but then wrongly concluded that the rules of a legal system must necessarily be connected with moral rules or principles of justice and that only on this footing could the phenomenon of legal rights be explained. Otherwise, Salmond thought, we would have to say that a mere 'verbal coincidence' connects the concepts of legal and moral right. Similarly, continental critics of the Utilitarians, always alive to the complexity of the notion of a subjective right, insisted that the command theory gave it no place. Hägerström insisted that if laws were merely commands the notion of an individual's right was really inexplicable, for commands are, as he said, something which we either obey or we do not obey; they do not confer rights.[6] But he, too, concluded that moral, or, as he put it, common-sense, notions of justice must therefore be necessarily involved in the analysis of any legal structure elaborate enough to confer rights.[7]

Yet, surely these arguments are confused. Rules that confer rights, though distinct from commands, need not be moral rules or coincide with them. Rights, after all, exist under the rules of ceremonies, games, and in many other spheres regulated by rules which are irrelevant to the question of justice or what the law ought to be. Nor need rules which confer rights be just or

[4] See, e.g., Kelsen, *General Theory of Law and State* (1945), pp. 58–61, 143–4. According to Kelsen, all laws, not only those conferring rights and powers, are reducible to such 'primary norms' conditionally stipulating sanctions.

[5] Salmond, *The First Principles of Jurisprudence* (1893), pp. 97–8. He protested against 'the creed of what is termed the English school of jurisprudence', because it 'attempted to deprive the idea of law of that ethical significance which is one of its most essential elements'. Id. at 9, 10.

[6] Hägerström, *Inquiries Into the Nature of Law and Morals* (Olivecrona edn., 1953), p. 217: '[T]he whole theory of the subjective rights of private individuals . . . is incompatible with the imperative theory'. See also id. at 221: 'The description of them [claims to legal protection] as rights is wholly derived from the idea that the law which is concerned with them is a true expression of rights and duties in the sense in which the popular notion of justice understands these terms.'

[7] Id. at 218.

morally good rules. The rights of a master over his slaves show us that. 'Their merit or demerit', as Austin termed it, depends on how rights are distributed in society and over whom or what they are exercised. These critics indeed revealed the inadequacy of the simple notions of command and habit for the analysis of law; at many points it is apparent that the social acceptance of a rule or standard of authority (even if it is motivated only by fear or superstition or rests on inertia) must be brought into the analysis and cannot itself be reduced to the two simple terms. Yet nothing in this showed the utilitarian insistence on the distinction between the existence of law and its 'merits' to be wrong.

II

I now turn to a distinctively American criticism of the separation of the law that is from the law that ought to be. It emerged from the critical study of the judicial process with which American jurisprudence has been on the whole so beneficially occupied. The most sceptical of these critics—the loosely named 'Realists' of the 1930s—perhaps too naïvely accepted the conceptual framework of the natural sciences as adequate for the characterization of law and for the analysis of rule-guided action of which a living system of law at least partly consists. But they opened men's eyes to what actually goes on when courts decide cases, and the contrast they drew between the actual facts of judicial decision and the traditional terminology for describing it as if it were a wholly logical operation was usually illuminating; for in spite of some exaggeration the 'Realists' made us acutely conscious of one cardinal feature of human language and human thought, emphasis on which is vital not only for the understanding of law but in areas of philosophy far beyond the confines of jurisprudence. The insight of this school may be presented in the following example. A legal rule forbids you to take a vehicle into the public park. Plainly this forbids an automobile, but what about bicycles, roller skates, toy automobiles? What about aeroplanes? Are these, as we say, to be called 'vehicles' for the purpose of the rule or not? If we are to communicate with each other at all, and if, as in the most elementary form of law, we are to express our intentions that a certain type of behaviour be regulated by rules, then the general words we use—like 'vehicle' in the case I consider—must have some standard instance in which no doubts are felt about its application. There must be a core of settled meaning, but there will be, as well, a penumbra of debatable cases in which words are neither obviously applicable nor obviously ruled out. These cases will each have some features in common with the standard case; they will lack others or be accompanied by features not present in the standard case. Human invention and natural processes continually throw up such variants on the familiar, and if we are to say that these ranges of facts do or do not fall under existing rules, then the classifier must make a decision which is not dictated to him, for the facts and phenomena to which we fit our words and apply our rules are as it were *dumb*. The toy automobile cannot speak up and say, 'I am a vehicle for the purpose of this legal rule', nor can the roller skates chorus, 'We are not a vehicle.' Fact situations do not await us neatly labelled, creased, and folded, nor is their legal classification written on them to be simply read off by the judge. Instead, in applying legal rules, someone must take the responsibility of deciding that words do or do not cover some case in hand with all the practical consequences involved in this decision.

We may call the problems which arise outside the hard core of standard instances or settled meaning 'problems of the penumbra'; they are always with us whether in relation to such trivial things as the regulation of the use of the public park or in relation to the multidimensional generalities of a constitution. If a penumbra of uncertainty must surround all legal rules, then their application to specific cases in the penumbral area cannot be a matter of logical deduction, and so deductive reasoning, which for generations has been cherished as the very perfection of human reasoning, cannot serve as a model for what judges, or indeed anyone, should do in bringing particular cases under general rules. In this area men cannot live by deduction alone. And it follows that if legal arguments and legal decisions of penumbral questions are to be rational, their rationality must lie in something other than a logical relation to premises. So if it is rational or 'sound' to argue and to decide that for the purposes of this rule an aeroplane is not a vehicle, this argument must be sound or rational without being logically conclusive. What is it then that makes such decisions correct or at least better than alternative decisions? Again, it seems true to say that the criterion which makes a decision sound in such cases is some concept of what the law ought to be; it is easy to slide from that into saying that it must be a moral judgment about what law ought to be. So here we touch upon a point of necessary 'intersection between law and morals' which demonstrates the falsity or, at any rate, the misleading character of the Utilitarians' emphatic insistence on the separation of law as it is and ought to be. Surely, Bentham and Austin could only have written as they did because they misunderstood or neglected this aspect of the judicial process, because they ignored the problems of the penumbra.

The misconception of the judicial process which ignores the problems of the penumbra and which views the process as consisting pre-eminently in deductive reasoning is often stigmatized as the error of 'formalism' or 'literalism'. My question now is, how and to what extent does the demonstration of this error show the utilitarian distinction to be wrong or misleading? Here there are many issues which have been confused, but I can only disentangle some. The charge of formalism has been levelled both at the 'positivist' legal theorist and at the courts, but of course it must be a very different charge in each case. Levelled at the legal theorist, the charge means that he has made a theoretical mistake about the character of legal decision; he has thought of the reasoning involved as consisting in deduction from premises in which the judges' practical choices or decisions play no part. It would be easy to show that Austin was guiltless of this error; only an entire misconception of what analytical jurisprudence is and why he thought it important has led to the view that he, or any other analyst, believed that the law was a closed logical system in which judges deduced their decisions from premises.[8] On the contrary, he was very much alive to the character of language, to its vagueness or open character;[9] he thought that in the penumbral situation judges must necessarily legislate,[10] and, in accents that sometimes recall those of the late Judge Jerome Frank, he berated the common-law judges for legislating feebly and timidly and for blindly relying on real or fancied analogies with past cases instead of adapting their decisions to the growing needs of society as revealed by the moral standard of utility.[11] The

[8] This misunderstanding of analytical jurisprudence is to be found in, among others, Stone, *The Province and Function of Law,*(1950), p. 141: 'In short, rejecting the implied assumption that all propositions of all parts of the law must be logically consistent with each other and proceed on a single set of definitions ... he [Cardozo, J.,] denied that the law is actually what the analytical jurist, *for his limited purposes,* assumes it to be.' See also id. at 49, 52, 138, 140; Friedmann, *Legal Theory* (3rd edn. 1953), p. 209. This misunderstanding seems to depend on the unexamined and false belief that analytical studies of the meaning of legal terms would be impossible or absurd if, to reach sound decisions in particular cases, more than a capacity for formal logical reasoning from unambiguous and clear predetermined premises is required.

[9] See the discussion of vagueness and uncertainty in law, in Austin, op. cit., at 202–5, 207, in which Austin recognized that, in consequence of this vagueness, often only 'fallible tests' can be provided for determining whether particular cases fall under general expressions.

[10] See Austin, op. cit., at 191: 'I cannot understand how any person who has considered the subject can suppose that society could possibly have gone on if judges had not legislated. . . .' As a corrective to the belief that the analytical jurist must take a 'slot machine' or 'mechanical' view of the judicial process it is worth noting the following observations made by Austin:

(1) Whenever law has to be applied, the '"competition of opposite analogies"' may arise, for the case 'may resemble in some of its points' cases to which the rule has been applied in the past and in other points 'cases from which the application of the law has been withheld'. 2 Austin, *Lectures on Jurisprudence* (5th edn., 1885), p. 633.

(2) Judges have commonly decided cases and so derived new rules by 'building' on a variety of grounds including sometimes (in Austin's opinion too rarely) their views of what law ought to be. Most commonly they have derived law from pre-existing law by 'consequence founded on analogy', i.e., they have made a new rule 'in *consequence* of the existence of a similar rule applying to subjects which are *analogous*. . . .' 2 id. at 638–9.

(3) '[I]f every rule in a system of law were perfectly definite or precise,' these difficulties incident to the application of law would not arise. 'But the ideal completeness and correctness I now have imagined is not attainable in fact ... though the system had been built and ordered with matchless solicitude and skill.' 2 id. at 997–8. Of course he thought that much could and should be done by codification to eliminate uncertainty. See 2 id. at 662–81.

[11] 2 id. at 641: 'Nothing, indeed, can be more natural, than that legislators, direct or judicial (especially if they be narrow-minded, timid and unskillful), should lean as much as they can on the examples set by their predecessors.'

See also 2 id. at 647: 'But it is much to be regretted that Judges of capacity, experience and weight, have not seized every opportunity of introducing a new rule (a rule beneficial for the future)

villains of this piece, responsible for the conception of the judge as an automaton, are not the Utilitarian thinkers. The responsibility, if it is to be laid at the door of any theorist, is with thinkers like Blackstone and, at an earlier stage, Montesquieu. The root of this evil is preoccupation with the separation of powers and Blackstone's 'childish fiction' (as Austin termed it) that judges only 'find', never 'make', law.

But we are concerned with 'formalism' as a vice not of jurists but of judges. What precisely is it for a judge to commit this error, to be a 'formalist', 'automatic', a 'slot machine'? Curiously enough the literature which is full of the denunciation of these vices never makes this clear in concrete terms; instead we have only descriptions which cannot mean what they appear to say: it is said that in the formalist error courts make an excessive use of logic, take a thing to 'a dryly logical extreme',[12] or make an excessive use of analytical methods. But just how in being a formalist does a judge make an excessive use of logic? It is clear that the essence of his error is to give some general term an interpretation which is blind to social values and consequences (or which is in some other way stupid or perhaps merely disliked by critics). But logic does not prescribe interpretation of terms; it dictates neither the stupid nor intelligent interpretation of any expression. Logic only tells you hypothetically that *if* you give a certain term a certain interpretation then a certain conclusion follows. Logic is silent on how to classify particulars— and this is the heart of a judicial decision. So this reference to logic and to logical extremes is a misnomer for something else, which must be this. A judge has to apply a rule to a concrete case—perhaps the rule that one may not take a stolen 'vehicle' across state lines, and in this case an aeroplane has been taken.[13] He either does not see or pretends not to see that the general terms of this rule are susceptible of different interpretations and that he has a choice left open uncontrolled by linguistic conventions. He ignores, or is blind to, the fact that he is in the area of the penumbra and is not dealing with a standard case. Instead of choosing in the light of social aims, the judge fixes the meaning in a different way. He either takes the meaning that the word most obviously suggests in its ordinary nonlegal context to ordinary men, or one which the word has been given in some other legal context, or, still worse, he thinks of a standard case and then arbitrarily identifies certain features in it—for example, in the case of a vehicle, (1) normally

... This is the reproach I should be inclined to make against Lord Eldon. .... [T]he Judges of the Common Law Courts would not do what they ought to have done, namely to model their rules of law and of procedure to the growing exigencies of society, instead of stupidly and sulkily adhering to the old and barbarous usages.'
[12] *Hynes* v. *New York Cent. R.R.*, 231 N.Y. 229, 235, 131 N.E. 898, 900 (1921); see Pound, *Interpretations of Legal History* (2nd edn., 1930) p. 123; Stone, op. cit., at 140-1.
[13] *Mr. Boyle* v. *United States*, 283 U.S. 25 (1931).

used on land, (2) capable of carrying a human person, (3) capable of being self-propelled—and treats these three as always necessary and always sufficient conditions for the use in all contexts of the word 'vehicle', irrespective of the social consequences of giving it this interpretation. This choice, not 'logic', would force the judge to include a toy motor car (if electrically propelled) and to exclude bicycles and the aeroplane. In all this there is possibly great stupidity but no more 'logic', and no less, than in cases in which the interpretation given to a general term and the consequent application of some general rule to a particular case is consciously controlled by some identified social aim.

Decisions made in a fashion as blind as this would scarcely deserve the name of decisions; we might as well toss a penny in applying a rule of law. But it is at least doubtful whether any judicial decisions (even in England) have been quite as automatic as this. Rather, either the interpretations stigmatized as automatic have resulted from the conviction that it is fairer in a criminal statute to take a meaning which would jump to the mind of the ordinary man at the cost even of defeating other values, and this itself is a social policy (though possibly a bad one); or much more frequently, what is stigmatized as 'mechanical' and 'automatic' is a determined choice made indeed in the light of a social aim but of a conservative social aim. Certainly many of the Supreme Court decisions at the turn of the century which have been so stigmatized[14] represent clear choices in the penumbral area to give effect to a policy of a conservative type. This is peculiarly true of Mr. Justice Peckham's opinions defining the spheres of police power and due process.[15]

But how does the wrongness of deciding cases in an automatic and mechanical way and the rightness of deciding cases by reference to social purposes show that the utilitarian insistence on the distinction between what the law is and what it ought to be is wrong? I take it that no one who wished to use these vices of formalism as proof that the distinction between what is and what ought to be is mistaken would deny that the decisions stigmatized as automatic are law; nor would he deny that the system in which such automatic decisions are made is a legal system. Surely he would say that they are law, but they are bad law, they ought not to be law. But this would be to use the distinction, not to refute it; and of course both Bentham and Austin used it to attack judges for failing to decide penumbral cases in accordance with the growing needs of society.

Clearly, if the demonstration of the errors of formalism is to show the

---

[14] See, e.g., Pound, 'Mechanical Jurisprudence' 8 Colum. L. Rev. 605, 615–16 (1908).
[15] See, e.g., *Lochner* v. *New York*, 198 U.S. 45 (1905). Justice Peckham's opinion that there were no reasonable grounds for interfering with the right of free contract by determining the hours of labour in the occupation of a baker may indeed be a wrongheaded piece of conservatism but there is nothing automatic or mechanical about it.

utilitarian distinction to be wrong, the point must be drastically restated. The point must be not merely that a judicial decision to be rational must be made in the light of some conception of what ought to be, but that the aims, the social policies and purposes to which judges should appeal if their decisions are to be rational, are themselves to be considered as part of the law in some suitably wide sense of 'law' which is held to be more illuminating than that used by the Utilitarians. This restatement of the point would have the following consequence: instead of saying that the recurrence of penumbral questions shows us that legal rules are essentially incomplete, and that, when they fail to determine decisions, judges must legislate and so exercise a creative choice between alternatives, we shall say that the social policies which guide the judges' choice are in a sense there for them to discover; the judges are only 'drawing out' of the rule what, if it is properly understood, is 'latent' within it. To call this judicial legislation is to obscure some essential continuity between the clear cases of the rule's application and the penumbral decisions. I shall question later whether this way of talking is salutary, but I wish at this time to point out something obvious, but likely, if not stated, to tangle the issues. It does not follow that, because the opposite of a decision reached blindly in the formalist or literalist manner is a decision intelligently reached by reference to some conception of what ought to be, we have a junction of law and morals. We must, I think, beware of thinking in a too simple-minded fashion about the word 'ought'. This is not because there is no distinction to be made between law as it is and ought to be. Far from it. It is because the distinction should be between what is and what from many different points of view ought to be. The word 'ought' merely reflects the presence of some standard of criticism; one of these standards is a moral standard but not all standards are moral. We say to our neighbour, 'You ought not to lie', and that may certainly be a moral judgment, but we should remember that the baffled poisoner may say, 'I ought to have given her a second dose.' The point here is that intelligent decisions which we oppose to mechanical or formal decisions are not necessarily identical with decisions defensible on moral grounds. We may say on many a decision: 'Yes, that is right; that is as it ought to be', and we may mean only that some accepted purpose or policy has been thereby advanced; we may not mean to endorse the moral propriety of the policy or the decision. So the contrast between the mechanical decision and the intelligent one can be reproduced inside a system dedicated to the pursuit of the most evil aims. It does not exist as a contrast to be found only in legal systems which, like our own, widely recognize principles of justice and moral claims of individuals.

An example may make this point plainer. With us the task of sentencing in criminal cases is the one that seems most obviously to demand from the judge the exercise of moral judgment. Here the factors to be weighed seem clearly to be moral factors: society must not be exposed to wanton attack; too much misery must not be inflicted on either the victim or his dependants; efforts must be made to enable him to lead a better life and regain a position in the society whose laws he has violated. To a judge striking the balance among these claims, with all the discretion and perplexities involved, his task seems as plain an example of the exercise of moral judgment as could be; and it seems to be the polar opposite of some mechanical application of a tariff of penalties fixing a sentence careless of the moral claims which in our system have to be weighed. So here intelligent and rational decision is guided however uncertainly by moral aims. But we have only to vary the example to see that this need not necessarily be so and surely, if it need not necessarily be so, the Utilitarian point remains unshaken. Under the Nazi regime men were sentenced by courts for criticism of the regime. Here the choice of sentence might be guided exclusively by consideration of what was needed to maintain the state's tyranny effectively. What sentence would both terrorize the public at large and keep the friends and family of the prisoner in suspense so that both hope and fear would co-operate as factors making for subservience? The prisoner of such a system would be regarded simply as an object to be used in pursuit of these aims. Yet, in contrast with a mechanical decision, decision on these grounds would be intelligent and purposive, and from one point of view the decision would be as it ought to be. Of course, I am not unaware that a whole philosophical tradition has sought to demonstrate the fact that we cannot correctly call decisions or behaviour truly rational unless they are in conformity with moral aims and principles. But the example I have used seems to me to serve at least as a warning that we cannot use the errors of formalism as something which *per se* demonstrates the falsity of the utilitarian insistence on the distinction between law as it is and law as *morally* it ought to be.

We can now return to the main point. If it is true that the intelligent decision of penumbral questions is one made not mechanically but in the light of aims, purposes, and policies, though not necessarily in the light of anything we would call moral principles, is it wise to express this important fact by saying that the firm utilitarian distinction between what the law is and what it ought to be should be dropped? Perhaps the claim that it is wise cannot be theoretically refuted for it is, in effect, an *invitation* to revise our conception of what a legal rule is. We are invited to include in the 'rule' the various aims and policies in the light of which its penumbral cases are decided on the ground that these aims have, because of their importance, as much right to be called law as the core of legal rules whose meaning is settled.

But though an invitation cannot be refuted, it may be refused and I would proffer two reasons for refusing this invitation. First, everything we have learned about the judicial process can be expressed in other less mysterious ways. We can say laws are incurably incomplete and we must decide the penumbral cases rationally by reference to social aims. I think Holmes, who had such a vivid appreciation of the fact that 'general propositions do not decide concrete cases', would have put it that way. Second to insist on the utilitarian distinction is to emphasize that the hard core of settled meaning is law in some centrally important sense and that even if there are border-lines, there must first be lines. If this were not so the notion of rules controlling courts' decisions would be senseless as some of the 'Realists'— in their most extreme moods, and, I think, on bad grounds—claimed.[16]

By contrast, to soften the distinction, to assert mysteriously that there is some fused identity between law as it is and as it ought to be, is to suggest that all legal questions are fundamentally like those of the penumbra. It is to assert that there is no central element of actual law to be seen in the core of central meaning which rules have, that there is nothing in the nature of a legal rule inconsistent with *all* questions being open to reconsideration in the light of social policy. Of course, it is good to be occupied with the penumbra. Its problems are rightly the daily diet of the law schools. But to be occupied with the penumbra is one thing, to be preoccupied with it another. And preoccupation with the penumbra is, if I may say so, as rich a source of confusion in the American legal tradition as formalism in the English. Of course we might abandon the notion that rules have authority; we might cease to attach force or even meaning to an argument that a case falls clearly within a rule and the scope of a precedent. We might call all such reasoning 'automatic' or 'mechanical', which is already the routine in-vective of the courts. But until we decide that this *is* what we want, we should not encourage it by obliterating the Utilitarian distinction.

III

The third criticism of the separation of law and morals is of a very different character; it certainly is less an intellectual argument against the Utilitarian

[16] One recantation of this extreme position is worth mention in the present context. In the first edition of *The Bramble Bush*, Professor Llewellyn committed himself wholeheartedly to the view that 'what these officials do about disputes is, to my mind, the law itself' and that '*rules* . . . are important so far as they help you . . . predict what judges will do. . . . That is all their importance, except as pretty playthings'. Llewellyn, *The Bramble Bush* (1st edn., 1930), pp. 3, 5. In the second edition he said that these were 'unhappy words when not more fully developed, and they are plainly at best a very partial statement of the whole truth. . . . [O]ne office of law is to control officials in some part, and to guide them even ... where no thoroughgoing control is possible, or is desired. . . . [T]he words fail to take proper account ... of the office of the institution of law as an instrument of conscious shaping. . . .' Llewellyn, *The Bramble Bush* (2nd edn., 1951), p. 9.

distinction than a passionate appeal supported not by detailed reasoning but by reminders of a terrible experience. For it consists of the testimony of those who have descended into Hell, and, like Ulysses or Dante, brought back a message for human beings. Only in this case the Hell was not beneath or beyond earth, but on it; it was a Hell created on earth by men for other men.

This appeal comes from those German thinkers who lived through the Nazi regime and reflected upon its evil manifestations in the legal system. One of these thinkers, Gustav Radbruch, had himself shared the 'positivist' doctrine until the Nazi tyranny, but he was converted by this experience and so his appeal to other men to discard the doctrine of the separation of law and morals has the special poignancy of a recantation. What is important about this criticism is that it really does confront the particular point which Bentham and Austin had in mind in urging the separation of law as it is and as it ought to be. These German thinkers put their insistence on the need to join together what the Utilitarians separated just where this separation was of most importance in the eyes of the Utilitarians; for they were concerned with the problem posed by the existence of morally evil laws.

Before his conversion Radbruch held that resistance to law was a matter for the personal conscience, to be thought out by the individual as a moral problem, and the validity of a law could not be disproved by showing that its requirements were morally evil or even by showing that the effect of compliance with the law would be more evil than the effect of disobedience. Austin, it may be recalled, was emphatic in condemning those who said that if human laws conflicted with the fundamental principles of morality then they cease to be laws, as talking 'stark nonsense'.

The most pernicious laws, and therefore those which are most opposed to the will of God, have been and are continually enforced as laws by judicial tribunals, Suppose an act innocuous, or positively beneficial, be prohibited by the sovereign under the penalty of death; if I commit this act, I shall be tried and condemned, and if I object to the sentence, that it is contrary to the law of God ... the court of justice will demonstrate the inconclusiveness of my reasoning by hanging me up, in pursuance of the law of which I have impugned the validity. An exception, demurrer, or plea, founded on the law of God was never heard in a Court of Justice, from the creation of the world down to the present moment.[17]

These are strong, indeed brutal words, but we must remember that they went along—in the case of Austin and, of course, Bentham—with the conviction that if laws reached a certain degree of iniquity then there would be a plain moral obligation to resist them and to withhold obedience. We shall see, when we consider the alternatives, that this simple presentation of the human dilemma which may arise has much to be said for it.

[17] Austin, *The Province of Jurisprudence Determined* (Library of Ideas edn., 1954), p. 185.

Radbruch, however, had concluded from the ease with which the Nazi regime had exploited subservience to mere law—or expressed, as he thought, in the 'positivist' slogan 'law as law' (*Gesetz als Gesetz*)—and from the failure of the German legal profession to protest against the enormities which they were required to perpetrate in the name of law, that 'positivism' (meaning here the insistence on the separation of law as it is from law as it ought to be) had powerfully contributed to the horrors. His considered reflections led him to the doctrine that the fundamental principles of humanitarian morality were part of the very concept of *Recht* or Legality and that no positive enactment or statute, however clearly it was expressed and however clearly it conformed with the formal criteria of validity of a given legal system, could be valid if it contravened basic principles of morality. This doctrine can be appreciated fully only if the nuances imported by the German word *Recht* are grasped. But it is clear that the doctrine meant that every lawyer and judge should denounce statutes that transgressed the fundamental principles not as merely immoral or wrong but as having no legal character, and enactments which on this ground lack the quality of law should not be taken into account in working out the legal position of any given individual in particular circumstances. The striking recantation of his previous doctrine is unfortunately omitted from the translation of his works, but it should be read by all who wish to think afresh on the question of the interconnection of law and morals.[18]

It is impossible to read without sympathy Radbruch's passionate demand that the German legal conscience should be open to the demands of morality and his complaint that this has been too little the case in the German tradition. On the other hand there is an extraordinary naïveté in the view that insensitiveness to the demands of morality and subservience to state power in a people like the Germans should have arisen from the belief that law might be law though it failed to conform with the minimum requirements of morality. Rather this terrible history prompts inquiry into why emphasis on the slogan 'law is law', and the distinction between law and morals, acquired a sinister character in Germany, but elsewhere, as with the Utilitarians themselves, went along with the most enlightened liberal attitudes. But something more disturbing than naïveté is latent in Radbruch's whole presentation of the issues to which the existence of morally iniquitous laws give rise. It is not, I think, uncharitable to say that we can see in his argument that he has only half digested the spiritual message of liberalism which he

---

[18] See Radbruch, 'Gesetzliches Unrecht und Übergesetzliches Recht', 1 Süddeutsche Juristen-Zeitung 105 (Germany, 1946) (reprinted in Radbruch, *Rechtsphilosophie* (4th edn., 1950), p. 347). I have used the translation of part of this essay and of Radbruch, 'Die Erneuerung des Rechts', 2 Die Wandlung 8 (Germany, 1947), prepared by Professor Lon Fuller of the Harvard Law School as a mimeographed supplement to the readings in jurisprudence used in his course at Harvard.

is seeking to convey to the legal profession. For everything that he says is really dependent upon an enormous overvaluation of the importance of the bare fact that a rule may be said to be a valid rule of law, as if this, once declared, was conclusive of the final moral question: 'Ought this rule of law to be obeyed?' Surely the truly liberal answer to any sinister use of the slogan 'law is law' or of the distinction between law and morals is, 'Very well, but that does not conclude the question. Law is not morality; do not let it supplant morality.'

However, we are not left to a mere academic discussion in order to evaluate the plea which Radbruch made for the revision of the distinction between law and morals. After the war Radbruch's conception of law as containing in itself the essential moral principle of humanitarianism was applied in practice by German courts in certain cases in which local war criminals, spies, and informers under the Nazi regime were punished. The special importance of these cases is that the persons accused of these crimes claimed that what they had done was not illegal under the laws of the regime in force at the time these actions were performed. This plea was met with the reply that the laws upon which they relied were invalid as contravening the fundamental principles of morality. Let me cite briefly one of these cases.[19]

In 1944 a woman, wishing to be rid of her husband, denounced him to the authorities for insulting remarks he had made about Hitler while home on leave from the German army. The wife was under no legal duty to report his acts, though what he had said was apparently in violation of statutes making it illegal to make statements detrimental to the government of the Third Reich or to impair by any means the military defence of the German people. The husband was arrested and sentenced to death, apparently pursuant to these statutes, though he was not executed but was sent to the front. In 1949 the wife was prosecuted in a West German court for an offence which we would describe as illegally depriving a person of his freedom (*rechtswidrige Freiheitsberaubung*). This was punishable as a crime under the German Criminal Code of 1871 which had remained in force continuously since its enactment. The wife pleaded that her husband's imprisonment was pursuant to the Nazi statutes and hence that she had committed no crime. The court of appeal to which the case ultimately came held that the wife was guilty of procuring the deprivation of her husband's liberty by denouncing him to the German courts, even though he had been sentenced by a court for having violated a statute, since, to quote the words of the court, the statute 'was contrary to the sound conscience and sense of justice of all decent

---

[19] Judgment of 27 July 1949, Oberlandesgericht, Bamberg, 5 Süddeutsche Juristen-Zeitung 207 (Germany, 1950), 64 Harv. L. Rev. 1005 (1951); see Friedmann, *Legal Theory* (3rd edn., 1953), p. 457.

human beings'. This reasoning was followed in many cases which have been hailed as a triumph of the doctrines of natural law and as signalling the overthrow of positivism. The unqualified satisfaction with this result seems to me to be hysteria. Many of us might applaud the objective—that of punishing a woman for an outrageously immoral act—but this was secured only by declaring a statute established since 1934 not to have the force of law, and at least the wisdom of this course must be doubted. There were, of course, two other choices. One was to let the woman go unpunished; one can sympathize with and endorse the view that this might have been a bad thing to do. The other was to face the fact that if the woman were to be punished it must be pursuant to the introduction of a frankly retrospective law and with a full consciousness of what was sacrificed in securing her punishment in this way. Odious as retrospective criminal legislation and punishment may be, to have pursued it openly in this case would at least have had the merits of candour. It would have made plain that in punishing the woman a choice had to be made between two evils, that of leaving her unpunished and that of sacrificing a very precious principle of morality endorsed by most legal systems. Surely if we have learned anything from the history of morals it is that the thing to do with a moral quandary is not to hide it. Like nettles, the occasions when life forces us to choose between the lesser of two evils must be grasped with the consciousness that they are what they are. The vice of this use of the principle that, at certain limiting points, what is utterly immoral cannot be law or lawful is that it will serve to cloak the true nature of the problems with which we are faced and will encourage the romantic optimism that all the values we cherish ultimately will fit into a single system, that no one of them has to be sacrificed or compromised to accommodate another.

> All Discord Harmony not understood
> All Partial Evil Universal Good.

This is surely untrue and there is an insincerity in any formulation of our problem which allows us to describe the treatment of the dilemma as if it were the disposition of the ordinary case.

It may seem perhaps to make too much of forms, even perhaps of words, to emphasize one way of disposing of this difficult case as compared with another which might have led, so far as the woman was concerned, to exactly the same result. Why should we dramatize the difference between them? We might punish the woman under a new retrospective law and declare overtly that we are doing something inconsistent with our principles as the lesser of two evils; or we might allow the case to pass as one in which we do not point out precisely where we sacrifice such a principle. But candour is not just one among many minor virtues of the administration of law, just as it is not merely a minor virtue of morality. For if we adopt Radbruch's view, and with him and the German courts make our protest against evil law in the form of an assertion that certain rules cannot be law because of their moral iniquity, we confuse one of the most powerful, because it is the simplest, forms of moral criticism. If with the Utilitarians we speak plainly, we say that laws may be law but too evil to be obeyed. This is a moral condemnation which everyone can understand and it makes an immediate and obvious claim to moral attention. If, on the other hand, we formulate our objection as an assertion that these evil things are not law, here is an assertion which many people do not believe, and if they are disposed to consider it at all, it would seem to raise a whole host of philosophical issues before it can be accepted. So perhaps the most important single lesson to be learned from this form of the denial of the Utilitarian distinction is the one that the Utilitarians were most concerned to teach: when we have the ample resources of plain speech we must not present the moral criticism of institutions as propositions of a disputable philosophy.

IV

I have endeavoured to show that, in spite of all that has been learned and experienced since the Utilitarians wrote, and in spite of the defects of other parts of their doctrine, their protest against the confusion of what is and what ought to be law has a moral as well as an intellectual value. Yet it may well be said that, though this distinction is valid and important if applied to any particular law of a system, it is at least misleading if we attempt to apply it to 'law', that is, to the notion of a legal system, and that if we insist, as I have, on the narrower truth (or truism), we obscure a wider (or deeper) truth. After all, it may be urged, we have learned that there are many things which are untrue of laws taken separately, but which are true and important in a legal system considered as a whole. For example, the connection between law and sanctions and between the existence of law and its 'efficacy' must be understood in this more general way. It is surely not arguable (without some desperate extension of the word 'sanction' or artificial narrowing of the word 'law') that every law in a municipal legal system must have a sanction, yet it is at least plausible to argue that a legal system must, to be a legal system, provide sanctions for certain of its rules. So too, a rule of law may be said to exist though enforced or obeyed in only a minority of cases, but this could not be said of a legal system as a whole. Perhaps the differences with respect to laws taken separately and a legal system as a whole are also true of the connection between moral (or some other) conceptions of what law ought to be and law in this wider sense.

This line of argument, found (at least in embryo form) in Austin, where he draws attention to the fact that every developed legal system contains certain fundamental notions which are 'necessary' and 'bottomed in the common nature of man',[20] is worth pursuing—up to a point—and I shall say briefly why and how far this is so.

We must avoid, if we can, the arid wastes of inappropriate definition, for, in relation to a concept as many-sided and vague as that of a legal system, disputes about the 'essential' character, or necessity to the whole, of any single element soon begin to look like disputes about whether chess could be 'chess' if played without pawns. There is a wish, which may be understandable, to cut straight through the question whether a legal system, to be a legal system, must measure up to some moral or other standard with simple statements of fact: for example, that no system which utterly failed in this respect has ever existed or could endure; that the normally fulfilled assumption that a legal system aims at some form of justice colours the whole way in which we interpret specific rules in particular cases, and if this normally fulfilled assumption were not fulfilled no one would have any reason to obey except fear (and probably not that) and still less, of course, any moral obligation to obey. The connection between law and moral standards and principles of justice is therefore as little arbitrary and as 'necessary' as the connection between law and sanctions, and the pursuit of the question whether this necessity is logical (part of the 'meaning' of law) or merely factual or causal can safely be left as an innocent pastime for philosophers.

Yet in two respects I should wish to go further (even though this involves the use of a philosophical fantasy) and show what could intelligibly be meant by the claim that certain provisions in a legal system are 'necessary'. The world in which we live, and we who live in it, may one day change in many different ways; and if this change were radical enough not only would certain statements of fact now true be false and vice versa, but whole ways of thinking and talking which constitute our present conceptual apparatus, through which we see the world and each other, would lapse. We have only to consider how the whole of our social, moral, and legal life as we understand it now, depends on the contingent fact that though our bodies do change in shape, size, and other physical properties they do not do this so drastically nor with such quicksilver rapidity and irregularity that we cannot identify each other as the same persistent individual over considerable spans of time. Though this is but a contingent fact which may one day be different, on

---

[20] Austin, 'Uses of the Study of Jurisprudence' in *The Province of Jurisprudence Determined* (Library of Ideas edn., 1954), pp. 365, 373, 367–8.

it at present rest huge structures of our thought and principles of action and social life. Similarly, consider the following possibility (not because it is more than a possibility but because it reveals why we think certain things necessary in a legal system and what we mean by this): suppose that men were to become invulnerable to attack by each other, were clad perhaps like giant land crabs with an impenetrable carapace, and could extract the food they needed from the air by some internal chemical process. In such circumstances (the details of which can be left to science fiction) rules forbidding the free use of violence and rules constituting the minimum form of property—with its rights and duties sufficient to enable food to grow and be retained until eaten—would not have the necessary nonarbitrary status which they have for us, constituted as we are in a world like ours. At present, and until such radical changes supervene, such rules are so fundamental that if a legal system did not have them there would be no point in having any other rules at all. Such rules overlap with basic moral principles vetoing murder, violence, and theft; and so we can add to the factual statement that all legal systems in fact coincide with morality at such vital points, the statement that this is, in this sense, necessarily so. And why not call it a 'natural' necessity?

Of course even this much depends on the fact that in asking what content a legal system must have we take this question to be worth asking only if we who consider it cherish the humble aim of survival in close proximity to our fellows. Natural-law theory, however, in all its protean guises, attempts to push the argument much further and to assert that human beings are equally devoted to and united in their conception of aims (the pursuit of knowledge, justice to their fellow men) other than that of survival, and these dictate a further necessary content to a legal system (over and above my humble minimum) without which it would be pointless. Of course we must be careful not to exaggerate the differences among human beings, but it seems to me that above this minimum the purposes men have for living in society are too conflicting and varying to make possible much extension of the argument that some fuller overlap of legal rules and moral standards is 'necessary' in this sense.

Another aspect of the matter deserves attention. If we attach to a legal system the minimum meaning that it must consist of general rules—general both in the sense that they refer to courses of action, not single actions, and to multiplicities of men, not single individuals—this meaning connotes the principle of treating like cases alike, though the criteria of when cases are alike will be, so far, only the general elements specified in the rules. It is, however, true that *one* essential element of the concept of justice is the principle of treating like cases alike. This is justice in the administration of the law, not justice of the law. So there is, in the very notion of law consisting of general rules, something which prevents us from treating it as if morally it is utterly neutral, without any necessary contact with moral principles. Natural procedural justice consists therefore of those principles of objectivity and impartiality in the administration of the law which implement just this aspect of law and which are designed to ensure that rules are applied only to what are genuinely cases of the rule or at least to minimize the risks of inequalities in this sense.

These two reasons (or excuses) for talking of a certain overlap between legal and moral standards as necessary and natural, of course, should not satisfy anyone who is really disturbed by the Utilitarian or 'positivist' insistence that law and morality are distinct. This is so because a legal system that satisfied these minimum requirements might apply, with the most pedantic impartiality as between the persons affected, laws which were hideously oppressive, and might deny to a vast rightless slave population the minimum benefits of protection from violence and theft. The stink of such societies is, after all, still in our nostrils and to argue that they have (or had) no legal system would only involve the repetition of the argument. Only if the rules failed to provide these essential benefits and protection for anyone—even for a slave-owning group—would the minimum be unsatisfied and the system sink to the status of a set of meaningless taboos. Of course no one denied those benefits would have any reason to obey except fear and would have every moral reason to revolt.

II

IS LAW A SYSTEM OF RULES?

R. M. DWORKIN

I. POSITIVISM

POSITIVISM has a few central and organizing propositions as its skeleton, and though not every philosopher who is called a positivist would subscribe to these in the way I present them, they do define the general position I want to examine. These key tenets may be stated as follows:

(a) The law of a community is a set of special rules used by the community directly or indirectly for the purpose of determining which behaviour will be punished or coerced by the public power. These special rules can be identified and distinguished by specific criteria, by tests having to do not with their content but with their *pedigree* or the manner in which they were adopted or developed. These tests of pedigree can be used to distinguish valid legal rules from spurious legal rules (rules which lawyers and litigants wrongly argue are rules of law) and also from other sorts of social rules (generally lumped together as 'moral rules') that the community follows but does not enforce through public power.

(b) The set of these valid legal rules is exhaustive of 'the law', so that if someone's case is not clearly covered by such a rule (because there is none that seems appropriate, or those that seem appropriate are vague, or for some other reason) then that case cannot be decided by 'applying the law'. It must be decided by some official, like a judge, 'exercising his discretion', which means reaching beyond the law for some other sort of standard to guide him in manufacturing a fresh legal rule or supplementing an old one.

(c) To say that someone has a 'legal obligation' is to say that his case falls under a valid legal rule that requires him to do or to forbear from doing something. (To say he has a legal right, or has a legal power of some sort, or a legal privilege or immunity, is to assert, in a shorthand way, that others have actual or hypothetical legal obligations to act or not to act in certain ways touching him.) In the absence of such a valid legal rule there is no

From 'The Model of Rules', 35 *U. Chi. L. R.* 14 (1967). Reprinted by permission of the author. Several articles have been written in reply to this essay. Many of these are identified, and some criticism of their arguments made, in Dworkin, 'Social Rules and Legal Theory', 81 *Yale Law Journal* 855 (1972).

legal obligation; it follows that when the judge decides an issue by exercising his discretion, he is not enforcing a legal obligation as to that issue.

This is only the skeleton of positivism. The flesh is arranged differently by different positivists, and some even tinker with the bones. Different versions differ chiefly in their description of the fundamental test of pedigree a rule must meet to count as a rule of law.

Austin, for example, framed his version of the fundamental test as a series of interlocking definitions and distinctions.[1] He defined having an obligation as lying under a rule, a rule as a general command, and a command as an expression of desire that others behave in a particular way, backed by the power and will to enforce that expression in the event of disobedience. He distinguished classes of rules (legal, moral, or religious) according to which person or group is the author of the general command the rule represents. In each political community, he thought, one will find a sovereign—a person or a determinate group whom the rest obey habitually, but who is not in the habit of obeying anyone else. The legal rules of a community are the general commands its sovereign has deployed. Austin's definition of legal obligation followed from this definition of law. One has a legal obligation, he thought, if one is among the addressees of some general order of the sovereign, and is in danger of suffering a sanction unless he obeys that order.

Of course, the sovereign cannot provide for all contingencies through any scheme of orders, and some of his orders will inevitably be vague or have furry edges. Therefore (according to Austin) the sovereign grants those who enforce the law (judges) discretion to make fresh orders when novel or troublesome cases are presented. The judges then make new rules or adapt old rules, and the sovereign either overturns their creations, or tacitly confirms them by failing to do so.

Austin's model is quite beautiful in its simplicity. It asserts the first tenet of positivism, that the law is a set of rules specially selected to govern public order, and offers a simple factual test—what has the sovereign commanded?—as the sole criterion for identifying those special rules. In time, however, those who studied and tried to apply Austin's model found it too simple. Many objections were raised, among which were two that seemed fundamental. First, Austin's key assumption that in each community a determinate group or institution can be found, which is in ultimate control of all other groups, seemed not to hold in a complex society. Political control in a modern nation is pluralistic and shifting, a matter of more or less, of compromise and co-operation and alliance, so that it is often impossible to say that any person or group has that dramatic control necessary to qualify as an Austinian sovereign. One wants to say, in the United States

[1] J. Austin, *The Provinces of Jurisprudence Determined* (1832).

for example, that the 'people' are sovereign. But this means almost nothing, and in itself provides no test for determining what the 'people' have commanded, or distinguishing their legal from their social or moral commands.

Second, critics began to realize that Austin's analysis fails entirely to account for, even to recognize, certain striking facts about the attitudes we take toward 'the law'. We make an important distinction between law and even the general orders of a gangster. We feel that the law's strictures—and its sanctions—are different in that they are obligatory in a way that the outlaw's commands are not. Austin's analysis has no place for any such distinction, because it defines an obligation as subjection to the threat of force, and so founds the authority of law entirely on the sovereign's ability and will to harm those who disobey. Perhaps the distinction we make is illusory—perhaps our feeling of some special authority attaching to the law is based on religious hangover or another sort of mass self-deception. But Austin does not demonstrate this, and we are entitled to insist that an analysis of our concept of law either acknowledge and explain our attitudes, or show why they are mistaken.

H. L. A. Hart's version of positivism is more complex than Austin's, in two ways. First, he recognizes, as Austin did not, that rules are of different logical kinds (Hart distinguishes two kinds, which he calls 'primary' and 'secondary' rules). Second, he rejects Austin's theory that a rule is a kind of command, and substitutes a more elaborate general analysis of what rules are. We must pause over each of these points, and then note how they merge in Hart's concept of law.

Hart's distinction between primary and secondary rules is of great importance.[2] Primary rules are those that grant rights or impose obligations upon members of the community. The rules of the criminal law that forbid us to rob, murder, or drive too fast are good examples of primary rules. Secondary rules are those that stipulate how, and by whom, such primary rules may be formed, recognized, modified, or extinguished. The rules that stipulate how Congress is composed, and how it enacts legislation, are examples of secondary rules. Rules about forming contracts and executing wills are also secondary rules because they stipulate how very particular rules governing particular legal obligations (i.e., the terms of a contract or the provisions of a will) come into existence and are changed.

His general analysis of rules is also of great importance.[3] Austin had said that every rule is a general command, and that a person is obligated under a rule if he is liable to be hurt should he disobey it. Hart points out that this obliterates the distinction between being *obliged* to do something and

---

[2] See Hart, *The Concept of Law* (1961), pp. 89—96.
[3] Op. cit., pp. 79–88.

being *obligated* to do it. If one is bound by a rule he is obligated, not merely obliged, to do what it provides, and therefore being bound by a rule must be different from being subject to an injury if one disobeys an order. A rule differs from an order, among other ways, by being *normative*, by setting a standard of behaviour that has a call on its subject beyond the threat that may enforce it. A rule can never be binding just because some person with physical power wants it to be so. He must have *authority* to issue the rule or it is no rule, and such authority can only come from another rule which is already binding on those to whom he speaks. That is the difference between a valid law and the orders of a gunman.

So Hart offers a general theory of rules that does not make their authority depend upon the physical power of their authors. If we examine the way different rules come into being, he tells us, and attend to the distinction between primary and secondary rules, we see that there are two possible sources of a rule's authority.[4]

(a) A rule may become binding upon a group of people because that group through its practices *accepts* the rule as a standard for its conduct. It is not enough that the group simply conforms to a pattern of behaviour: even though most Englishmen may go to the cinema on Saturday evening, they have not accepted a rule requiring that they do so. A practice constitutes the acceptance of a rule only when those who follow the practice regard the rule as binding, and recognize the rule as a reason or justification for their own behaviour and as a reason for criticizing the behaviour of others who do not obey it.

(b) A rule may also become binding in quite a different way, namely by being enacted in conformity with some *secondary* rule that stipulates that rules so enacted shall be binding. If the constitution of a club stipulates, for example, that by-laws may be adopted by a majority of the members, then particular by-laws so voted are binding upon all the members, not because of any practice of acceptance of these particular by-laws, but because the constitution says so. We use the concept of *validity* in this connection: rules binding because they have been created in a manner stipulated by some secondary rule are called 'valid' rules. Thus we can record Hart's fundamental distinction this way: a rule may be binding (a) because it is accepted or (b) because it is valid.

Hart's concept of law is a construction of these various distinctions.[5] Primitive communities have only primary rules, and these are binding entirely because of practices of acceptance. Such communities cannot be said to have 'law', because there is no way to distinguish a set of legal rules from

[4] Op. cit., pp. 97–107.
[5] Op. cit., *passim*, particularly Ch. VI.

amongst other social rules, as the first tenet of positivism requires. But when a particular community has developed a fundamental secondary rule that stipulates how legal rules are to be identified, the idea of a distinct set of legal rules, and thus of law, is born.

Hart calls such a fundamental secondary rule a 'rule of recognition'. The rule of recognition of a given community may be relatively simple ('What the king enacts is law') or it may be very complex (the United States Constitution, with all its difficulties of interpretation, may be considered a single rule of recognition). The demonstration that a particular rule is valid may therefore require tracing a complicated chain of validity back from that particular rule ultimately to the fundamental rule. Thus a parking ordinance of the city of New Haven is valid because it is adopted by a city council, pursuant to the procedures and within the competence specified by the municipal law adopted by the state of Connecticut, in conformity with the procedures and within the competence specified by the constitution of the state of Connecticut, which was in turn adopted consistently with the requirements of the United States Constitution.

Of course, a rule of recognition cannot itself be valid, because by hypothesis it is ultimate, and so cannot meet tests stipulated by a more fundamental rule. The rule of recognition is the sole rule in a legal system whose binding force depends upon its acceptance. If we wish to know what rule of recognition a particular community has adopted or follows, we must observe how its citizens, and particularly its officials, behave. We must observe what ultimate arguments they accept as showing the validity of a particular rule, and what ultimate arguments they use to criticize other officials or institutions. We can apply no mechanical test, but there is no danger of our confusing the rule of recognition of a community with its rules of morality. The rule of recognition is identified by the fact that its province is the operation of the governmental apparatus of legislatures, courts, agencies, policemen, and the rest.

In this way Hart rescues the fundamentals of positivism from Austin's mistakes. Hart agrees with Austin that valid rules of law may be created through the acts of officials and public institutions. But Austin thought that the authority of these institutions lay only in their monopoly of power. Hart finds their authority in the background of constitutional standards against which they act, constitutional standards that have been accepted, in the form of a fundamental rule of recognition, by the community which they govern. This background legitimates the decisions of government and gives them the cast and call of obligation that the naked commands of Austin's sovereign lacked. Hart's theory differs from Austin's also, in recognizing that different communities use different ultimate tests of law, and that some allow other means of creating law than the deliberate act of a legislative institution. Hart mentions 'long customary practice' and 'the relation [of a rule] to judicial decisions' as other criteria that are often used, though generally along with and subordinate to the test of legislation.

So Hart's version of positivism is more complex than Austin's, and his test for valid rules of law is more sophisticated. In one respect, however, the two models are very similar. Hart, like Austin, recognizes that legal rules have furry edges (he speaks of them as having 'open texture') and, again like Austin, he accounts for troublesome cases by saying that judges have and exercise discretion to decide these cases by fresh legislation.[6] (I shall later try to show why one who thinks of law as a special set of rules is almost inevitably drawn to account for difficult cases in terms of someone's exercise of discretion.)

II. RULES, PRINCIPLES, AND POLICIES

I want to make a general attack on positivism, and I shall use H. L. A. Hart's version as a target, when a particular target is needed. My strategy will be organized around the fact that when lawyers reason or dispute about legal rights and obligations, particularly in those hard cases when our problems with these concepts seem most acute, they make use of standards that do not function as rules, but operate differently as principles, policies, and other sorts of standards. Positivism, I shall argue, is a model of and for a system of rules, and its central notion of a single fundamental test for law forces us to miss the important roles of these standards that are not rules.

I just spoke of 'principles, policies, and other sorts of standards'. Most often I shall use the term 'principle' generically, to refer to the whole set of these standards other than rules; occasionally, however, I shall be more precise, and distinguish between principles and policies. Although nothing in the present argument will turn on the distinction, I should state how I draw it. I call a 'policy' that kind of standard that sets out a goal to be reached, generally an improvement in some economic, political, or social feature of the community (though some goals are negative, in that they stipulate that some present feature is to be protected from adverse change). I call a 'principle' a standard that is to be observed, not because it will advance or secure an economic, political, or social situation deemed desirable, but because it is a requirement of justice or fairness or some other dimension of morality. Thus the standard that automobile accidents are to be decreased is a policy, and the standard that no man may profit by his own wrong a principle. The distinction can be collapsed by construing a principle as stating a social goal (i.e., the goal of a society in which no man profits by his own wrong), or by construing a policy as stating a principle (i.e., the principle that the goal the policy embraces is a worthy one) or by adopting the utilitarian thesis that principles of justice are disguised statements of goals (securing the greatest happiness of the greatest number). In some contexts the distinction has uses which are lost if it is thus collapsed.[7]

My immediate purpose, however, is to distinguish principles in the generic sense from rules, and I shall start by collecting some examples of the former. The examples I offer are chosen haphazardly; almost any case in a law school casebook would provide examples that would serve as well. In 1889 a New York court, in the famous case of *Riggs* v. *Palmer*,[8] had to decide whether an heir named in the will of his grandfather could inherit under that will, even though he had murdered his grandfather to do so. The court began its reasoning with this admission: 'It is quite true that statutes regulating the making, proof and effect of wills, and the devolution of property, if literally construed, and if their force and effect can in no way and under no circumstances be controlled or modified, give this property to the murderer.[9] But the court continued to note that 'all laws as well as all contracts may be controlled in their operation and effect by general, fundamental maxims of the common law. No one shall be permitted to profit by his own fraud, or to take advantage of his own wrong, or to found any claim upon his own iniquity, or to acquire property by his own crime.'[10] The murderer did not receive his inheritance.

In 1960, a New Jersey court was faced in *Henningsen* v. *Bloomfield Motors, Inc.*,[11] with the important question of whether (or how much) an automobile manufacturer may limit his liability in case the automobile is defective. Henningsen had bought a car, and signed a contract which said that the manufacturer's liability for defects was limited to 'making good' defective parts — 'this warranty being expressly in lieu of all other warranties, obligations or liabilities'. Henningsen argued that, at least in the circumstances of his case, the manufacturer ought not to be protected by this limitation, and ought to be liable for the medical and other expenses of persons injured in a crash. He was not able to point to any statute, or to any established rule of law, that prevented the manufacturer from standing on the contract. The court nevertheless agreed with Henningsen. At various points in the court's argument the following appeals to standards are made: (a) '[W]e

---

[7] See Dworkin, 'Wasserstrom: The Judicial Decision', 75 *Ethics* 47 (1964).
[8] 115 N.Y. 506, 22 N.E. 188 (1889).
[9] Id. at 509, 22 N.E. at 189.
[10] Id. at 511, 22 N.E. at 190.
[11] 32 N.J. 358, 161 A. 2d 69 (1960).

must keep in mind the general principle that, in the absence of fraud, one who does not choose to read a contract before signing it cannot later relieve himself of its burdens.'[12] (b) 'In applying that principle, the basic tenet of freedom of competent parties to contract is a factor of importance.'[13] (c) 'Freedom of contract is not such an immutable doctrine as to admit of no qualification in the area in which we are concerned'.[14] (d) 'In a society such as ours, where the automobile is a common and necessary adjunct of daily life, and where its use is so fraught with danger to the driver, passengers and the public, the manufacturer is under a special obligation in connection with the construction, promotion and sale of his cars. Consequently, the courts must examine purchase agreements closely to see if consumer and public interests are treated fairly.'[15] (e) ' "[I]s there any principle which is more familiar or more firmly embedded in the history of Anglo-American law than the basic doctrine that the courts will not permit themselves to be used as instruments of inequity and injustice?" '[16] (f) ' "More specifically, the courts generally refuse to lend themselves to the enforcement of a 'bargain' in which one party has unjustly taken advantage of the economic necessities of the other. ..." '[17]

The standards set out in these quotations are not the sort we think of as legal rules. They seem very different from propositions like 'The maximum legal speed on the turnpike is sixty miles an hour' or 'A will is invalid unless signed by three witnesses'. They are different because they are legal principles rather than legal rules.

The difference between legal principles and legal rules is a logical distinction. Both sets of standards point to particular decisions about legal obligation in particular circumstances, but they differ in the character of the direction they give. Rules are applicable in an all-or-nothing fashion. If the facts a rule stipulates are given, then either the rule is valid, in which case the answer it supplies must be accepted, or it is not, in which case it contributes nothing to the decision.

This all-or-nothing is seen most plainly if we look at the way rules operate, not in law, but in some enterprise they dominate—a game, for example. In baseball a rule provides that if the batter has had three strikes, he is out. An official cannot consistently acknowledge that this is an accurate statement of a baseball rule, and decide that a batter who has had three strikes is not out. Of course, a rule may have exceptions (the batter who has taken

---

[12] Id. at 386, 161 A. 2d at 84.
[13] Id.
[14] Id. at 388, 161 A. 2d at 86.
[15] Id. at 387, 161 A. 2d at 85.
[16] Id. at 389, 161 A. 2d at 86 (quoting Frankfurter J. in *United States* v. *Bethlehem Steel* 315 U.S. 289, 326 (1942)).
[17] Id.

three strikes is not out if the catcher drops the third strike). However, an accurate statement of the rule would take this exception into account, and any that did not would be incomplete. If the list of exceptions is very large, it would be too clumsy to repeat them each time the rule is cited; there is, however, no reason in theory why they could not all be added on, and the more that are, the more accurate is the statement of the rule.

If we take baseball rules as a model, we find that rules of law, like the rule that a will is invalid unless signed by three witnesses, fit the model well. If the requirement of three witnesses is a valid legal rule, then it cannot be that a will has been signed by only two witnesses and is valid. The rule might have exceptions, but if it does it is inaccurate and incomplete to state the rule so simply, without enumerating the exceptions. In theory, at least, the exceptions could all be listed, and the more of them that are, the more complete is the statement of the rule.

But this is not the way the sample principles in the quotations operate. Even those which look most like rules do not set out legal consequences that follow automatically when the conditions provided are met. We say that our law respects the principle that no man may profit from his own wrong, but we do not mean that the law never permits a man to profit from wrongs he commits. In fact, people often profit, perfectly legally, from their legal wrongs. The most notorious case is adverse possession—if I trespass on your land long enough, some day I will gain a right to cross your land whenever I please. There are many less dramatic examples. If a man leaves one job, breaking a contract, to take a much higher paying job, he may have to pay damages to his first employer, but he is usually entitled to keep his new salary. If a man jumps bail and crosses state lines to make a brilliant investment in another state, he may be sent back to jail, but he will keep his profits.

We do not treat these—and countless other counter-instances that can easily be imagined—as showing that the principle about profiting from one's wrongs is not a principle of our legal system, or that it is incomplete and needs qualifying exceptions. We do not treat counter-instances as exceptions (at least not exceptions in the way in which a catcher's dropping the third strike is an exception) because we could not hope to capture these counter-instances simply by a more extended statement of the principle. They are not, even in theory, subject to enumeration, because we would have to include not only these cases (like adverse possession) in which some institution has already provided that profit can be gained through a wrong, but also those numberless imaginary cases in which we know in advance that the principle would not hold. Listing some of these might sharpen our sense of the principle's weight (I shall mention that dimension in a moment), but it would not make for a more accurate or complete statement of the principle.

A principle like 'No man may profit from his own wrong' does not even purport to set out conditions that make its application necessary. Rather, it states a reason that argues in one direction, but does not necessitate a particular decision. If a man has or is about to receive something, as a direct result of something illegal he did to get it, then that is a reason which the law will take into account in deciding whether he should keep it. There may be other principles or policies arguing in the other direction—a policy of securing title, for example, or a principle limiting punishment to what the legislature has stipulated. If so, our principle may not prevail, but that does not mean that it is not a principle of our legal system, because in the next case, when these contravening considerations are absent or less weighty, the principle may be decisive. All that is meant, when we say that a particular principle is a principle of our law, is that the principle is one which officials must take into account, if it is relevant, as a consideration inclining in one direction or another.

The logical distinction between rules and principles appears more clearly when we consider principles that do not even look like rules. Consider the proposition, set out under (d) in the excerpts from the *Henningsen* opinion, the 'the manufacturer is under a special obligation in connection with the construction, promotion and sale of his cars'. This does not even purport to define the specific duties such a special obligation entails, or to tell us what rights automobile consumers acquire as a result. It merely states— and this is an essential link in the *Henningsen* argument—that automobile manufacturers must be held to higher standards than other manufacturers, and are less entitled to rely on the competing principle of freedom of contract. It does not mean that they may never rely on that principle, or that courts may rewrite automobile purchase contracts at will; it means only that if a particular clause seems unfair or burdensome, courts have less reason to enforce the clause than if it were for the purchase of neckties. The 'special obligation' counts in favour, but does not in itself necessitate, a decision refusing to enforce the terms of an automobile purchase contract.

This first difference between rules and principles entails another. Principles have a dimension that rules do not—the dimension of weight or importance. When principles intersect (the policy of protecting automobile consumers intersecting with principles of freedom of contract, for example), one who must resolve the conflict has to take into account the relative weight of each. This cannot be, of course, an exact measurement, and the judgment that a particular principle or policy is more important than another will often be a controversial one. Nevertheless, it is an integral part of the concept of a principle that it has this dimension, that it makes sense to ask how important or how weighty it is.

Rules do not have this dimension. We can speak of rules as being *functionally* important or unimportant (the baseball rule that three strikes are out is more important than the rule that runners may advance on a balk, because the game would be much more changed with the first rule altered than the second). In this sense, one legal rule may be more important than another because it has a greater or more important role in regulating behaviour. But we cannot say that one rule is more important than another within the system of rules, so that when two rules conflict one supersedes the other by virtue of its greater weight. If two rules conflict, one of them cannot be a valid rule. The decision as to which is valid, and which must be abandoned or recast, must be made by appealing to considerations beyond the rules themselves. A legal system might regulate such conflicts by other rules, which prefer the rule enacted by the higher authority, or the rule enacted later, or the more specific rule, or something of that sort. A legal system may also prefer the rule supported by the more important principles. (Our own legal system uses both of these techniques.)

It is not always clear from the form of a standard whether it is a rule or a principle. 'A will is invalid unless signed by three witnesses' is not very different in form from 'A man may not profit from his own wrong', but one who knows something of American law knows that he must take the first as stating a rule and the second as stating a principle. In many cases the distinction is difficult to make—it may not have been settled how the standard should operate, and this issue may itself be a focus of controversy. The First Amendment to the United States Constitution contains the provision that Congress shall not abridge freedom of speech. Is this a rule, so that if a particular law does abridge freedom of speech, it follows that it is unconstitutional? Those who claim that the first amendment is 'an absolute' say that it must be taken in this way, that is, as a rule. Or does it merely state a principle, so that when an abridgement of speech is discovered, it is unconstitutional unless the context presents some other policy or principle which in the circumstances is weighty enough to permit the abridgement? That is the position of those who argue for what is called the 'clear and present danger' test or some other form of 'balancing'.

Sometimes a rule and a principle can play the same role, and the difference between them is almost a matter of form alone. The first section of the Sherman Act states that every contract in restraint of trade shall be void. The Supreme Court had to make the decision whether this provision should be treated as a rule in its own terms (striking down every contract 'which restrains trade', which almost any contract does) or as a principle, providing a reason for striking down a contract in the absence of effective contrary policies. The Court construed the provision as a rule, but treated that rule as containing the word 'unreasonable', and as prohibiting only 'unreasonable' restraints of trade.[18] This allowed the provision to function logically as a rule (whenever a court finds that the restraint is 'unreasonable' it is bound to hold the contract invalid) and substantially as a principle (a court must take into account a variety of other principles and policies in determining whether a particular restraint in particular economic circumstances is 'unreasonable').

Words like 'reasonable', 'negligent', 'unjust', and 'significant' often perform just this function. Each of these terms makes the application of the rule which contains it depend to some extent upon principles or policies lying beyond the rule, and in this way makes that rule itself more like a principle. But they do not quite turn the rule into a principle, because even the least confining of these terms restricts the *kind* of other principles and policies on which the rule depends. If we are bound by a rule that says that 'unreasonable' contracts are void, or that grossly 'unfair' contracts will not be enforced, much more judgment is required than if the quoted terms were omitted. But suppose a case in which some consideration of policy or principle suggests that a contract should be enforced even though its restraint is not reasonable, or even though it is grossly unfair. Enforcing these contracts would be forbidden by our rules, and thus permitted only if these rules were abandoned or modified. If we were dealing, however, not with a rule but with a policy against enforcing unreasonable contracts, or a principle that unfair contracts ought not to be enforced, the contracts could be enforced without alteration of the law.

III. PRINCIPLES AND THE CONCEPT OF LAW

Once we identify legal principles as separate sorts of standards, different from legal rules, we are suddenly aware of them all around us. Law teachers teach them, lawbooks cite them, legal historians celebrate them. But they seem most energetically at work, carrying most weight, in difficult lawsuits like *Riggs* and *Henningsen*. In cases like these, principles play an essential part in arguments supporting judgments about particular legal rights and obligations. After the case is decided, we may say that the case stands for a particular rule (e.g., the rule that one who murders is not eligible to take under the will of his victim). But the rule does not exist before the case is decided; the court cites principles as its justification for adopting and applying

[18] *Standard Oil* v. *United States*, 221 U.S. 1, 60 (1911); *United States* v. *American Tobacco Co.*, 221 U.S. 106, 180 (1911).

a new rule. In *Riggs*, the court cited the principle that no man may profit from his own wrong as a background standard against which to read the statute of wills, and in this way justified a new interpretation of that statute. In *Henningsen*, the court cited a variety of intersecting principles and policies as authority for a new rule respecting manufacturers' liability for automobile defects.

An analysis of the concept of legal obligation must therefore account for the important role of principles in reaching particular decisions of law. There are two very different tacks we might take.

(a) We might treat legal principles the way we treat legal rules and say that some principles are binding as law and must be taken into account by judges and lawyers who make decisions of legal obligation. If we took this tack, we should say that in the United States, at least, the 'law' includes principles as well as rules.

(b) We might, on the other hand, deny that principles can be binding the way some rules are. We would say, instead, that in cases like *Riggs* or *Henningsen* the judge reaches beyond the rules that he is bound to apply (reaches, that is, beyond the 'law') for extra-legal principles he is free to follow if he wishes.

One might think that there is not very much difference between these two lines of attack, that it is only a verbal question of how one wants to use the word 'law'. But that is a mistake, because the choice between these two accounts has the greatest consequences for an analysis of legal obligation. It is a choice between two *concepts* of a legal principle, a choice we can clarify by comparing it to a choice we might make between two concepts of a legal rule. We sometimes say of someone that he 'makes it a rule' to do something, when we mean that he has chosen to follow a certain practice. We might say that someone has made it a rule, for example, to run a mile before breakfast because he wants to be healthy and believes in a regimen. We do not mean, when we say this, that he is *bound* by the rule that he must run a mile before breakfast, or even that he regards it as binding upon him. Accepting a rule as binding is something different from making it a rule to do something. If we use Hart's example again, there is a difference between saying that Englishmen make it a rule to see a movie once a week, and saying that the English have a rule that one must see a movie once a week. The second implies that if an Englishman does not follow the rule, he is subject to criticism or censure, but the first does not. The first does not exclude the possibility of a *sort* of criticism—we can say that one who does not see movies is neglecting his education—but we do not suggest that he is doing something wrong *just* in not following the rule.[19]

[19] The distinction is in substance the same as that made by Rawls, 'Two Concepts of Rules', 64 *Philosophical Review* 3 (1955).

If we think of the judges of a community as a group, we could describe the rules of law they follow in these two different ways. We could say, for instance, that in a certain state the judges make it a rule not to enforce wills unless there are three witnesses. This would not imply that the rare judge who enforces such a rule is doing anything wrong just for that reason. On the other hand we can say that in that state a rule of law requires judges not to enforce such wills; this does imply that a judge who enforces them is doing something wrong. Hart, Austin, and other positivists, of course, would insist on this latter account of legal rules; they would not at all be satisfied with the 'make it a rule' account. It is not a verbal question of which account is right. It is a question of which describes the social situation more accurately. Other important issues turn on which description we accept. If judges simply 'make it a rule' not to enforce certain contracts, for example, then we cannot say, before the decision, that anyone is 'entitled' to that result, and that proposition cannot enter into any justification we might offer for the decision.

The two lines of attack on principles parallel these two accounts of rules. The first tack treats principles as binding upon judges, so that they are wrong not to apply the principles when they are pertinent. The second tack treats principles as summaries of what most judges 'make it a principle' to do when forced to go beyond the standards that bind them. The choice between these approaches will affect, perhaps even determine, the answer we can give to the question whether the judge in a hard case like *Riggs* or *Henningsen* is attempting to enforce pre-existing legal rights and obligations. If we take the first tack, we are still free to argue that because such judges are applying binding legal standards they are enforcing legal rights and obligations. But if we take the second, we are out of court on that issue, and we must acknowledge that the murderer's family in *Riggs* and the manufacturer in *Henningsen* were deprived of their property by an act of judicial discretion applied *ex post facto*. This may not shock many readers—the notion of judicial discretion has percolated through the legal community—but it does illustrate one of the most nettlesome of the puzzles that drive philosophers to worry about legal obligation. If taking property away in cases like these cannot be justified by appealing to an established obligation, another justification must be found, and nothing satisfactory has yet been supplied.

In my skeleton diagram of positivism, previously set out, I listed the doctrine of judicial discretion as the second tenet. Positivists hold that when a case is not covered by a clear rule, a judge must exercise his discretion to decide that case by what amounts to a fresh piece of legislation. There may be an important connection between this doctrine and the question of which of the two approaches to legal principles we must take. We shall therefore want to ask whether the doctrine is correct, and whether it implies the second approach, as it seems on its face to do. *En route* to these issues, however, we shall have to polish our understanding of the concept of discretion. I shall try to show how certain confusions about that concept, and in particular a failure to discriminate different senses in which it is used, account for the popularity of the doctrine of discretion. I shall argue that in the sense in which the doctrine does have a bearing on our treatment of principles, it is entirely unsupported by the arguments the positivists use to defend it.

IV. DISCRETION

The concept of discretion was lifted by the positivists from ordinary language, and to understand it we must put it back *in habitat* for a moment. What does it mean, in ordinary life, to say that someone 'has discretion'? The first thing to notice is that the concept is out of place in all but very special contexts. For example, you would not say that I either do or do not have discretion to choose a house for my family. It is not true that I have 'no discretion' in making that choice, and yet it would be almost equally misleading to say that I do have discretion. The concept of discretion is at home in only one sort of context: when someone is in general charged with making decisions subject to standards set by a particular authority. It makes sense to speak of the discretion of a sergeant who is subject to orders of superiors, or the discretion of a sports official or contest judge who is governed by a rule book or the terms of the contest. Discretion, like the hole in a doughnut, does not exist except as an area left open by a surrounding belt of restriction. It is therefore a relative concept. It always makes sense to ask, 'Discretion under which standards?' or 'Discretion as to which authority?' Generally the context will make the answer to this plain, but in some cases the official may have discretion from one standpoint though not from another.

Like almost all terms, the precise meaning of 'discretion' is affected by features of the context. The term is always coloured by the background of understood information against which it is used. Although the shadings are many, it will be helpful for us to recognize some gross distinctions.

Sometimes we use 'discretion' in a weak sense, simply to say that for some reason the standards an official must apply cannot be applied mechanically but demand the use of judgment. We use this weak sense when the context does not already make that clear, when the background our audience assumes does not contain that piece of information. Thus we might say, 'The sergeant's orders left him a great deal of discretion', to those who do not know what the sergeant's orders were or who do not know something that made those orders vague or hard to carry out. It would make perfect sense to add, by way of amplification, that the lieutenant had ordered the sergeant to take his five most experienced men on patrol but that it was hard to determine which were the most experienced.

Sometimes we use the term in a different weak sense, to say only that some official has final authority to make a decision which cannot be reversed by any other official. We speak this way when the official is part of a hierarchy of officials structured so that some have higher authority but in which the patterns of authority are different for different classes of decision. Thus we might say that in baseball certain decisions, like the decision whether the ball or the runner reached second base first, are left to the discretion of the second base umpire, if we mean that on this issue the head umpire has no power to substitute his own judgment if he disagrees.

I call both of these senses weak to distinguish them from a stronger sense. We use 'discretion' sometimes not merely to say that an official must use judgment in applying the standards set him by authority, or that no one will review that exercise of judgment, but to say that on some issue he is simply not bound by standards set by the authority in question. In this sense we say that a sergeant has discretion if he has been told to pick any five men for patrol he chooses or that a judge in a dog show has discretion to judge airedales before boxers if the rules do not stipulate an order of events. We use this sense not to comment on the vagueness or difficulty of the standards, or on who has the final word in applying them, but on their range and the decisions they purport to control. If the sergeant is told to take the five most experienced men, he does not have discretion in this strong sense because that order purports to govern his decision. The boxing referee who must decide which fighter has been the more aggressive does not have discretion, in the strong sense for the same reason.[20]

If anyone said that the sergeant or the referee had discretion in these cases, we should have to understand him, if the context permitted, as using the term in one of the weak senses. Suppose, for example, the lieutenant ordered the sergeant to select the five men he deemed most experienced, and then added that the sergeant had discretion to choose them. Or the rules provided that the referee should award the round to the more aggressive fighter, with discretion in selecting him. We should have to understand these statements in the second weak sense, as speaking to the question of review of the de-

---

[20] I have not spoken of that jurisprudential favourite, 'limited' discretion, because that concept presents no special difficulties if we remember the relativity of discretion. Suppose the sergeant is told to choose from 'amongst' experienced men, or to 'take experience into account'. We might say either that he has (limited) discretion in picking his patrol, or (full) discretion either to pick amongst experienced men or to decide what else to take into account.

cision. The first weak sense—that the decisions take judgment—would be otiose, and the third, strong sense is excluded by the statements themselves.

We must avoid one tempting confusion. The strong sense of discretion is not tantamount to licence, and does not exclude criticism. Almost any situation in which a person acts (including those in which there is no question of decision under special authority, and so no question of discretion) makes relevant certain standards of rationality, fairness, and effectiveness. We criticize each other's acts in terms of these standards, and there is no reason not to do so when the acts are within the centre rather than beyond the perimeter of the doughnut of special authority. So we can say that the sergeant who was given discretion (in the strong sense) to pick a patrol did so stupidly or maliciously or carelessly, or that the judge who had discretion in the order of viewing dogs made a mistake because he took boxers first although there were only three airedales and many more boxers. An official's discretion means not that he is free to decide without recourse to standards of sense and fairness, but only that his decision is not controlled by a standard furnished by the particular authority we have in mind when we raise the question of discretion. Of course this latter sort of freedom is important; that is why we have the strong sense of discretion. Someone who has discretion in this third sense can be criticized, but not for being disobedient, as in the case of the soldier. He can be said to have made a mistake, but not to have deprived a participant of a decision to which he was entitled, as in the case of a sports official or contest judge.

We may now return, with these observations in hand, to the positivists' doctrine of judicial discretion. That doctrine argues that if a case is not controlled by an established rule, the judge must decide it by exercising discretion. We want to examine this doctrine and to test its bearing on our treatment of principles; but first we must ask in which sense of discretion we are to understand it.

Some nominalists argue that judges always have discretion, even when a clear rule is in point, because judges are ultimately the final arbiters of the law. This doctrine of discretion uses the second weak sense of that term, because it makes the point that no higher authority reviews the decisions of the highest court. It therefore has no bearing on the issue of how we account for principles, any more than it bears on how we account for rules.

The positivists do not mean their doctrine this way, because they say that a judge has no discretion when a clear and established rule is available. If we attend to the positivists' arguments for the doctrine we may suspect that they use discretion in the first weak sense to mean only that judges must sometimes exercise judgment in applying legal standards. Their arguments call attention to the fact that some rules of law are vague (Professor Hart, for example, says that all rules of law have 'open texture'), and that some cases arise (like *Henningsen*) in which no established rule seems to be suitable. They emphasize that judges must sometimes agonize over points of law, and that two equally trained and intelligent judges will often disagree.

These points are easily made; they are commonplace to anyone who has any familiarity with law. Indeed, that is the difficulty with assuming that positivists mean to use 'discretion' in this weak sense. The proposition that when no clear rule is available discretion in the sense of judgment must be used is a tautology. It has no bearing, moreover, on the problem of how to account for legal principles. It is perfectly consistent to say that the judge in *Riggs*, for example, had to use judgment, and that he was bound to follow the principle that no man may profit from his own wrong. The positivists speak as if their doctrine of judicial discretion is an insight rather than a tautology, and as if it does have a bearing on the treatment of principles. Hart, for example, says that when the judge's discretion is in play, we can no longer speak of his being bound by standards, but must speak rather of what standards he 'characteristically uses'.[21] Hart thinks that when judges have discretion, the principles they cite must be treated on our second approach, as what courts 'make it a principle' to do.

It therefore seems that positivists, at least sometimes, take their doctrine in the third, strong sense of discretion. In that sense it does bear on the treatment of principles; indeed, in that sense it is nothing less than a restatement of our second approach. It is the same thing to say that when a judge runs out of rules he has discretion, in the sense that he is not bound by any standards from the authority of law, as to say that the legal standards judges cite other than rules are not binding on them.

So we must examine the doctrine of judicial discretion in the strong sense. (I shall henceforth use the term 'discretion' in that sense.) Do the principles judges cite in cases like *Riggs* or *Henningsen* control their decisions, as the sergeant's orders to take the most experienced men or the referee's duty to choose the more aggressive fighter control the decisions of these officials? What arguments could a positivist supply to show that they do not?

(1) A positivist might argue that principles cannot be binding or obligatory. That would be a mistake. It is always a question, of course, whether any particular principle is *in fact* binding upon some legal official. But there is nothing in the logical character of a principle that renders it incapable of binding him. Suppose that the judge in *Henningsen* had failed to take any account of the principle that automobile manufacturers have a special obligation to their consumers, or the principle that the courts seek to protect those whose bargaining position is weak, but had simply decided for the

[21] Hart, *The Concept of Law* (1961), p. 144.

defendant by citing the principle of freedom of contract without more ado. His critics would not have been content to point out that he had not taken account of considerations that other judges have been attending to for some time. Most would have said that it was his duty to take the measure of these principles and that the plaintiff was entitled to have him do so. We mean no more, when we say that a *rule* is binding upon a judge, than that he must follow it if it applies, and that if he does not he will on that account have made a mistake.

It will not do to say that in a case like *Henningsen* the court is only 'morally' obligated to take particular principles into account, or that it is 'institutionally' obligated, or obligated as a matter of judicial 'craft', or something of that sort. The question will still remain why this type of obligation (whatever we call it) is different from the obligation that rules impose upon judges, and why it entitles us to say that principles and policies are not part of the law but are merely extra-legal standards 'courts characteristically use'.

(2) A positivist might argue that even though some principles are binding, in the sense that the judge must take them into account, they cannot determine a particular result. This is a harder argument to assess because it is not clear what it means for a standard to 'determine' a result. Perhaps it means that the standard *dictates* the result whenever it applies so that nothing else counts. If so, then it is certainly true that individual principles do not determine results, but that is only another way of saying that principles are not rules. Only rules dictate results, come what may. When a contrary result has been reached, the rule has been abandoned or changed. Principles do not work that way; they incline a decision one way, though not conclusively, and they survive intact when they do not prevail. This seems no reason for concluding that judges who must reckon with principles have discretion because a set of principles *can* dictate a result. If a judge believes that principles he is bound to recognize point in one direction and that principles pointing in the other direction, if any, are not of equal weight, then he must decide accordingly, just as he must follow what he believes to be a binding rule. He may, of course, be wrong in his assessment of the principles, but he may also be wrong in his judgment that the rule is binding. The sergeant and the referee, we might add, are often in the same boat. No one factor dictates which soldiers are the most experienced or which fighter the more aggressive. These officials must make judgments of the relative weights of these various factors; they do not on that account have discretion.

(3) A positivist might argue that principles cannot count as law because their authority, and even more so their weight, are congenitally *controversial*. It is true that generally we cannot *demonstrate* the authority or weight of a particular principle as we can sometimes demonstrate the validity of a

rule by locating it in an act of Congress or in the opinion of an authoritative court. Instead, we make a case for a principle, and for its weight, by appealing to an amalgam of practice and other principles in which the implications of legislative and judicial history figure along with appeals to community practices and understandings. There is no litmus paper for testing the sound- ness of such a case—it is a matter of judgment, and reasonable men may disagree. But again this does not distinguish the judge from other officials who do not have discretion. The sergeant has no litmus paper for experience, the referee none for aggressiveness. Neither of these has discretion, because he is bound to reach an understanding, controversial or not, of what his orders or the rules require, and to act on that understanding. That is the judge's duty as well.

Of course, if the positivists are right in another of their doctrines—the theory that in each legal system there is an ultimate *test* for binding law like Professor Hart's rule of recognition—it follows that principles are not binding law. But the incompatibility of principles with the positivists' theory can hardly be taken as an argument that principles must be treated any par- ticular way. That begs the question; we are interested in the status of prin- ciples because we want to evaluate the positivists' model. The positivist can- not defend his theory of a rule of recognition by fiat; if principles are not amenable to a test he must show some other reason why they cannot count as law. Since principles seem to play a role in arguments about legal obliga- tion (witness, again, *Riggs* and *Henningsen*), a model that provides for that role has some initial advantage over one that excludes it, and the latter can- not properly be inveighed in its own support.

These are the most obvious of the arguments a positivist might use for the doctrine of discretion in the strong sense, and for the second approach to principles. I shall mention one strong counter-argument against that doc- trine and in favour of the first approach. Unless at least some principles are acknowledged to be binding upon judges, requiring them as a set to reach particular decisions, then no rules, or very few rules, can be said to be binding upon them either.

In most American jurisdictions, and now in England also, the higher courts not infrequently reject established rules. Common-law rules—those developed by earlier court decisions—are sometimes overruled directly, and sometimes radically altered by further development. Statutory rules are sub- jected to interpretation and reinterpretation, sometimes even when the result is not to carry out what is called the 'legislative intent'.[22] If courts had dis- cretion to change established rules, then these rules would of course not be

[22] See Wellington and Albert, 'Statutory Interpretation and the Political Process: A Comment on *Sinclair* v. *Atkinson*', 72 Yale L.J. 1547 (1963).

binding upon them, and so would not be law on the positivists' model. The positivist must therefore argue that there are standards, themselves binding upon judges, that determine when a judge may overrule or alter an established rule, and when he may not.

When, then, is a judge permitted to change an existing rule of law? Principles figure in the answer in two ways. First, it is necessary, though not sufficient, that the judge find that the change would advance some policy or serve some principle, which policy or principle thus justifies the change. In *Riggs* the change (a new interpretation of the statute of wills) was justified by the principle that no man should profit from his own wrong; in *Henningsen* certain rules about automobile manufacturer's liability were altered on the basis of the principles and policies I quoted from the opinion of the court.

But not any principle will do to justify a change, or no rule would ever be safe. There must be some principles that count and others that do not, and there must be some principles that count for more than others. It could not depend on the judge's own preferences amongst a sea of respectable extra-legal standards, any one in principle eligible, because if that were the case we could not say that any rules were binding. We could always imagine a judge whose preferences amongst extra-legal standards were such as would justify a shift or radical re-interpretation of even the most entrenched rule.

Second, any judge who proposes to change existing doctrine must take account of some important standards that argue against departures from established doctrine, and these standards are also for the most part principles. They include the doctrine of 'legislative supremacy', a set of principles and policies that require the courts to pay a qualified deference to the acts of the legislature. They also include the doctrine of precedent, another set of principles and policies reflecting the equities and efficiencies of consistency. The doctrines of legislative supremacy and precedent incline toward the *status quo*, each within its sphere, but they do not command it. Judges are not free, however, to pick and choose amongst the principles and policies that make up these doctrines—if they were, again, no rule could be said to be binding.

Consider, therefore, what someone implies who says that a particular rule is binding. He may imply that the rule is affirmatively supported by principles the court is not free to disregard, and which are collectively more weighty than other principles that argue for a change. If not, he implies that any change would be condemned by a combination of conservative principles of legislative supremacy and precedent that the court is not free to ignore. Very often, he will imply both, for the conservative principles, being principles and not rules, are usually not powerful enough to save a common law rule or an aging statute that is entirely unsupported by substantive principles the court is bound to respect.

Either of these implications, of course, treats a body of principles and policies as law in the sense that rules are; it treats them as standards binding upon the officials of a community, controlling their decisions of legal right and obligation.

We are left with this issue. If the positivists' theory of judicial discretion is either trivial because it uses 'discretion' in a weak sense, or unsupported because the various arguments we can supply in its defence fall short, why have so many careful and intelligent lawyers embraced it? We can have no confidence in our treatment of that theory unless we can deal with that question. It is not enough to note (although perhaps it contributes to the explanation) that 'discretion' has different senses that may be confused. We do not confuse these senses when we are not thinking about law.

Part of the explanation, at least, lies in a lawyer's natural tendency to associate laws and rules, and to think of 'the law' as a collection or system of rules. Roscoe Pound, who diagnosed this tendency long ago, thought that English-speaking lawyers were tricked into it by the fact that English uses the same word, changing only the article, for 'a law'.[23] (Other languages, on the contrary, use two words: 'loi' and 'droit', for example, and 'Gesetz' and 'Recht'.) This may have had its effect, with the English speaking positivists, because the expression 'a law' certainly does suggest a rule. But the principal reason for associating law with rules runs deeper, and lies, I think, in the fact that legal education has for a long time consisted of teaching and examining those established rules that form the cutting edge of law.

In any event, if a lawyer thinks of law as a system of rules, and yet recognizes, as he must, that judges change old rules and introduce new ones, he will come naturally to the theory of judicial discretion in the strong sense. In those other systems of rules with which he has experience (like games), the rules are the only special authority that govern official decisions, so that if an umpire could change a rule, he would have discretion as to the subject matter of that rule. Any principles umpires might mention when changing the rules would represent only their 'characteristic' preferences. Positivists treat law like baseball revised in this way.

There is another, more subtle consequence of this initial assumption that law is a system of rules. When the positivists do attend to principles and policies, they treat them as rules *manqué*. They assume that *if* they are standards of law they must be rules, and so they read them as standards that are trying to be rules. When a positivist hears someone argue that legal principles are part of the law, he understands this to be an argument for what

[23] R. Pound, *An Introduction to the Philosophy of Law* (rev. edn., 1954), p. 56.

he calls the 'higher law' theory, that these principles are the rules of a law above the law.[24] He refutes this theory by pointing out that these 'rules' are sometimes followed and sometimes not, that for every 'rule' like 'no man shall profit from his own wrong' there is another competing 'rule' like 'the law favours security of title', and that there is no way to test the validity of 'rules' like these. He concludes that these principles and policies are not valid rules of a law above the law, which is true, because they are not rules at all. He also concludes that they are extra-legal standards which each judge selects according to his own lights in the exercise of his discretion, which is false. It is as if a zoologist had proved that fish are not mammals, and then concluded that they are really only plants.

V. THE RULE OF RECOGNITION

This discussion was provoked by our two competing accounts of legal principles. We have been exploring the second account, which the positivists seem to adopt through their doctrine of judicial discretion, and we have discovered grave difficulties. It is time to return to the fork in the road. What if we adopt the first approach? What would the consequences of this be for the skeletal structure of positivism? Of course we should have to drop the second tenet, the doctrine of judicial discretion (or, in the alternative, to make plain that the doctrine is to be read merely to say that judges must often exercise judgment). Would we also have to abandon or modify the first tenet, the proposition that law is distinguished by tests of the sort that can be set out in a master rule like Professor Hart's rule of recognition? If principles of the *Riggs* and *Henningsen* sort are to count as law, and we are nevertheless to preserve the notion of a master rule for law, then we must be able to deploy some test that all (and only) the principles that do count as law meet. Let us begin with the test Hart suggests for identifying valid *rules* of law, to see whether these can be made to work for principles as well.

Most rules of law, according to Hart, are valid because some competent institution enacted them. Some were created by a legislature, in the form of statutory enactments. Others were created by judges who formulated them to decide particular cases, and thus established them as precedents for the future. But this test of pedigree will not work for the *Riggs* and *Henningsen* principles. The origin of these as legal principles lies not in a particular decision of some legislature or court, but in a sense of appropriateness developed in the profession and the public over time. Their continued power depends upon this sense of appropriateness being sustained. If it no longer seemed unfair to allow people to profit by their wrongs, or fair to place

[24] See e.g., Dickinson, 'The Law Behind Law' (pts. 1 and 2), 29 Colum. L. Rev. 112, 254 (1929).

special burdens upon oligopolies that manufacture potentially dangerous machines, these principles would no longer play much of a role in new cases, even if they had never been overruled or repealed. (Indeed, it hardly makes sense to speak of principles like these as being 'overruled' or 'repealed'. When they decline they are eroded, not torpedoed.)

True, if we were challenged to back up our claim that some principle is a principle of law, we would mention any prior cases in which that principle was cited, or figured in the argument. We would also mention any statute that seemed to exemplify that principle (even better if the principle was cited in the preamble of the statute, or in the committee reports or other legislative documents that accompanied it). Unless we could find some such institutional support, we would probably fail to make out our case, and the more support we found, the more weight we could claim for the principle.

Yet we could not devise any formula for testing how much and what kind of institutional support is necessary to make a principle a legal principle, still less to fix its weight at a particular order of magnitude. We argue for a particular principle by grappling with a whole set of shifting, developing, and interacting standards (themselves principles rather than rules) about institutional responsibility, statutory interpretation, the persuasive force of various sorts of precedent, the relation of all these to contemporary moral practices, and hosts of other such standards. We could not bolt all of these together into a single 'rule', even a complex one, and if we could the result would bear little relation to Hart's picture of a rule of recognition, which is the picture of a fairly stable master rule specifying 'some feature or features possession of which by a suggested rule is taken as a conclusive affirmative indication that it is a rule'.[25]

Moreover, the techniques we apply in arguing for another principle do not stand (as Hart's rule of recognition is designed to) on an entirely different level from the principles they support. Hart's sharp distinction between acceptance and validity does not hold. If we are arguing for the principle that a man should not profit from his own wrong, we could cite the acts of courts and legislatures that exemplify it, but this speaks as much to the principle's acceptance as its validity. (It seems odd to speak of a principle as being valid at all, perhaps because validity is an all-or-nothing concept, appropriate for rules, but inconsistent with a principle's dimension of weight.) If we are asked (as we might well be) to defend the particular doctrine of precedent, or the particular technique of statutory interpretation, that we used in this argument, we should certainly cite the practice of others in using that doctrine or technique. But we should also cite other general principles that we believe support that practice, and this introduces a note of validity into the chord

[25] Hart, op. cit., p. 92.

of acceptance. We might argue, for example, that the use we make of earlier cases and statutes is supported by a particular analysis of the point of the practice of legislation or the doctrine of precedent, or by the principles of democratic theory, or by a particular position on the proper division of authority between national and local institutions, or something else of that sort. Nor is this path of support a one-way street leading to some ultimate principle resting on acceptance alone. Our principles of legislation, precedent, democracy, or federalism might be challenged too; and if they were we should argue for them, not only in terms of practice, but in terms of each other and in terms of the implications of trends of judicial and legislative decisions, even though this last would involve appealing to those same doctrines of interpretation we justified through the principles we are now trying to support. At this level of abstraction, in other words, principles rather hang together than link together.

So even though principles draw support from the official acts of legal institutions, they do not have a simple or direct enough connection with these acts to frame that connection in terms of criteria specified by some ultimate master rule of recognition. Is there any other route by which principles might be brought under such a rule?

Hart does say that a master rule might designate as law not only rules enacted by particular legal institutions, but rules established by custom as well. He has in mind a problem that bothered other positivists, including Austin. Many of our most ancient legal rules were never explicitly created by a legislature or a court. When they made their first appearance in legal opinions and texts, they were treated as already being part of the law because they represented the customary practice of the community, or some specialized part of it, like the business community. (The examples ordinarily given are rules of mercantile practice, like the rules governing what rights arise under a standard form of commercial paper.)[26] Since Austin thought that all law was the command of a determinate sovereign, he held that these customary practices were not law until the courts (as agents of the sovereign) recognized them, and that the courts were indulging in a fiction in pretending otherwise. But that seemed arbitrary. If everyone thought custom might in itself be law, the fact that Austin's theory said otherwise was not persuasive.

Hart reversed Austin on this point. The master rule, he says, might stipulate that some custom counts as law even before the courts recognize it. But he does not face the difficulty this raises for his general theory because he

---

[26] See Note, 'Custom and Trade Usage: Its Application to Commercial Dealings and the Common Law', 55 Colum. L. Rev. 1192 (1955), and materials cited therein at 1193 n. 1. As that note makes plain, the actual practices of courts in recognizing trade customs follow the pattern of applying a set of general principles and policies rather than a test that could be captured as part of a rule of recognition.

does not attempt to set out the criteria a master rule might use for this purpose. It cannot use, as its only criterion, the provision that the community regard the practice as *morally* binding, for this would not distinguish legal customary rules from moral customary rules, and of course not all of the community's long-standing customary moral obligations are enforced at law. If, on the other hand, the test is whether the community regards the customary practice as *legally* binding, the whole point of the master rule is undercut, at least for this class of legal rules. The master rule, says Hart, marks the transformation from a primitive society to one with law, because it provides a test for determining social rules of law other than by measuring their acceptance. But if the master rule says merely that whatever other rules the community accepts as legally binding are legally binding, then it provides no such test at all, beyond the test we should use were there no master rule. The master rule becomes (for these cases) a non-rule of recognition; we might as well say that every primitive society has a secondary rule of recognition, namely the rule that whatever is accepted as binding is binding. Hart himself, in discussing international law, ridicules the idea that such a rule could be a rule of recognition, by describing the proposed rule as 'an empty repetition of the mere fact that the society concerned . . . observes certain standards of conduct as obligatory rules.'[27]

Hart's treatment of custom amounts, indeed, to a confession that there are at least some rules of law that are not binding because they are valid under standards laid down by a master rule but are binding—like the master rule—because they are accepted as binding by the community. This chips at the neat pyramidal architecture we admired in Hart's theory: we can no longer say that only the master rule is binding because of its acceptance, all other rules being valid under its terms.

This is perhaps only a chip, because the customary rules Hart has in mind are no longer a very significant part of the law. But it does suggest that Hart would be reluctant to widen the damage by bringing under the head of 'custom' all those crucial principles and policies we have been discussing. If he were to call these part of the law and yet admit that the only test of their force lies in the degree to which they are accepted as law by the community or some part thereof, he would very sharply reduce that area of the law over which his master rule held any dominion. It is not just that all the principles and policies would escape its sway, though that would be bad enough. Once these principles and policies are accepted as law, and thus as standards judges must follow in determining legal obligations, it would follow that *rules* like those announced for the first time in *Riggs* and *Henningsen* owe

[27] Hart, op. cit., p. 230.

their force at least in part to the authority of principles and policies, and so not entirely to the master rule of recognition.

So we cannot adapt Hart's version of positivism by modifying his rule of recognition to embrace principles. No tests of pedigree, relating principles to acts of legislation, can be formulated, nor can his concept of customary law, itself an exception to the first tenet of positivism, be made to serve without abandoning that tenet altogether. One more possibility must be considered, however. If no rule of recognition can provide a test for identifying principles, why not say that principles are ultimate, and *form* the rule of recognition of our law? The answer to the general question 'What is valid law in an American jurisdiction?' would then require us to state all the principles (as well as ultimate constitutional rules) in force in that jurisdiction at the time, together with appropriate assignments of weight. A positivist might then regard the complete set of these standards as the rule of recognition of the jurisdiction. This solution has the attraction of paradox, but of course it is an unconditional surrender. If we simply designate our rule of recognition by the phrase 'the complete set of principles in force', we achieve only the tautology that law is law. If, instead, we tried actually to list all the principles in force we would fail. They are controversial, their weight is all important, they are numberless, and they shift and change so fast that the start of our list would be obsolete before we reached the middle. Even if we succeeded, we would not have a key for law because there would be nothing left for our key to unlock.

I conclude that if we treat principles as law we must reject the positivists' first tenet, that the law of a community is distinguished from other social standards by some test in the form of a master rule. We have already decided that we must then abandon the second tenet—the doctrine of judicial discretion—or clarify it into triviality. What of the third tenet, the positivists' theory of legal obligation?

This theory holds that a legal obligation exists when (and only when) an established rule of law imposes such an obligation. It follows from this that in a hard case—when no such established rule can be found—there is no legal obligation until the judge creates a new rule for the future. The judge may apply that new rule to the parties in the case, but this is *ex post facto* legislation, not the enforcement of an existing obligation.

The positivists' doctrine of discretion (in the strong sense) required this view of legal obligation, because if a judge has discretion there can be no legal right or obligation—no entitlement—that he must enforce. Once we abandon that doctrine, however, and treat principles as law, we raise the possibility, that a legal obligation might be imposed by a constellation of principles as well as by an established rule. We might want to say that a legal obligation exists whenever the case supporting such an obligation, in terms of binding legal principles of different sorts, is stronger than the case against it.

Of course, many questions would have to be answered before we could accept that view of legal obligation. If there is no rule of recognition, no test for law in that sense, how do we decide which principles are to count, and how much, in making such a case? How do we decide whether one case is better than another? If legal obligation rests on an undemonstrable judgment of that sort, how can it provide a justification for a judicial decision that one party had a legal obligation? Does this view of obligation square with the way lawyers, judges, and laymen speak, and is it consistent with our attitudes about moral obligation? Does this analysis help us to deal with the classical jurisprudential puzzles about the nature of law?

These questions must be faced, but even the questions promise more than positivism provides. Positivism, on its own thesis, stops short of just those puzzling, hard cases that send us to look for theories of law. When we reach these cases, the positivist remits us to a doctrine of discretion that leads nowhere and tells nothing. His picture of law as a system of rules has exercised a tenacious hold on our imagination, perhaps through its very simplicity. If we shake ourselves loose from this model of rules, we may be able to build a model truer to the complexity and sophistication of our own practices.

III

MORALS AND THE CRIMINAL LAW

LORD PATRICK DEVLIN

THE Report of the Committee on Homosexual Offences and Prostitution, generally known as the Wolfenden Report, is recognized to be an excellent study of two very difficult legal and social problems. But it has also a particular claim to the respect of those interested in jurisprudence; it does what law reformers so rarely do; it sets out clearly and carefully what in relation to its subjects it considers the function of the law to be.[1] Statutory additions to the criminal law are too often made on the simple principle that 'there ought to be a law against it'. The greater part of the law relating to sexual offences is the creation of statute and it is difficult to ascertain any logical relationship between it and the moral ideas which most of us uphold. Adultery, fornication, and prostitution are not, as the Report[2] points out, criminal offences: homosexuality between males is a criminal offence, but between females it is not. Incest was not an offence until it was declared so by statute only fifty years ago. Does the legislature select these offences haphazardly or are there some principles which can be used to determine what part of the moral law should be embodied in the criminal? There is, for example, being now considered a proposal to make A.I.D., that is, the practice of artificial insemination of a woman with the seed of a man who is not her husband, a criminal offence; if, as is usually the case, the woman is married, this is in substance, if not in form, adultery. Ought it to be made punishable when adultery is not? This sort of question is of practical importance, for a law that appears to be arbitrary and illogical, in the end and after the wave of moral indignation that has put it on the statute book subsides, forfeits respect. As a practical question it arises more frequently in the field of sexual morals than in any other, but there is no special answer to be found

---

[1] The Committee's 'statement of juristic philosophy' (to quote Lord Pakenham) was considered by him in a debate in the House of Lords on 4 December 1957, reported in *Hansard Lords Debates*, vol. ccvi at 738; and also in the same debate by the Archbishop of Canterbury at 753 and Lord Denning at 806. The subject has also been considered by Mr. J. E. Hall Williams in the *Law Quarterly Review*, January 1958, vol. lxxiv, p. 76.

[2] Para. 14.

in that field. The inquiry must be general and fundamental. What is the connection between crime and sin and to what extent, if at all, should the criminal law of England concern itself with the enforcement of morals and punish sin or immorality as such?

The statements of principle in the Wolfenden Report provide an admirable and modern starting-point for such an inquiry. In the course of my examination of them I shall find matter for criticism. If my criticisms are sound, it must not be imagined that they point to any shortcomings in the Report. Its authors were not, as I am trying to do, composing a paper on the jurisprudence of morality; they were evolving a working formula to use for reaching a number of practical conclusions. I do not intend to express any opinion one way or the other about these; that would be outside the scope of a lecture on jurisprudence. I am concerned only with general principles; the statement of these in the Report illuminates the entry into the subject and I hope that its authors will forgive me if I carry the lamp with me into places where it was not intended to go.

Early in the Report[3] the Committee put forward:

Our own formulation of the function of the criminal law so far as it concerns the subjects of this enquiry. In this field, its function, as we see it, is to preserve public order and decency, to protect the citizen from what is offensive or injurious, and to provide sufficient safeguards against exploitation and corruption of others, particularly those who are specially vulnerable because they are young, weak in body or mind, inexperienced, or in a state of special physical, official or economic dependence.

It is not, in our view, the function of the law to intervene in the private lives of citizens, or to seek to enforce any particular pattern of behaviour, further than is necessary to carry out the purposes we have outlined.

The Committee preface their most important recommendation[4]

that homosexual behaviour between consenting adults in private should no longer be a criminal offence, [by stating the argument[5]] which we believe to be decisive, namely, the importance which society and the law ought to give to individual freedom of choice and action in matters of private morality. Unless a deliberate attempt is to be made by society, acting through the agency of the law, to equate the sphere of crime with that of sin, there must remain a realm of private morality and immorality which is, in brief and crude terms, not the law's business. To say this is not to condone or encourage private immorality.

Similar statements of principle are set out in the chapters of the Report which deal with prostitution. No case can be sustained, the Report says, for attempting to make prostitution itself illegal.[6] The Committee refer to

[3] Para. 13
[4] Para. 62.
[5] Para. 61.
[6] Para. 224.

the general reasons already given and add: 'We are agreed that private immorality should not be the concern of the criminal law except in the special circumstances therein mentioned.' They quote[7] with approval the report of the Street Offences Committee,[8] which says: 'As a general proposition it will be universally accepted that the law is not concerned with private morals or with ethical sanctions.' It will be observed that the emphasis is on *private* immorality. By this is meant immorality which is not offensive or injurious to the public in the ways defined or described in the first passage which I quoted. In other words, no act of immorality should be made a criminal offence unless it is accompanied by some other feature such as indecency, corruption, or exploitation. This is clearly brought out in relation to prostitution: 'It is not the duty of the law to concern itself with immorality as such ... it should confine itself to those activities which offend against public order and decency or expose the ordinary citizen to what is offensive or injurious.[9]

These statements of principle are naturally restricted to the subject-matter of the Report. But they are made in general terms and there seems to be no reason why, if they are valid, they should not be applied to the criminal law in general. They separate very decisively crime from sin, the divine law from the secular, and the moral from the criminal. They do not signify any lack of support for the law, moral or criminal, and they do not represent an attitude that can be called either religious or irreligious. There are many schools of thought among those who may think that morals are not the law's business. There is first of all the agnostic or free-thinker. He does not of course disbelieve in morals, nor in sin if it be given the wider of the two meanings assigned to it in the *Oxford English Dictionary* where it is defined as 'transgression against divine law or the principles of morality'. He cannot accept the divine law; that does not mean that he might not view with suspicion any departure from moral principles that have for generations been accepted by the society in which he lives; but in the end he judges for himself. Then there is the deeply religious person who feels that the criminal law is sometimes more of a hindrance than a help in the sphere of morality, and that the reform of the sinner--at any rate when he injures only himself-- should be a spiritual rather than a temporal work. Then there is the man who without any strong feeling cannot see why, where there is freedom in religious belief, there should not logically be freedom in morality as well. All these are powerfully allied against the equating of crime with sin.

I must disclose at the outset that I have as a judge an interest in the result

[7] Para. 227.
[8] Cmd. 3231 (1928).
[9] Para. 257.

of the inquiry which I am seeking to make as a jurisprudent. As a judge who administers the criminal law and who has often to pass sentence in a criminal court, I should feel handicapped in my task if I thought that I was addressing an audience which had no sense of sin or which thought of crime as something quite different. Ought one, for example, in passing sentence upon a female abortionist to treat her simply as if she were an un-licenced midwife? If not, why not? But if so, is all the panoply of the law erected over a set of social regulations? I must admit that I begin with a feeling that a complete separation of crime from sin (I use the term through-out this lecture in the wider meaning) would not be good for the moral law and might be disastrous for the criminal. But can this sort of feeling be justi-fied as a matter of jurisprudence? And if it be a right feeling, how should the relationship between the criminal and the moral law be stated? Is there a good theoretical basis for it, or is it just a practical working alliance, or is it a bit of both? That is the problem which I want to examine, and I shall begin by considering the standpoint of the strict logician. It can be supported by cogent arguments, some of which I believe to be unanswerable and which I put as follows.

Morals and religion are inextricably joined—the moral standards gener-ally accepted in Western civilization being those belonging to Christianity. Outside Christendom other standards derive from other religions. None of these moral codes can claim any validity except by virtue of the religion on which it is based. Old Testament morals differ in some respects from New Testament morals. Even within Christianity there are differences. Some hold that contraception is an immoral practice and that a man who has carnal knowledge of another woman while his wife is alive is in all circum-stances a fornicator; others, including most of the English-speaking world, deny both these propositions. Between the great religions of the world, of which Christianity is only one, there are much wider differences. It may or may not be right for the State to adopt one of these religions as the truth, to found itself upon its doctrines, and to deny to any of its citizens the liberty to practise any other. If it does, it is logical that it should use the secular law wherever it thinks it necessary to enforce the divine. If it does not, it is illogical that it should concern itself with morals as such. But if it leaves matters of religion to private judgment, it should logically leave matters of morals also. A State which refuses to enforce Christian beliefs has lost the right to enforce Christian morals.

If this view is sound, it means that the criminal law cannot justify any of its provisions by reference to the moral law. It cannot say, for example, that murder and theft are prohibited because they are immoral or sinful. The State must justify in some other way the punishments which it imposes on wrongdoers and a function for the criminal law independent of morals must be found. This is not difficult to do. The smooth functioning of society and the preservation of order require that a number of activities should be regulated. The rules that are made for that purpose and are enforced by the criminal law are often designed simply to achieve uniformity and convenience and rarely involve any choice between good and evil. Rules that impose a speed limit or prevent obstruction on the highway have nothing to do with morals. Since so much of the criminal law is composed of rules of this sort, why bring morals into it at all? Why not define the function of the criminal law in simple terms as the preservation of order and decency and the protection of the lives and property of citizens, and elaborate those terms in relation to any particular subject in the way in which it is done in the Wolfenden Report? The criminal law in carrying out these objects will undoubtedly overlap the moral law. Crimes of violence are morally wrong and they are also offences against good order; therefore they offend against both laws. But this is simply because the two laws in pursuit of different objectives happen to cover the same area. Such is the argument.

Is the argument consistent or inconsistent with the fundamental principles of English criminal law as it exists today? That is the first way of testing it, though by no means a conclusive one. In the field of jurisprudence one is at liberty to overturn even fundamental conceptions if they are theoretically unsound. But to see how the argument fares under the existing law is a good starting-point.

It is true that for many centuries the criminal law was much concerned with keeping the peace and little, if at all, with sexual morals. But it would be wrong to infer from that that it had no moral content or that it would ever have tolerated the idea of a man being left to judge for himself in matters of morals. The criminal law of England has from the very first concerned itself with moral principles. A simple way of testing this point is to consider the attitude which the criminal law adopts towards consent.

Subject to certain exceptions inherent in the nature of particular crimes, the criminal law has never permitted consent of the victim to be used as a defence. In rape, for example, consent negatives an essential element. But consent of the victim is no defence to a charge of murder. It is not a defence to any form of assault that the victim thought his punishment well deserved and submitted to it; to make a good defence the accused must prove that the law gave him the right to chastise and that he exercised it reasonably. Likewise, the victim may not forgive the aggressor and require the prosecution to desist; the right to enter a *nolle prosequi* belongs to the Attorney-General alone.

Now, if the law existed for the protection of the individual, there would be no reason why he should avail himself of it if he did not want it. The reason why a man may not consent to the commission of an offence against himself beforehand or forgive it afterwards is because it is an offence against society. It is not that society is physically injured; that would be impossible. Nor need any individual be shocked, corrupted, or exploited; everything may be done in private. Nor can it be explained on the practical ground that a violent man is a potential danger to others in the community who have therefore a direct interest in his apprehension and punishment as being necessary to their own protection. That would be true of a man whom the victim is prepared to forgive but not of one who gets his consent first; a murderer who acts only upon the consent, and maybe the request, of his victim is no menace to others, but he does threaten one of the great moral principles upon which society is based, that is, the sanctity of human life. There is only one explanation of what has hitherto been accepted as the basis of the criminal law and that is that there are certain standards of behaviour or moral principles which society requires to be observed; and the breach of them is an offence not merely against the person who is injured but against society as a whole.

Thus, if the criminal law were to be reformed so as to eliminate from it everything that was not designed to preserve order and decency or to protect citizens (including the protection of youth from corruption), it would overturn a fundamental principle. It would also end a number of specific crimes. Euthanasia or the killing of another at his own request, suicide, attempted suicide, and suicide pacts, duelling, abortion, incest between brother and sister, are all acts which can be done in private and without offence to others and need not involve the corruption or exploitation of others. Many people think that the law on some of these subjects is in need of reform, but no one hitherto has gone so far as to suggest that they should all be left outside the criminal law as matters of private morality. They can be brought within it only as a matter of moral principle. It must be remembered also that although there is much immorality that is not punished by the law, there is none that is condoned by the law. The law will not allow its processes to be used by those engaged in immorality of any sort. For example, a house may not be let for immoral purposes; the lease is invalid and would not be enforced. But if what goes on inside there is a matter of private morality and not the law's business, why does the law inquire into it all?

I think it is clear that the criminal law as we know it is based upon moral principle. In a number of crimes its function is simply to enforce a moral principle and nothing else. The law, both criminal and civil, claims to be able to speak about morality and immorality generally. Where does it get its authority to do this and how does it settle the moral principles which it enforces? Undoubtedly, as a matter of history, it derived both from Christian teaching. But I think that the strict logician is right when he says that the law can no longer rely on doctrines in which citizens are entitled to disbelieve. It is necessary therefore to look for some other source.

In jurisprudence, as I have said, everything is thrown open to discussion and, in the belief that they cover the whole field, I have framed three inter-rogatories addressed to myself to answer:

1. Has society the right to pass judgment at all on matters of morals? Ought there, in other words, to be a public morality, or are morals always a matter for private judgment?

2. If society has the right to pass judgment, has it also the right to use the weapon of the law to enforce it?

3. If so, ought it to use that weapon in all cases or only in some; and if only in some, on what principles should it distinguish?

I shall begin with the first interrogatory and consider what is meant by the right of society to pass a moral judgment, that is, a judgment about what is good and what is evil. The fact that a majority of people may disapprove of a practice does not of itself make it a matter for society as a whole. Nine men out of ten may disapprove of what the tenth man is doing and still say that it is not their business. There is a case for a collective judgment (as distinct from a large number of individual opinions which sensible people may even refrain from pronouncing at all if it is upon somebody else's private affairs) only if society is affected. Without a collective judgment there can be no case at all for intervention. Let me take as an illustration the English-man's attitude to religion as it is now and as it has been in the past. His attitude now is that a man's religion is his private affair; he may think of another man's religion that it is right or wrong, true or untrue, but not that it is good or bad. In earlier times that was not so; a man was denied the right to practise what was thought of as heresy, and heresy was thought of as destructive of society.

The language used in the passages I have quoted from the Wolfenden Report suggests the view that there ought not to be a collective judgment about immorality *per se*. Is this what is meant by 'private morality' and 'in-dividual freedom of choice and action'? Some people sincerely believe that homosexuality is neither immoral nor unnatural. Is the 'freedom of choice and action' that is offered to the individual, freedom to decide for himself what is moral or immoral, society remaining neutral; or is it freedom to be immoral if he wants to be? The language of the Report may be open to question, but the conclusions at which the Committee arrive answer this question unambiguously. If society is not prepared to say that homosexuality is morally wrong, there would be no basis for a law protecting youth from 'corruption' or punishing a man for living on the 'immoral' earnings of a homosexual prostitute, as the Report recommends.[10] This attitude the Committee make even clearer when they come to deal with prostitution. In truth, the Report takes it for granted that there is in existence a public morality which condemns homosexuality and prostitution. What the Report seems to mean by private morality might perhaps be better described as private behaviour in matters of morals.

This view—that there is such a thing as public morality—can also be justified by *a priori* argument. What makes a society of any sort is community of ideas, not only political ideas but also ideas about the way its members should behave and govern their lives; these latter ideas are its morals. Every society has a moral structure as well as a political one: or rather, since that might suggest two independent systems, I should say that the structure of every society is made up both of politics and morals. Take, for example, the institution of marriage. Whether a man should be allowed to take more than one wife is something about which every society has to make up its mind one way or the other. In England we believe in the Christian idea of marriage and therefore adopt monogamy as a moral principle. Consequently the Christian institution of marriage has become the basis of family life and so part of the structure of our society. It is there not because it is Christian. It has got there because it is Christian, but it remains there because it is built into the house in which we live and could not be removed without bringing it down. The great majority of those who live in this country accept it because it is the Christian idea of marriage and for them the only true one. But a non-Christian is bound by it, not because it is part of Christianity but because, rightly or wrongly, it has been adopted by the society in which he lives. It would be useless for him to stage a debate designed to prove that polygamy was theologically more correct and socially preferable; if he wants to live in the house, he must accept it as built in the way in which it is.

We see this more clearly if we think of ideas or institutions that are purely political. Society cannot tolerate rebellion; it will not allow argument about the rightness of the cause. Historians a century later may say that the rebels were right and the Government was wrong and a percipient and conscientious subject of the State may think so at the time. But it is not a matter which can be left to individual judgment.

The institution of marriage is a good example for my purpose because it bridges the division, if there is one, between politics and morals. Marriage is part of the structure of our society and it is also the basis of a moral code which condemns fornication and adultery. The institution of marriage would

[10] Para. 76.

be gravely threatened if individual judgments were permitted about the morality of adultery; on these points there must be a public morality. But public morality is not to be confined to those moral principles which support institutions such as marriage. People do not think of monogamy as something which has to be supported because our society has chosen to organize itself upon it; they think of it as something that is good in itself and offering a good way of life and that it is for that reason that our society has adopted it. I return to the statement that I have already made, that society means a community of ideas; without shared ideas on politics, morals, and ethics no society can exist. Each one of us has ideas about what is good and what is evil; they cannot be kept private from the society in which we live. If men and women try to create a society in which there is no fundamental agreement about good and evil they will fail; if, having based it on common agreement, the agreement goes, the society will disintegrate. For society is not something that is kept together physically; it is held by the invisible bonds of common thought. If the bonds were too far relaxed the members would drift apart. A common morality is part of the bondage. The bondage is part of the price of society; and mankind, which needs society, must pay its price.

Common lawyers used to say that Christianity was part of the law of the land. That was never more than a piece of rhetoric as Lord Sumner said in *Bowman* v. *The Secular Society*.[11] What lay behind it was the notion which I have been seeking to expound, namely that morals—and until a century or so ago no one thought it worth distinguishing between religion and morals—were necessary to the temporal order. In 1675 Chief Justice Hale said: 'To say that religion is a cheat is to dissolve all those obligations whereby civil society is preserved.'[12] In 1797 Mr. Justice Ashurst said of blasphemy that it was 'not only an offence against God but against all law and government from its tendency to dissolve all the bonds and obligations of civil society'.[13] By 1908 Mr. Justice Phillimore was able to say: 'A man is free to think, to speak and to teach what he pleases as to religious matters, but not as to morals'.[14]

You may think that I have taken far too long in contending that there is such a thing as public morality, a proposition which most people would readily accept, and may have left myself too little time to discuss the next question which to many minds may cause greater difficulty: to what extent should society use the law to enforce its moral judgments? But I believe that the answer to the first question determines the way in which the second

[11] (1917), A.C. 406, at 457.
[12] *Taylor's Case*, 1 Vent. 293.
[13] *R.* v. *Williams*, 26 St. Tr. 653, at 715.
[14] *R.* v. *Boulter*, 72 J.P. 188.

should be approached and may indeed very nearly dictate the answer to the second question. If society has no right to make judgments on morals, the law must find some special justification for entering the field of morality: if homosexuality and prostitution are not in themselves wrong, then the onus is very clearly on the lawgiver who wants to frame a law against certain aspects of them to justify the exceptional treatment. But if society has the right to make a judgment and has it on the basis that a recognized morality is as necessary to society as, say, a recognized government, then society may use the law to preserve morality in the same way as it uses it to safeguard anything else that is essential to its existence. If therefore the first proposition is securely established with all its implications, society has a prima facie right to legislate against immorality as such.

The Wolfenden Report, notwithstanding that it seems to admit the right of society to condemn homosexuality and prostitution as immoral, requires special circumstances to be shown to justify the intervention of the law. I think that this is wrong in principle and that any attempt to approach my second interrogatory on these lines is bound to break down. I think that the attempt by the Committee does break down and that this is shown by the fact that it has to define or describe its special circumstances so widely that they can be supported only if it is accepted that the law *is* concerned with immorality as such.

The widest of the special circumstances are described as the provision of 'sufficient safeguards against exploitation and corruption of others, particularly those who are specially vulnerable because they are young, weak in body or mind, inexperienced, or in a state of special physical, official or economic dependence'.[15] The corruption of youth is a well-recognized ground for intervention by the State and for the purpose of any legislation the young can easily be defined. But if similar protection were to be extended to every other citizen, there would be no limit to the reach of the law. The 'corruption and exploitation of others' is so wide that it could be used to cover any sort of immorality which involves, as most do, the co-operation of another person. Even if the phrase is taken as limited to the categories that are particularized as 'specially vulnerable', it is so elastic as to be practically no restriction. This is not merely a matter of words. For if the words used are stretched almost beyond breaking-point, they still are not wide enough to cover the recommendations which the Committee make about prostitution.

Prostitution is not in itself illegal and the Committee do not think that it ought to be made so.[16] If prostitution is private immorality and not the law's business, what concern has the law with the ponce or the brothel-keeper

---

[15] Para. 13.
[16] Paras. 224, 285, and 318.

or the householder who permits habitual prostitution? The Report recommends that the laws which make these activities criminal offences should be maintained or strengthened and brings them (so far as it goes into principle; with regard to brothels it says simply that the law rightly frowns on them) under the head of exploitation.[17] There may be cases of exploitation in this trade, as there are or used to be in many others, but in general a ponce exploits a prostitute no more than an impressario exploits an actress. The Report finds that 'the great majority of prostitutes are women whose psychological makeup is such that they choose this life because they find in it a style of living which is to them easier, freer and more profitable than would be provided by any other occupation. . . . In the main the association between prostitute and ponce is voluntary and operates to mutual advantage'.[18] The Committee would agree that this could not be called exploitation in the ordinary sense. They say: 'It is in our view an over-simplification to think that those who live on the earnings of prostitution are exploiting the prostitute as such. What they are really exploiting is the whole complex of the relationship between prostitute and customer; they are, in effect, exploiting the human weaknesses which cause the customer to seek the prostitute and the prostitute to meet the demand'.[19]

All sexual immorality involves the exploitation of human weaknesses. The prostitute exploits the lust of her customers and the customer the moral weakness of the prostitute. If the exploitation of human weaknesses is-considered to create a special circumstance, there is virtually no field of morality which can be defined in such a way as to exclude the law.

I think, therefore, that it is not possible to set theoretical limits to the power of the State to legislate against immorality. It is not possible to settle in advance exceptions to the general rule or to define inflexibly areas of morality into which the law is in no circumstances to be allowed to enter. Society is entitled by means of its laws to protect itself from dangers, whether from within or without. Here again I think that the political parallel is legitimate. The law of treason is directed against aiding the king's enemies and against sedition from within. The justification for this is that established government is necessary for the existence of society and therefore its safety against violent overthrow must be secured. But an established morality is as necessary as good government to the welfare of society. Societies disintegrate from within more frequently than they are broken up by external pressures. There is disintegration when no common morality is observed and history shows that the loosening of moral bonds is often the first stage

[17] Paras. 302 and 320.
[18] Para. 223.
[19] Para. 306.

of disintegration, so that society is justified in taking the same steps to preserve its moral code as it does to preserve its government and other essential institutions.[20] The suppression of vice is as much the law's business as the suppression of subversive activities; it is no more possible to define a sphere of private morality than it is to define one of private subversive activity. It is wrong to talk of private morality or of the law not being concerned with immorality as such or to try to set rigid bounds to the part which the law may play in the suppression of vice. There are no theoretical limits to the power of the State to legislate against treason and sedition, and likewise I think there can be no theoretical limits to legislation against immorality. You may argue that if a man's sins affect only himself it cannot be the concern of society. If he chooses to get drunk every night in the privacy of his own home, is any one except himself the worse for it? But suppose a quarter or a half of the population got drunk every night, what sort of society would

[20] It is somewhere about this point in the argument that Professor Hart in *Law, Liberty and Morality* discerns a proposition which he describes as central to my thought. He states the proposition and his objection to it as follows (p. 51). 'He appears to move from the acceptable proposition that *some* shared morality is essential to the existence of any society [this I take to be the proposition on p. 75] to the unacceptable proposition that a society is identical with its morality as that is at any given moment of its history so that a change in its morality is tantamount to the destruction of a society. The former proposition might be even accepted as a necessary rather than an empirical truth depending on a quite plausible definition of society as a body of men who hold certain moral views in common. But the latter proposition is absurd. Taken strictly, it would prevent us saying that the morality of a given society had changed, and would compel us instead to say that one society had disappeared and another one taken its place. But it is only on this absurd criterion of what it is for the same society to continue to exist that it could be asserted without evidence that any deviation from a society's shared morality threatens its existence.' In conclusion (p. 82) Professor Hart condemns the whole thesis in the lecture as based on 'a confused definition of what a society is'.

I do not assert that *any* deviation from a society's shared morality threatens its existence any more than I assert that *any* subversive activity threatens its existence. I assert that they are both activities which are capable in their nature of threatening the existence of society so that neither can be put beyond the law.

For the rest, the objection appears to me to be all a matter of words. I would venture to assert, for example, that you cannot have a game without rules and that if there were no rules there would be no game. If I am asked whether that means that the game is 'identical' with the rules, I would be willing for the question to be answered either way in the belief that the answer would lead to nowhere. If I am asked whether a change in the rules means that one game has disappeared and another has taken its place, I would reply probably not, but that it would depend on the extent of the change.

Likewise I should venture to assert that there cannot be a contract without terms. Does this mean that an 'amended' contract is a 'new' contract in the eyes of the law? I once listened to an argument by an ingenious counsel that a contract, because of the substitution of one clause for another, had 'ceased to have effect' within the meaning of a statutory provision. The judge did not accept the argument; but if most of the fundamental terms had been changed, I daresay he would have done.

The proposition that I make in the text is that if (as I understand Professor Hart to agree, at any rate for the purposes of the argument) you cannot have a society without morality, the law can be used to enforce morality as something that is essential to a society. I cannot see why this proposition (whether it is right or wrong) should mean that morality can never be changed without the destruction of society. If morality is changed, the law can be changed. Professor Hart refers (p. 72) to the proposition as 'the use of legal punishment to freeze into immobility the morality dominant at a particular time in a society's existence.' One might as well say that the inclusion of a penal section into a statute prohibiting certain acts freezes the whole statute into immobility and prevents the prohibitions from ever being modified.

it be? You cannot set a theoretical limit to the number of people who can get drunk before society is entitled to legislate against drunkenness. The same may be said of gambling. The Royal Commission on Betting, Lotteries, and Gaming took as their test the character of the citizen as a member of society. They said: 'Our concern with the ethical significance of gambling is confined to the effect which it may have on the character of the gambler as a member of society. If we were convinced that whatever the degree of gambling this effect must be harmful we should be inclined to think that it was the duty of the State to restrict gambling to the greatest extent practicable.[21]

In what circumstances the State should exercise its power is the third of the interrogatories I have framed. But before I get to it I must raise a point which might have been brought up in any one of the three. How are the moral judgments of society to be ascertained? By leaving it until now, I can ask it in the more limited form that is now sufficient for my purpose. How is the law-maker to ascertain the moral judgments of society? It is surely not enough that they should be reached by the opinion of the majority; it would be too much to require the individual assent of every citizen. English law has evolved and regularly uses a standard which does not depend on the counting of heads. It is that of the reasonable man. He is not to be confused with the rational man. He is not expected to reason about anything and his judgment may be largely a matter of feeling. It is the viewpoint of the man in the street—or to use an archaism familiar to all lawyers—the man in the Clapham omnibus. He might also be called the right-minded man. For my purpose I should like to call him the man in the jury box, for the moral judgment of society must be something about which any twelve men or women drawn at random might after discussion be expected to be unanimous. This was the standard the judges applied in the days before Parliament was as active as it is now and when they laid down rules of public policy. They did not think of themselves as making law but simply as stating principles which every right-minded person would accept as valid. It is what Pollock called 'practical morality', which is based not on theological or philosophical foundations but 'in the mass of continuous experience half-consciously or unconsciously accumulated and embodied in the morality of common sense'. He called it also 'a certain way of thinking on questions of morality which we expect to find in a reasonable civilized man or a reasonable Englishman, taken at random'.[22]

Immorality then, for the purpose of the law, is what every right-minded person is presumed to consider to be immoral. Any immorality is capable

[21] (1951) Cmd. 8190, para. 159.
[22] *Essays in Jurisprudence and Ethics* (Macmillan, 1882), pp. 278 and 353.

of affecting society injuriously and in effect to a greater or lesser extent it usually does; this is what gives the law its *locus standi*. It cannot be shut out. But—and this brings me to the third question—the individual has a *locus standi* too; he cannot be expected to surrender to the judgment of society the whole conduct of his life. It is the old and familiar question of striking a balance between the rights and interests of society and those of the individual. This is something which the law is constantly doing in matters large and small. To take a very down-to-earth example, let me consider the right of the individual whose house adjoins the highway to have access to it; that means in these days the right to have vehicles stationary in the highway, sometimes for a considerable time if there is a lot of loading or unloading. There are many cases in which the courts have had to balance the private right of access against the public right to use the highway without obstruction. It cannot be done by carving up the highway into public and private areas. It is done by recognizing that each have rights over the whole; that if each were to exercise their rights to the full, they would come into conflict; and therefore that the rights of each must be curtailed so as to ensure as far as possible that the essential needs of each are safeguarded.

I do not think that one can talk sensibly of a public and private morality any more than one can of a public or private highway. Morality is a sphere in which there is a public interest and a private interest, often in conflict, and the problem is to reconcile the two. This does not mean that it is impossible to put forward any general statements about how in our society the balance ought to be struck. Such statements cannot of their nature be rigid or precise; they would not be designed to circumscribe the operation of the law-making power but to guide those who have to apply it. While every decision which a court of law makes when it balances the public against the private interest is an *ad hoc* decision, the cases contain statements of principle to which the court should have regard when it reaches its decision. In the same way it is possible to make general statements of principle which it may be thought the legislature should bear in mind when it is considering the enactment of laws enforcing morals.

I believe that most people would agree upon the chief of these elastic principles. There must be toleration of the maximum individual freedom that is consistent with the integrity of society. It cannot be said that this is a principle that runs all through the criminal law. Much of the criminal law that is regulatory in character—the part of it that deals with *malum prohibitum* rather than *malum in se*—is based upon the opposite principle, that is, that the choice of the individual must give way to the convenience of the many. But in all matters of conscience the principle I have stated is generally held to prevail. It is not confined to thought and speech; it extends to action, as is shown by the recognition of the right to conscientious objection in war-time; this example shows also that conscience will be respected even in times of national danger. The principle appears to me to be peculiarly appropriate to all questions of morals. Nothing should be punished by the law that does not lie beyond the limits of tolerance. It is not nearly enough to say that a majority dislike a practice; there must be a real feeling of reprobation. Those who are dissatisfied with the present law on homosexuality often say that the opponents of reform are swayed simply by disgust. If that were so it would be wrong, but I do not think one can ignore disgust if it is deeply felt and not manufactured. Its presence is a good indication that the bounds of toleration are being reached. Not everything is to be tolerated. No society can do without intolerance, indignation, and disgust; they are the forces behind the moral law, and indeed it can be argued that if they or something like them are not present, the feelings of society cannot be weighty enough to deprive the individual of freedom of choice. I suppose that there is hardly anyone nowadays who would not be disgusted by the thought of deliberate cruelty to animals. No one proposes to relegate that or any other form of sadism to the realm of private morality or to allow it to be practised in public or in private. It would be possible no doubt to point out that until a compara-tively short while ago nobody thought very much of cruelty to animals and also that pity and kindliness and the unwillingness to inflict pain are virtues more generally esteemed now than they have ever been in the past. But matters of this sort are not determined by rational argument. Every moral judgment, unless it claims a divine source, is simply a feeling that no right-minded man could behave in any other way without admitting that he was doing wrong. It is the power of a common sense and not the power of reason that is behind the judgments of society. But before a society can put a practice beyond the limits of tolerance there must be a deliberate judgment that the practice is injurious to society. There is, for example, a general abhorrence of homosexuality. We should ask ourselves in the first instance whether, looking at it calmly and dispassionately, we regard it as a vice so abominable that its mere presence is an offence. If that is the genuine feeling of the society in which we live, I do not see how society can be denied the right to eradicate it. Our feeling may not be so intense as that. We may feel about it that, if confined, it is tolerable, but that if it spread it might be gravely injurious; it is in this way that most societies look upon fornication, seeing it as a natural weakness which must be kept within bounds but which cannot be rooted out. It becomes then a question of balance, the danger to society in one scale and the extent of the restriction in the other. On this sort of point the value of an investigation by such a body as the Wolfenden Com-mittee and of its conclusions is manifest.

The limits of tolerance shift. This is supplementary to what I have been saying but of sufficient importance in itself to deserve statement as a separate principle which law-makers have to bear in mind. I suppose that moral standards do not shift; so far as they come from divine revelation they do not, and I am willing to assume that the moral judgments made by a society always remain good for that society. But the extent to which society will tolerate—I mean tolerate, not approve—departures from moral standards varies from generation to generation. It may be that over-all tolerance is always increasing. The pressure of the human mind, always seeking greater freedom of thought, is outwards against the bonds of society forcing their gradual relaxation. It may be that history is a tale of contraction and expansion and that all developed societies are on their way to dissolution. I must not speak of things I do not know; and anyway as a practical matter no society is willing to make provision for its own decay. I return therefore to the simple and observable fact that in matters of morals the limits of tolerance shift. Laws, especially those which are based on morals, are less easily moved. It follows as another good working principle that in any new matter of morals the law should be slow to act. By the next generation the swell of indignation may have abated and the law be left without the strong backing which it needs. But it is then difficult to alter the law without giving the impression that moral judgment is being weakened. This is now one of the factors that is strongly militating against any alteration to the law on homosexuality.

A third elastic principle must be advanced more tentatively. It is that as far as possible privacy should be respected. This is not an idea that has ever been made explicit in the criminal law. Acts or words done or said in public or in private are all brought within its scope without distinction in principle. But there goes with this a strong reluctance on the part of judges and legislators to sanction invasions of privacy in the detection of crime. The police have no more right to trespass than the ordinary citizen has; there is no general right of search; to this extent an Englishman's home is still his castle. The Government is extremely careful in the exercise even of those powers which it claims to be undisputed. Telephone tapping and interference with the mails afford a good illustration of this. A Committee of three Privy Councillors who recently inquired[23] into these activities found that the Home Secretary and his predecessors had already formulated strict rules governing the exercise of these powers and the Committee were able to recommend that they should be continued to be exercised substantially on the same terms. But they reported that the power was 'regarded with general disfavour'.

[23] (1957) Cmd. 283.

This indicates a general sentiment that the right to privacy is something to be put in the balance against the enforcement of the law. Ought the same sort of consideration to play any part in the formation of the law? Clearly only in a very limited number of cases. When the help of the law is invoked by an injured citizen, privacy must be irrelevant; the individual cannot ask that his right to privacy should be measured against injury criminally done to another. But when all who are involved in the deed are consenting parties and the injury is done to morals, the public interest in the moral order can be balanced against the claims of privacy. The restriction on police powers of investigation goes further than the affording of a parallel; it means that the detection of crime committed in private and when there is no complaint is bound to be rather haphazard and this is an additional reason for moderation. These considerations do not justify the exclusion of all private immorality from the scope of the law. I think that, as I have already suggested, the test of 'private behaviour' should be substituted for 'private morality' and the influence of the factor should be reduced from that of a definite limitation to that of a matter to be taken into account. Since the gravity of the crime is also a proper consideration, a distinction might well be made in the case of homosexuality between the lesser acts of indecency and the full offence, which on the principles of the Wolfenden Report it would be illogical to do.

The last and the biggest thing to be remembered is that the law is concerned with the minimum and not with the maximum; there is much in the Sermon on the Mount that would be out of place in the Ten Commandments. We all recognize the gap between the moral law and the law of the land. No man is worth much who regulates his conduct with the sole object of escaping punishment, and every worthy society sets for its members standards which are above those of the law. We recognize the existence of such higher standards when we use expressions such as 'moral obligation' and 'morally bound'. The distinction was well put in the judgment of African elders in a family dispute: 'We have power to make you divide the crops, for this is our law, and we will see this is done. But we have not power to make you behave like an upright man.'[24]

---

[24] A case in the Saa-Katengo at Lialiu, August 1942, quoted in *The Judicial Process among the Barotse of Northern Rhodesia* by Max Gluckman (Manchester University Press, 1955), p. 172.

IV
IMMORALITY AND TREASON

H. L. A. HART

THE most remarkable feature of Sir Patrick's lecture is his view of the nature of morality—the morality which the criminal law may enforce. Most previous thinkers who have repudiated the liberal point of view have done so because they thought that morality consisted either of divine commands or of rational principles of human conduct discoverable by human reason. Since morality for them had this elevated divine or rational status as the law of God or reason, it seemed obvious that the state should enforce it, and that the function of human law should not be merely to provide men with the opportunity for leading a good life, but actually to see that they lead it. Sir Patrick does not rest his repudiation of the liberal point of view on these religious or rationalist conceptions. Indeed much that he writes reads like an abjuration of the notion that reasoning or thinking has much to do with morality. English popular morality has no doubt its historical connection with the Christian religion: 'That', says Sir Patrick, 'is how it got there.' But it does not owe its present status or social significance to religion any more than to reason.

What, then, is it? According to Sir Patrick it is primarily a matter of feeling. 'Every moral judgment', he says, 'is a feeling that no right-minded man could act in any other way without admitting that he was doing wrong.' Who then must feel this way if we are to have what Sir Patrick calls a public morality? He tells us that it is 'the man in the street', 'the man in the jury box', or (to use the phrase so familiar to English lawyers) 'the man on the Clapham omnibus'. For the moral judgments of society so far as the law is concerned are to be ascertained by the standards of the reasonable man, and he is not to be confused with the rational man. Indeed, Sir Patrick says 'he is not expected to reason about anything and his judgment may be largely a matter of feeling.'

INTOLERANCE, INDIGNATION, AND DISGUST

But what precisely are the relevant feelings, the feelings which may justify

From *The Listener*, 30 July 1959, pp. 162–3. Reprinted by permission of the author. For a fuller development of the ideas expressed here see Hart, *Law, Liberty, and Morality*, Oxford, 1963.

use of the criminal law? Here the argument becomes a little complex. Widespread dislike of a practice is not enough. There must, says Sir Patrick, be 'a real feeling of reprobation'. Disgust is not enough either. What is crucial is a combination of intolerance, indignation, and disgust. These three are the forces behind the moral law, without which it is not 'weighty enough to deprive the individual of freedom of choice'. Hence there is, in Sir Patrick's outlook, a crucial difference between the mere adverse moral judgment of society and one which is inspired by feeling raised to the concert pitch of intolerance, indignation, and disgust.

This distinction is novel and also very important. For on it depends the weight to be given to the fact that when morality is enforced individual liberty is necessarily cut down. Though Sir Patrick's abstract formulation of his views on this point is hard to follow, his examples make his position fairly clear. We can see it best in the contrasting things he says about fornication and homosexuality. In regard to fornication, public feeling in most societies is not now of the concert-pitch intensity. We may feel that it is tolerable if confined: only its spread might be gravely injurious. In such cases the question whether individual liberty should be restricted is for Sir Patrick a question of balance between the danger to society in the one scale, and the restriction of the individual in the other. But if, as may be the case with homosexuality, public feeling is up to concert pitch, if it expresses a 'deliberate judgment' that a practice as such is injurious to society, if there is 'a genuine feeling that it is a vice so abominable that its mere presence is an offence', then it is beyond the limits of tolerance, and society may eradicate it. In this case, it seems, no further balancing of the claims of individual liberty is to be done, though as a matter of prudence the legislator should remember that the popular limits of tolerance may shift: the concert-pitch feeling may subside. This may produce a dilemma for the law; for the law may then be left without the full moral backing that it needs, yet it cannot be altered without giving the impression that the moral judgment is being weakened.

A SHARED MORALITY

If this is what morality is—a compound of indignation, intolerance, and disgust—we may well ask what justification there is for taking it, and turning it as such, into criminal law with all the misery which criminal punishment entails. Here Sir Patrick's answer is very clear and simple. A collection of individuals is not a society; what makes them into a society is among other things a shared or public morality. This is as necessary to its existence as an organized government. So society may use the law to preserve its morality like anything else essential to it. 'The suppression of vice is as much the law's business as the suppression of subversive activities'. The liberal point of view which denies this is guilty of 'an error in jurisprudence': for it is no more possible to define an area of private morality than an area of private subversive activity. There can be no 'theoretical limits' to legislation against immorality just as there are no such limits to the power of the state to legislate against treason and sedition.

Surely all this, ingenious as it is, is misleading. Mill's formulation of the liberal point of view may well be too simple. The grounds for interfering with human liberty are more various than the single criterion of 'harm to others' suggests: cruelty to animals or organizing prostitution for gain do not, as Mill himself saw, fall easily under the description of harm to others. Conversely, even where there is harm to others in the most literal sense, there may well be other principles limiting the extent to which harmful activities should be repressed by law. So there are multiple criteria, not a single criterion, determining when human liberty may be restricted. Perhaps this is what Sir Patrick means by a curious distinction which he often stresses between theoretical and practical limits. But with all its simplicities the liberal point of view is a better guide than Sir Patrick to clear thought on the proper relation of morality to the criminal law: for it stresses what he obscures—namely, the points at which thought is needed before we turn popular morality into criminal law.

SOCIETY AND MORAL OPINION

No doubt we would all agree that a consensus of moral opinion on certain matters is essential if society is to be worth living in. Laws against murder, theft, and much else would be of little use if they were not supported by a widely diffused conviction that what these laws forbid is also immoral. So much is obvious. But it does not follow that everything to which the moral vetoes of accepted morality attach is of equal importance to society; nor is there the slightest reason for thinking of morality as a seamless web: one which will fall to pieces carrying society with it, unless all its emphatic vetoes are enforced by law. Surely even in the face of the moral feeling that is up to concert pitch—the trio of intolerance, indignation, and disgust—we must pause to think. We must ask a question at two different levels which Sir Patrick never clearly enough identifies or separates. First, we must ask whether a practice which offends moral feeling is harmful, independently of its repercussion on the general moral code. Secondly, what about repercussion on the moral code? Is it really true that failure to translate this item of general morality into criminal law will jeopardize the whole fabric of morality and so of society?

We cannot escape thinking about these two different questions merely by repeating to ourselves the vague nostrum: 'This is part of public morality and public morality must be preserved if society is to exist.' Sometimes Sir Patrick seems to admit this, for he says in words which both Mill and the Wolfenden Report might have used, that there must be the maximum respect for individual liberty consistent with the integrity of society. Yet this, as his contrasting examples of fornication and homosexuality show, turns out to mean only that the immorality which the law may punish must be generally felt to be intolerable. This plainly is no adequate substitute for a reasoned estimate of the damage to the fabric of society likely to ensue if it is not suppressed.

Nothing perhaps shows more clearly the inadequacy of Sir Patrick's approach to this problem than his comparison between the suppression of sexual immorality and the suppression of treason or subversive activity. Private subversive activity is, of course, a contradiction in terms because 'subversion' means overthrowing government, which is a public thing. But it is grotesque, even where moral feeling against homosexuality is up to concert pitch, to think of the homosexual behaviour of two adults in private as in any way like treason or sedition either in intention or effect. We can make it *seem* like treason only if we assume that deviation from a general moral code is bound to affect that code, and to lead not merely to its modification but to its destruction. The analogy could begin to be plausible only if it was clear that offending against this item of morality was likely to jeopardize the whole structure. But we have ample evidence for believing that people will not abandon morality, will not think any better of murder, cruelty, and dishonesty, merely because some private sexual practice which they abominate is not punished by the law.

Because this is so the analogy with treason is absurd. Of course 'No man is an island': what one man does in private, if it is known, may affect others in many different ways. Indeed it may be that deviation from general sexual morality by those whose lives, like the lives of many homosexuals, are noble ones and in all other ways exemplary will lead to what Sir Patrick calls the shifting of the limits of tolerance. But if this has any analogy in the sphere of government it is not the overthrow of ordered government, but a peaceful change in its form. So we may listen to the promptings of common sense and of logic, and say that though there could not logically be a sphere of private treason there is a sphere of private morality and immorality.

Sir Patrick's doctrine is also open to a wider, perhaps a deeper, criticism. In his reaction against a rationalist morality and his stress on feeling, he has I think thrown out the baby and kept the bath water; and the bath water may turn out to be very dirty indeed. When Sir Patrick's lecture was first delivered *The Times* greeted it with these words: 'There is a moving and welcome humility in the conception that society should not be asked to give its reason for refusing to tolerate what in its heart it feels intolerable.' This drew from a correspondent in Cambridge the retort: 'I am afraid that we are less humble than we used to be. We once burnt old women because, without giving our reasons, we felt in our hearts that witchcraft was intolerable.'

This retort is a bitter one, yet its bitterness is salutary. We are not, I suppose, likely, in England, to take again to the burning of old women for witchcraft or to punishing people for associating with those of a different race or colour, or to punishing people again for adultery. Yet if these things were viewed with intolerance, indignation, and disgust, as the second of them still is in some countries, it seems that on Sir Patrick's principles no rational criticism could be opposed to the claim that they should be punished by law. We could only pray, in his words, that the limits of tolerance might shift.

CURIOUS LOGIC

It is impossible to see what curious logic has led Sir Patrick to this result. For him a practice is immoral if the thought of it makes the man on the Clapham omnibus sick. So be it. Still, why should we not summon all the resources of our reason, sympathetic understanding, as well as critical intelligence, and insist that before general moral feeling is turned into criminal law it is submitted to scrutiny of a different kind from Sir Patrick's? Surely, the legislator should ask whether the general morality is based on ignorance, superstition, or misunderstanding; whether there is a false conception that those who practise what it condemns are in other ways dangerous or hostile to society; and whether the misery to many parties, the blackmail and the other evil consequences of criminal punishment, especially for sexual offences, are well understood. It is surely extraordinary that among the things which Sir Patrick says are to be considered before we legislate against immorality these appear nowhere; not even as 'practical considerations', let alone 'theoretical limits'. To any theory which, like this one, asserts that the criminal law may be used on the vague ground that the preservation of morality is essential to society and yet omits to stress the need for critical scrutiny, our reply should be: 'Morality, what crimes may be committed in thy name!'

As Mill saw, and de Tocqueville showed in detail long ago in his critical but sympathetic study of democracy, it is fatally easy to confuse the democratic principle that power should be in the hands of the majority with the utterly different claim that the majority with power in their hands need respect no limits. Certainly there is a special risk in a democracy that the majority may dictate how all should live. This is the risk we run, and should gladly run; for it is the price of all that is so good in democratic rule. But loyalty to democratic principles does not require us to maximize this risk: yet this is what we shall do if we mount the man in the street on the top of the Clapham omnibus and tell him that if only he feels sick enough about what other people do in private to demand its suppression by law no theoretical criticism can be made of his demand.

V

A THEORY OF CIVIL DISOBEDIENCE

J. RAWLS

55. THE DEFINITION OF CIVIL DISOBEDIENCE

I NOW wish to illustrate the content of the principles of natural duty and obligation by sketching a theory of civil disobedience. As I have already indicated, this theory is designed only for the special case of a nearly just society, one that is well ordered for the most part but in which some serious violations of justice nevertheless do occur. Since I assume that a state of near justice requires a democratic regime, the theory concerns the role and the appropriateness of civil disobedience to legitimately established democratic authority. It does not apply to the other forms of government nor, except incidentally, to other kinds of dissent or resistance. I shall not discuss this mode of protest, along with militant action and resistance, as a tactic for transforming or even overturning an unjust and corrupt system. There is no difficulty about such action in this case. If any means to this end are justified, then surely nonviolent opposition is justified. The problem of civil disobedience, as I shall interpret it, arises only within a more or less just democratic state for those citizens who recognize and accept the legitimacy of the constitution. The difficulty is one of a conflict of duties. At what point does the duty to comply with laws enacted by a legislative majority (or with executive acts supported by such a majority) cease to be binding in view of the right to defend one's liberties and the duty to oppose injustice? This question involves the nature and limits of majority rule. For this reason the problem of civil disobedience is a crucial test case for any theory of the moral basis of democracy.

A constitutional theory of civil disobedience has three parts. First, it defines this kind of dissent and separates it from other forms of opposition to democratic authority. These range from legal demonstrations and infractions of law designed to raise test cases before the courts to militant action and organized resistance. A theory specifies the place of civil disobedience in this spectrum of possibilities. Next, it sets out the grounds of civil

From *A Theory of Justice* by John Rawls, Cambridge, Mass.: The Belknap Press of Harvard University Press. Copyright © 1971 by the President and Fellows of Harvard College. Reprinted by permission of Harvard University Press and Oxford University Press.

disobedience and the conditions under which such action is justified in a (more or less) just democratic regime. And finally, a theory should explain the role of civil disobedience within a constitutional system and account for the appropriateness of this mode of protest within a free society.

Before I take up these matters, a word of caution. We should not expect too much of a theory of civil disobedience, even one framed for special circumstances. Precise principles that straightway decide actual cases are clearly out of the question. Instead, a useful theory defines a perspective within which the problem of civil disobedience can be approached; it identifies the relevant considerations and helps us to assign them their correct weights in the more important instances. If a theory about these matters appears to us, on reflection, to have cleared our vision and to have made our considered judgments more coherent, then it has been worthwhile. The theory has done what, for the present, one may reasonably expect it to do: namely, to narrow the disparity between the conscientious convictions of those who accept the basic principles of a democratic society.

I shall begin by defining civil disobedience as a public, nonviolent, conscientious yet political act contrary to law usually done with the aim of bringing about a change in the law or policies of the government.[1] By acting in this way one addresses the sense of justice of the majority of the community and declares that in one's considered opinion the principles of social cooperation among free and equal men are not being respected. A preliminary gloss on this definition is that it does not require that the civilly disobedient act breach the same law that is being protested.[2] It allows for what some have called indirect as well as direct civil disobedience. And this a definition should do, as there are sometimes strong reasons for not infringing on the law or policy held to be unjust. Instead, one may disobey traffic ordinances or laws of trespass as a way of presenting one's case. Thus, if the government enacts a vague and harsh statute against treason, it would not be appropriate to commit treason as a way of objecting to it, and in any event, the penalty might be far more than one should reasonably be ready to accept. In other cases there is no way to violate the government's policy directly, as when

---

[1] Here I follow H. A. Bedau's definition of civil disobedience. See his 'On Civil Disobedience', *Journal of Philosophy*, vol. 58 (1961), pp. 653–61. It should be noted that this definition is narrower than the meaning suggested by Thoreau's essay, as I note in the next section. A statement of a similar view is found in Martin Luther King's 'Letter from Birmingham City Jail' (1963), reprinted in H. A. Bedau, ed., *Civil Disobedience* (New York, Pegasus, 1969), pp. 72–89. The theory of civil disobedience in the text tries to set this sort of conception into a wider framework. Some recent writers have also defined civil disobedience more broadly. For example, Howard Zinn, *Disobedience and Democracy* (New York, Random House, 1968), pp. 119f, defines it as 'the deliberate, discriminate violation of law for a vital social purpose'. I am concerned with a more restricted notion. I do not at all mean to say that only this form of dissent is ever justified in a democratic state.

[2] This and the following gloss are from Marshall Cohen, 'Civil Disobedience in a Constitutional Democracy', *The Massachusetts Review*, vol. 10 (1969), pp. 224–6, 218–21, respectively.

it concerns foreign affairs, or affects another part of the country. A second gloss is that the civilly disobedient act is indeed thought to be contrary to law, at least in the sense that those engaged in it are not simply presenting a test case for a constitutional decision; they are prepared to oppose the statute even if it should be upheld. To be sure, in a constitutional regime, the courts may finally side with the dissenters and declare the law or policy objected to unconstitutional. It often happens, then, that there is some uncertainty as to whether the dissenter's action will be held illegal or not. But this is merely a complicating element. Those who use civil disobedience to protest unjust laws are not prepared to desist should the courts eventually disagree with them, however pleased they might have been with the opposite decision.

It should also be noted that civil disobedience is a political act not only in the sense that it is addressed to the majority that holds political power, but also because it is an act guided and justified by political principles, that is, by the principles of justice which regulate the constitution and social institutions generally. In justifying civil disobedience one does not appeal to principles of personal morality or to religious doctrines, though these may coincide with and support one's claims; and it goes without saying that civil disobedience cannot be grounded solely on group- or self-interest. Instead one invokes the commonly shared conception of justice that underlies the political order. It is assumed that in a reasonably just democratic regime there is a public conception of justice by reference to which citizens regulate their political affairs and interpret the constitution. The persistent and deliberate violation of the basic principles of this conception over any extended period of time, especially the infringement of the fundamental equal liberties, invites either submission or resistance. By engaging in civil disobedience a minority forces the majority to consider whether it wishes to have its actions construed in this way, or whether, in view of the common sense of justice, it wishes to acknowledge the legitimate claims of the minority.

A further point is that civil disobedience is a public act. Not only is it addressed to public principles, it is done in public. It is engaged in openly with fair notice; it is not covert or secretive. One may compare it to public speech, and being a form of address, an expression of profound and conscientious political conviction, it takes place in the public forum. For this reason, among others, civil disobedience is nonviolent. It tries to avoid the use of violence, especially against persons, not from the abhorrence of the use of force in principle, but because it is a final expression of one's case. To engage in violent acts likely to injure and to hurt is incompatible with civil disobedience as a mode of address. Indeed, any interference with the civil liberties of others tends to obscure the civilly disobedient quality of one's act. Sometimes if the appeal fails in its purpose, forceful resistance may later be entertained. Yet civil disobedience is giving voice to conscientious and deeply held convictions; while it may warn and admonish, it is not itself a threat.

Civil disobedience is nonviolent for another reason. It expresses disobedience to law within the limits of fidelity to law, although it is at the outer edge thereof.[3] The law is broken, but fidelity to law is expressed by the public and nonviolent nature of the act, by the willingness to accept the legal consequences of one's conduct.[4] This fidelity to law helps to establish to the majority that the act is indeed politically conscientious and sincere, and that it is intended to address the public's sense of justice. To be completely open and nonviolent is to give bond of one's sincerity, for it is not easy to convince another that one's acts are conscientious, or even to be sure of this before oneself. No doubt it is possible to imagine a legal system in which conscientious belief that the law is unjust is accepted as a defence for noncompliance. Men of great honesty with full confidence in one another might make such a system work. But as things are, such a scheme would presumably be unstable even in a state of near justice. We must pay a certain price to convince others that our actions have, in our carefully considered view, a sufficient moral basis in the political convictions of the community.

Civil disobedience has been defined so that it falls between legal protest and the raising of test cases on the one side, and conscientious refusal and the various forms of resistance on the other. In this range of possibilities it stands for that form of dissent at the boundary of fidelity to law. Civil disobedience, so understood, is clearly distinct from militant action and obstruction; it is far removed from organized forcible resistance. The militant, for example, is much more deeply opposed to the existing political system. He does not accept it as one which is nearly just or reasonably so; he believes either that it departs widely from its professed principles or that it pursues a mistaken conception of justice altogether. While his action is conscientious in its own terms, he does not appeal to the sense of justice of the majority (or those having effective political power), since he thinks that their sense of justice is erroneous, or else without effect. Instead, he seeks by well-framed militant acts of disruption and resistance and the like to

---

[3] For a fuller discussion of this point, see Charles Fried, 'Moral Causation', 77 *Harv. L. Rev.*, 1268 (1964). For clarification below of the notion of militant action, I am indebted to Gerald Loev.

[4] Those who define civil disobedience more broadly might not accept this description. See, for example, Zinn, *Disobedience and Democracy*, pp. 27–31, 39, 119f. Moreover, he denies that civil disobedience need be nonviolent. Certainly one does not accept the punishment as right, that is, as deserved for an unjustified act. Rather one is willing to undergo the legal consequences for the sake of fidelity to law, which is a different matter. There is room for latitude here in that the definition allows that the charge may be contested in court, should this prove appropriate. But there comes a point beyond which dissent ceases to be civil disobedience as defined here.

attack the prevalent view of justice or to force a movement in the desired direction. Thus the militant may try to evade the penalty, since he is not prepared to accept the legal consequences of his violation of the law; this would not only be to play into the hands of forces that he believes cannot be trusted, but also to express a recognition of the legitimacy of the constitution to which he is opposed. In this sense militant action is not within the bounds of fidelity to law, but represents a more profound opposition to the legal order. The basic structure is thought to be so unjust or else to depart so widely from its own professed ideals that one must try to prepare the way for radical or even revolutionary change. And this is to be done by trying to arouse the public to an awareness of the fundamental reforms that need to be made. Now in certain circumstances militant action and other kinds of resistance are surely justified. I shall not, however, consider these cases. As I have said, my aim here is the limited one of defining a concept of civil disobedience and understanding its role in a nearly just constitutional regime.

56. THE DEFINITION OF CONSCIENTIOUS REFUSAL

Although I have distinguished civil disobedience from conscientious refusal, I have yet to explain the latter notion. This will now be done. It must be recognized, however, that to separate these two ideas is to give a narrower definition to civil disobedience than is traditional; for it is customary to think of civil disobedience in a broader sense as any noncompliance with law for conscientious reasons, at least when it is not covert and does not involve the use of force. Thoreau's essay is characteristic, if not definitive, of the traditional meaning.[5] The usefulness of the narrower sense will, I believe, be clear once the definition of conscientious refusal is examined.

Conscientious refusal is noncompliance with a more or less direct legal injunction or administrative order. It is refusal since an order is addressed to us and, given the nature of the situation, whether we accede to it is known to the authorities. Typical examples are the refusal of the early Christians to perform certain acts of piety prescribed by the pagan state, and the refusal of the Jehovah's Witnesses to salute the flag. Other examples are the unwillingness of a pacifist to serve in the armed forces, or of a soldier to obey an order that he thinks is manifestly contrary to the moral law as it applies to war. Or again, in Thoreau's case, the refusal to pay a tax on the grounds that to do so would make him an agent of grave injustice to another. One's action is assumed to be known to the authorities, however much one might

[5] See Henry David Thoreau, 'Civil Disobedience' (1848), reprinted in H. A. Bedau, ed., *Civil Disobedience*, pp. 27–48. For a critical discussion, see Bedau's remarks, pp. 15–26.

wish, in some cases, to conceal it. Where it can be covert, one might speak of conscientious evasion rather than conscientious ʹrefusal. Covert infractions of a fugitive slave law are instances of conscientious evasion.[6]

There are several contrasts between conscientious refusal (or evasion) and civil disobedience. First of all, conscientious refusal is not a form of address appealing to the sense of justice of the majority. To be sure, such acts are not generally secretive or covert, as concealment is often impossible anyway. One simply refuses on conscientious grounds to obey a command or to comply with a legal injunction. One does not invoke the convictions of the community, and in this sense conscientious refusal is not an act in the public forum. Those ready to withhold obedience recognize that there may be no basis for mutual understanding; they do not seek out occasions for disobedience as a way to state their cause. Rather, they bide their time hoping that the necessity to disobey will not arise. They are less optimistic than those undertaking civil disobedience and they may entertain no expectation of changing laws or policies. The situation may allow no time for them to make their case, or again there may not be any chance that the majority will be receptive to their claims.

Conscientious refusal is not necessarily based on political principles; it may be founded on religious or other principles at variance with the constitutional order. Civil disobedience is an appeal to a commonly shared conception of justice, whereas conscientious refusal may have other grounds. For example, assuming that the early Christians would not justify their refusal to comply with the religious customs of the Empire by reasons of justice but simply as being contrary to their religious convictions, their argument would not be political; nor, with similar qualifications, are the views of a pacifist, assuming that wars of self-defence at least are recognized by the conception of justice that underlies a constitutional regime. Conscientious refusal may, however, be grounded on political principles. One may decline to go along with a law thinking that it is so unjust that complying with it is simply out of the question. This would be the case if, say, the law were to enjoin our being the agent of enslaving another, or to require us to submit to a similar fate. These are patent violations of recognized political principles.

It is a difficult matter to find the right course when some men appeal to religious principles in refusing to do actions which, it seems, are required by principles of political justice. Does the pacifist possess an immunity from military service in a just war, assuming that there are such wars? Or is the state permitted to impose certain hardships for noncompliance? There is a temptation to say that the law must always respect the dictates of con-

[6] For these distinctions I am indebted to Burton Dreben.

science, but this cannot be right. As we have seen in the case of the intolerant, the legal order must regulate men's pursuit of their religious interests so as to realize the principle of equal liberty; and it may certainly forbid religious practices such as human sacrifice, to take an extreme case. Neither religiosity nor conscientiousness suffice to protect this practice. A theory of justice must work out from its own point of view how to treat those who dissent from it. The aim of a well-ordered society, or one in a state of near justice, is to preserve and strengthen the institutions of justice. If a religion is denied its full expression, it is presumably because it is in violation of the equal liberties of others. In general, the degree of tolerance accorded opposing moral conceptions depends upon the extent to which they can be allowed an equal place within a just system of liberty.

If pacificism is to be treated with respect and not merely tolerated, the explanation must be that it accords reasonably well with the principles of justice, the main exception arising from its attitude toward engaging in a just war (assuming here that in some situations wars of self-defence are justified). The political principles recognized by the community have a certain affinity with the doctrine the pacifist professes. There is a common abhorrence of war and the use of force, and a belief in the equal status of men as moral persons. And given the tendency of nations, particularly great powers, to engage in war unjustifiably and to set in motion the apparatus of the state to suppress dissent, the respect accorded to pacifism serves the purpose of alerting citizens to the wrongs that governments are prone to commit in their name. Even though his views are not altogether sound, the warnings and protests that a pacifist is disposed to express may have the result that on balance the principles of justice are more rather than less secure. Pacifism as a natural departure from the correct doctrine conceivably compensates for the weakness of men in living up to their professions.

It should be noted that there is, of course, in actual situations no sharp distinction between civil disobedience and conscientious refusal. Moreover the same action (or sequence of actions) may have strong elements of both. While there are clear cases of each, the contrast between them is intended as a way of elucidating the interpretation of civil disobedience and its role in a democratic society. Given the nature of this way of acting as a special kind of political appeal, it is not usually justified until other steps have been taken within the legal framework. By contrast this requirement often fails in the obvious cases of legitimate conscientious refusal. In a free society no one may be compelled, as the early Christians were, to perform religious acts in violation of equal liberty, nor must a soldier comply with inherently evil commands while waiting an appeal to higher authority. These remarks lead up to the question of justification.

57. THE JUSTIFICATION OF CIVIL DISOBEDIENCE

With these various distinctions in mind, I shall consider the circumstances under which civil disobedience is justified. For simplicity I shall limit the discussion to domestic institutions and so to injustices internal to a given society. The somewhat narrow nature of this restriction will be mitigated a bit by taking up the contrasting problem of conscientious refusal in connection with the moral law as it applies to war. I shall begin by setting out what seem to be reasonable conditions for engaging in civil disobedience, and then later connect these conditions more systematically with the place of civil disobedience in a state of near justice. Of course, the conditions enumerated should be taken as presumptions; no doubt there will be situations when they do not hold, and other arguments could be given for civil disobedience.

The first concerns the kinds of wrongs that are appropriate objects of civil disobedience. Now if one views such disobedience as a political act addressed to the sense of justice of the community, then it seems reasonable, other things being equal, to limit it to instances of substantial and clear injustice, and preferably to those which block the way to removing other injustices. For this reason there is a presumption in favour of restricting civil disobedience to serious infringements of the first principle of justice, the principle of equal liberty, and to blatant violations of the second part of the second principle, the principle of fair equality of opportunity. Of course, it is not always easy to tell whether these principles are satisfied. Still, if we think of them as guaranteeing the basic liberties, it is often clear that these freedoms are not being honoured. After all, they impose certain strict requirements that must be visibly expressed in institutions. Thus when certain minorities are denied the right to vote or to hold office, or to own property and to move from place to place, or when certain religious groups are repressed and others denied various opportunities, these injustices may be obvious to all. They are publicly incorporated into the recognized practice, if not the letter, of social arrangements. The establishment of these wrongs does not presuppose an informed examination of institutional effects.

By contrast infractions of the difference principle are more difficult to ascertain. There is usually a wide range of conflicting yet rational opinion as to whether this principle is satisfied. The reason for this is that it applies primarily to economic and social institutions and policies. A choice among these depends upon theoretical and speculative beliefs as well as upon a wealth of statistical and other information, all of this seasoned with shrewd judgment and plain hunch. In view of the complexities of these questions, it is difficult to check the influence of self-interest and prejudice; and even if we can do this in our own case, it is another matter to convince others of our good faith. Thus unless tax laws, for example, are clearly designed to attack or to abridge a basic equal liberty, they should not normally be protested by civil disobedience. The appeal to the public's conception of justice is not sufficiently clear. The resolution of these issues is best left to the political process provided that the requisite equal liberties are secure. In this case a reasonable compromise can presumably be reached. The violation of the principle of equal liberty is, then, the more appropriate object of civil disobedience. This principle defines the common status of equal citizenship in a constitutional regime and lies at the basis of the political order. When it is fully honoured the presumption is that other injustices, while possibly persistent and significant, will not get out of hand.

A further condition for civil disobedience is the following. We may suppose that the normal appeals to the political majority have already been made in good faith and that they have failed. The legal means of redress have proved to no avail. Thus, for example, the existing political parties have shown themselves indifferent to the claims of the minority or have proved unwilling to accommodate them. Attempts to have the laws repealed have been ignored and legal protests and demonstrations have had no success. Since civil disobedience is a last resort, we should be sure that it is necessary. Note that it has not been said, however, that legal means have been exhausted. At any rate, further normal appeals can be repeated; free speech is always possible. But if past actions have shown the majority immovable or apathetic, further attempts may reasonably be thought fruitless, and a second condition for justified civil disobedience is met. This condition is, however, a presumption. Some cases may be so extreme that there may be no duty to use first only legal means of political opposition. If, for example, the legislature were to enact some outrageous violation of equal liberty, say by forbidding the religion of a weak and defenceless minority, we surely could not expect that sect to oppose the law by normal political procedures. Indeed, even civil disobedience might be much too mild, the majority having already convicted itself of wantonly unjust and overtly hostile aims.

The third and last condition I shall discuss can be rather complicated. It arises from the fact that while the two preceding conditions are often sufficient to justify civil disobedience, this is not always the case. In certain circumstances the natural duty of justice may require a certain restraint. We can see this as follows. If a certain minority is justified in engaging in civil disobedience, then any other minority in relevantly similar circumstances is likewise justified. Using the two previous conditions as the criteria of relevantly similar circumstances, we can say that, other things equal, two minorities are similarly justified in resorting to civil disobedience if they have suffered for the same length of time from the same degree of injustice and if their equally sincere and normal political appeals have likewise been to no avail. It is conceivable, however, even if it is unlikely, that there should be many groups with an equally sound case (in the sense just defined) for being civilly disobedient; but that, if they were all to act in this way, serious disorder would follow which might well undermine the efficacy of the just constitution. I assume here that there is a limit on the extent to which civil disobedience can be engaged in without leading to a breakdown in the respect for law and the constitution, thereby setting in motion consequences unfortunate for all. There is also an upper bound on the ability of the public forum to handle such forms of dissent; the appeal that civilly disobedient groups wish to make can be distorted and their intention to appeal to the sense of justice of the majority lost sight of. For one or both of these reasons, the effectiveness of civil disobedience as a form of protest declines beyond a certain point; and those contemplating it must consider these constraints.

The ideal solution from a theoretical point of view calls for a co-operative political alliance of the minorities to regulate the over-all level of dissent. For consider the nature of the situation: there are many groups each equally entitled to engage in civil disobedience. Moreover they all wish to exercise this right, equally strong in each case; but if they all do so, lasting injury may result to the just constitution to which they each recognize a natural duty of justice. Now when there are many equally strong claims which if taken together exceed what can be granted, some fair plan should be adopted so that all are equitably considered. In simple cases of claims to goods that are indivisible and fixed in number, some rotation or lottery scheme may be the fair solution when the number of equally valid claims is too great.[7] But this sort of device is completely unrealistic here. What seems called for is a political understanding among the minorities suffering from injustice. They can meet their duty to democratic institutions by co-ordinating their actions so that while each has an opportunity to exercise its right, the limits on the degree of civil disobedience are not exceeded. To be sure, an alliance of this sort is difficult to arrange; but with perceptive leadership, it does not appear impossible.

Certainly the situation envisaged is a special one, and it is quite possible

[7] For a discussion of the conditions when some fair arrangement is called for, see Kurt Baier, *The Moral Point of View* (Ithaca, N.Y., Cornell University Press, 1958), pp. 207–13; and David Lyons, *Forms and Limits of Utilitarianism* (Oxford, The Clarendon Press, 1965), pp. 160–76. Lyons gives an example of a fair rotation scheme and he also observes that (waiving costs of setting them up) such fair procedures may be reasonably efficient. See pp. 169–71. I accept the conclusions of his account, including his contention that the notion of fairness cannot be explained by assimilating it to utility (pp. 176f). The earlier discussion by C. D. Broad, 'On the Function of False Hypotheses in Ethics', *International Journal of Ethics*, vol. 26 (1916), esp. pp. 385–90, should also be noted here.

that these sorts of considerations will not be a bar to justified civil disobedience. There are not likely to be many groups similarly entitled to engage in this form of dissent while at the same time recognizing a duty to a just constitution. One should note, however, that an injured minority is tempted to believe its claim as strong as that of any other; and therefore, whether the reasons that different groups have for engaging in civil disobedience are equally compelling, it may often be wise to presume that their claims are indistinguishable. Adopting this maxim, the circumstance imagined seems more likely to happen. This kind of case is also instructive in showing that the exercise of the right to dissent, like the exercise of rights generally, is sometimes limited by others having the very same right. Everyone's exercising this right would have deleterious consequences for all, and some equitable plan is called for.

Suppose that in the light of the three conditions, one has a right to appeal one's case by civil disobedience. The injustice one protests is a clear violation of the liberties of equal citizenship, or of equality of opportunity, this violation having been more or less deliberate over an extended period of time in the face of normal political opposition, and any complications raised by the question of fairness are met. These conditions are not exhaustive; some allowance still has to be made for the possibility of injury to third parties, to the innocent, so to speak. But I assume that they cover the main points. There is still, of course, the question whether it is wise or prudent to exercise this right. Having established the right, one is now free, as one is not before, to let these matters decide the issue. We may be acting within our rights but nevertheless unwisely if our conduct only serves to provoke the harsh retaliation of the majority. To be sure, in a state of near justice, vindictive repression of legitimate dissent is unlikely, but it is important that the action be properly designed to make an effective appeal to the wider community. Since civil disobedience is a mode of address taking place in the public forum, care must be taken to see that it is understood. Thus the exercise of the right to civil disobedience should, like any other right, be rationally framed to advance one's ends or the ends of those one wishes to assist. The theory of justice has nothing specific to say about these practical considerations. In any event questions of strategy and tactics depend upon the circumstances of each case. But the theory of justice should say at what point these matters are properly raised.

Now in this account of the justification of civil disobedience I have not mentioned the principle of fairness. The natural duty of justice is the primary basis of our political ties to a constitutional regime. As we noted before (§52), only the more favoured members of society are likely to have a clear political obligation as opposed to a political duty. They are better situated to win public office and find it easier to take advantage of the political system. And having done so, they have acquired an obligation owed to citizens generally to uphold the just constitution. But members of subjected minorities, say, who have a strong case for civil disobedience will not generally have a political obligation of this sort. This does not mean, however, that the principle of fairness will not give rise to important obligations in their case.[8] For not only do many of the requirements of private life derive from this principle, but it comes into force when persons or groups come together for common political purposes. Just as we acquire obligations to others with whom we have joined in various private associations, those who engage in political action assume obligatory ties to one another. Thus while the political obligation of dissenters to citizens generally is problematical, bonds of loyalty and fidelity still develop between them as they seek to advance their cause. In general, free association under a just constitution gives rise to obligations provided that the ends of the group are legitimate and its arrangements fair. This is as true of political as it is of other associations. These obligations are of immense significance and they constrain in many ways what individuals can do. But they are distinct from an obligation to comply with a just constitution. My discussion of civil disobedience is in terms of the duty of justice alone; a fuller view would note the place of these other requirements.

58   THE JUSTIFICATION OF CONSCIENTIOUS REFUSAL

In examining the justification of civil disobedience I assumed for simplicity that the laws and policies protested concerned domestic affairs. It is natural to ask how the theory of political duty applies to foreign policy. Now in order to do this it is necessary to extend the theory of justice to the law of nations. I shall try to indicate how this can be done. To fix ideas I shall consider briefly the justification of conscientious refusal to engage in certain acts of war, or to serve in the armed forces. I assume that this refusal is based upon political and not upon religious or other principles; that is, the principles cited by way of justification are those of the conception of justice underlying the constitution. Our problem, then, is to relate the just political principles regulating the conduct of states to the contract doctrine and to explain the moral basis of the law of nations from this point of view.

Let us assume that we have already derived the principles of justice as these apply to societies as units and to the basic structure. Imagine also that the various principles of natural duty and of obligation that apply to individuals have been adopted. Thus the persons in the original position have

---

[8] For a discussion of these obligations, see Michael Walzer, *Obligations: Essays on Disobedience, War, and Citizenship* (Cambridge, Harvard University Press, 1970), Ch. III.

agreed to the principles of right as these apply to their own society and to themselves as members of it. Now at this point one may extend the interpretation of the original position and think of the parties as representatives of different nations who must choose together the fundamental principles to adjudicate conflicting claims among states. Following out the conception of the initial situation, I assume that these representatives are deprived of various kinds of information. While they know that they represent different nations each living under the normal circumstances of human life, they know nothing about the particular circumstances of their own society, its power and strength in comparison with other nations, nor do they know their place in their own society. Once again the contracting parties, in this case representatives of states, are allowed only enough knowledge to make a rational choice to protect their interests but not so much that the more fortunate among them can take advantage of their special situation. This original position is fair between nations; it nullifies the contingencies and biases of historical fate. Justice between states is determined by the principles that would be chosen in the original position so interpreted. These principles are political principles, for they govern public policies toward other nations.

I can give only an indication of the principles that would be acknowledged. But, in any case, there would be no surprises, since the principles chosen would, I think, be familiar ones.[9] The basic principle of the law of nations is a principle of equality. Independent peoples organized as states have certain fundamental equal rights. This principle is analogous to the equal rights of citizens in a constitutional regime. One consequence of this equality of nations is the principle of self-determination, the right of a people to settle its own affairs without the intervention of foreign powers. Another consequence is the right of self-defence against attack, including the right to form defensive alliances to protect this right. A further principle is that treaties are to be kept, provided they are consistent with the other principles governing the relations of states. Thus treaties for self-defence, suitably interpreted, would be binding, but agreements to co-operate in an unjustified attack are void *ab initio*.

These principles define when a nation has a just cause in war or, in the traditional phrase, its *jus ad bellum*. But there are also principles regulating the means that a nation may use to wage war, its *jus in bello*.[10] Even in a just war certain forms of violence are strictly inadmissible; and where a country's right to war is questionable and uncertain, the constraints on the

[9] See J. L. Brierly, *The Law of Nations*, 6th edn. (Oxford, The Clarendon Press, 1963), esp. Chs. IV–V. This work contains all that we need here.

[10] For a recent discussion, see Paul Ramsey, *War and the Christian Conscience* (Durham, N.C., The Duke University Press, 1961); and also R. B. Potter, *War and Moral Discourse* (Richmond, Va., John Knox Press, 1969). The latter contains a useful bibliographical essay, pp. 87–123.

means it can use are all the more severe. Acts permissible in a war of legiti-mate self-defence, when these are necessary, may be flatly excluded in a more doubtful situation. The aim of war is a just peace, and therefore the means employed must not destroy the possibility of peace or encourage a contempt for human life that puts the safety of ourselves and of mankind in jeopardy. The conduct of war is to be constrained and adjusted to this end. The repre-sentatives of states would recognize that their national interest, as seen from the original position, is best served by acknowledging these limits on the means of war. This is because the national interest of a just state is defined by the principles of justice that have already been acknowledged. Therefore such a nation will aim above all to maintain and to preserve its just institu-tions and the conditions that make them possible. It is not moved by the desire for world power or national glory; nor does it wage war for purposes of economic gain or the acquisition of territory. These ends are contrary to the conception of justice that defines a society's legitimate interest, how-ever prevalent they have been in the actual conduct of states. Granting these presumptions, then, it seems reasonable to suppose that the traditional pro-hibitions incorporating the natural duties that protect human life would be chosen.

Now if conscientious refusal in time of war appeals to these principles, it is founded upon a political conception, and not necessarily upon religious or other notions. While this form of denial may not be a political act, since it does not take place in the public forum, it is based upon the same theory of justice that underlies the constitution and guides its interpretation. More-over, the legal order itself presumably recognizes in the form of treaties the validity of at least some of these principles of the law of nations. Therefore if a soldier is ordered to engage in certain illicit acts of war, he may refuse if he reasonably and conscientiously believes that the principles applying to the conduct of war are plainly violated. He can maintain that, all things considered, his natural duty not to be made the agent of grave injustice and evil to another outweighs his duty to obey. I cannot discuss here what con-stitutes a manifest violation of these principles. It must suffice to note that certain clear cases are perfectly familiar. The essential point is that the justifi-cation cites political principles that can be accounted for by the contract doctrine. The theory of justice can be developed, I believe, to cover this case.

A somewhat different question is whether one should join the armed forces at all during some particular war. The answer is likely to depend upon the aim of the war as well as upon its conduct. In order to make the situation definite, let us suppose that conscription is in force and that the individual has to consider whether to comply with his legal duty to enter military ser-vice. Now I shall assume that since conscription is a drastic interference with the basic liberties of equal citizenship, it cannot be justified by any needs less compelling than those of national security.[11] In a well-ordered society (or in one nearly just) these needs are determined by the end of preserving just institutions. Conscription is permissible only if it is demanded for the defence of liberty itself, including here not only the liberties of the citizens of the society in question, but also those of persons in other societies as well. Therefore if a conscript army is less likely to be an instrument of unjustified foreign adventures, it may be justified on this basis alone despite the fact that conscription infringes upon the equal liberties of citizens. But in any case, the priority of liberty (assuming serial order to obtain) requires that conscription be used only as the security of liberty necessitates. Viewed from the standpoint of the legislature (the appropriate stage for this question), the mechanism of the draft can be defended only on this ground. Citizens agree to this arrangement as a fair way of sharing in the burdens of national defence. To be sure, the hazards that any particular individual must face are in part the result of accident and historical happenstance. But in a well-ordered society anyway, these evils arise externally, that is, from unjustified attacks from the outside. It is impossible for just institutions to eliminate these hardships entirely. The most that they can do is to try to make sure that the risks of suffering from these imposed misfortunes are more or less evenly shared by all members of society over the course of their life, and that there is no avoidable class bias in selecting those who are called for duty.

Imagine, then, a democratic society in which conscription exists. A person may conscientiously refuse to comply with his duty to enter the armed forces during a particular war on the grounds that the aims of the conflict are unjust. It may be that the objective sought by war is economic advantage or national power. The basic liberty of citizens cannot be interfered with to achieve these ends. And, of course, it is unjust and contrary to the law of nations to attack the liberty of other societies for these reasons. Therefore a just cause for war does not exist, and this may be sufficiently evident that a citizen is justified in refusing to discharge his legal duty. Both the law of nations and the principles of justice for his own society uphold him in his claim. There is sometimes a further ground for refusal based not on the aim of the war but upon its conduct. A citizen may maintain that once it is clear that the moral law of war is being regularly violated, he has a right to decline military service on the ground that he is entitled to insure that he honours his natural duty. Once he is in the armed forces, and in a situation where he finds himself ordered to do acts contrary to the moral law of war, he may not be able to resist the demand to obey. Actually, if the aims of the

---

[11] I am indebted to R. G. Albritton for clarification on this and other matters in this paragraph.

conflict are sufficiently dubious and the likelihood of receiving flagrantly unjust commands sufficiently great, one may have a duty and not only a right to refuse. Indeed, the conduct and aims of states in waging war, especially large and powerful ones, are in some circumstances so likely to be unjust that one is forced to conclude that in the foreseeable future one must abjure military service altogether. So understood a form of contingent pacifism may be a perfectly reasonable position: the possibility of a just war is conceded but not under present circumstances.[12]

What is needed, then, is not a general pacifism but a discriminating conscientious refusal to engage in war in certain circumstances. States have not been loath to recognize pacifism and to grant it a special status. The refusal to take part in all war under any conditions is an unworldly view bound to remain a sectarian doctrine. It no more challenges the state's authority than the celibacy of priests challenges the sanctity of marriage.[13] By exempting pacifists from its prescriptions the state may even seem to display a certain magnanimity. But conscientious refusal based upon the principles of justice between peoples as they apply to particular conflicts is another matter. For such refusal is an affront to the government's pretensions, and when it becomes widespread, the continuation of an unjust war may prove impossible. Given the often predatory aims of state power, and the tendency of men to defer to their government's decision to wage war, a general willingness to resist the state's claims is all the more necessary.

59. THE ROLE OF CIVIL DISOBEDIENCE

The third aim of a theory of civil disobedience is to explain its role within a constitutional system and to account for its connection with a democratic policy. As always, I assume that the society in question is one that is nearly just; and this implies that it has some form of democratic government, although serious injustices may nevertheless exist. In such a society I assume that the principles of justice are for the most part publicly recognized as the fundamental terms of willing co-operation among free and equal persons. By engaging in civil disobedience one intends, then, to address the sense of justice of the majority and to serve fair notice that in one's sincere and considered opinion the conditions of free co-operation are being violated. We are appealing to others to reconsider, to put themselves in our position, and to recognize that they cannot expect us to acquiesce indefinitely in the terms they impose upon us.

Now the force of this appeal depends upon the democratic conception

[12] See *Nuclear Weapons and Christian Conscience*, ed. Walter Stein (London, The Merlin Press, 1965), for a presentation of this sort of doctrine in connection with nuclear war.

[13] I borrow this point from Walzer, *Obligations*, p. 127.

of society as a system of co-operation among equal persons. If one thinks of society in another way, this form of protest may be out of place. For example, if the basic law is thought to reflect the order of nature and if the sovereign is held to govern by divine right as God's chosen lieutenant, then his subjects have only the right of suppliants. They can plead their cause but they cannot disobey should their appeal be denied. To do this would be to rebel against the final legitimate moral (and not simply legal) authority. This is not to say that the sovereign cannot be in error but only that the situation is not one for his subjects to correct. But once society is interpreted as a scheme of co-operation among equals, those injured by serious injustice need not submit. Indeed, civil disobedience (and conscientious refusal as well) is one of the stabilizing devices of a constitutional system, although by definition an illegal one. Along with such things as free and regular elections and an independent judiciary empowered to interpret the constitution (not necessarily written), civil disobedience used with due restraint and sound judgment helps to maintain and strengthen just institutions. By resisting injustice within the limits of fidelity to law, it serves to inhibit departures from justice and to correct them when they occur. A general disposition to engage in justified civil disobedience introduces stability into a well-ordered society, or one that is nearly just.

It is necessary to look at this doctrine from the standpoint of the persons in the original position. There are two related problems which they must consider. The first is that, having chosen principles for individuals, they must work out guidelines for assessing the strength of the natural duties and obligations, and, in particular, the strength of the duty to comply with a just constitution and one of its basic procedures, that a majority rule. The second problem is that of finding reasonable principles for dealing with unjust situations, or with circumstances in which the compliance with just principles is only partial. Now it seems that, given the assumptions characterizing a nearly just society, the parties would agree to the presumptions (previously discussed) that specify when civil disobedience is justified. They would acknowledge these criteria as spelling out when this form of dissent is appropriate. Doing this would indicate the weight of the natural duty of justice in one important special case. It would also tend to enhance the realization of justice throughout the society by strengthening men's self-esteem as well as their respect for one another. As the contract doctrine emphasizes, the principles of justice are the principles of willing co-operation among equals. To deny justice to another is either to refuse to recognize him as an equal (one in regard to whom we are prepared to constrain our actions by principles that we would choose in a situation of equality that is fair), or to manifest a willingness to exploit the contingencies of natural fortune and happenstance for our own advantage. In either case deliberate injustice invites submission or resistance. Submission arouses the contempt of those who perpetuate injustice and confirms their intention, whereas resistance cuts the ties of community. If after a decent period of time to allow for reasonable political appeals in the normal way, citizens were to dissent by civil disobedience when infractions of the basic liberties occurred, these liberties would, it seems, be more rather than less secure. For these reasons, then, the parties would adopt the conditions defining justified civil disobedience as a way of setting up, within the limits of fidelity to law, a final device to maintain the stability of a just constitution. Although this mode of action is strictly speaking contrary to law, it is nevertheless a morally correct way of maintaining a constitutional regime.

In a fuller account the same kind of explanation could presumably be given for the justifying conditions of conscientious refusal (again assuming the context of a nearly just state). I shall not, however, discuss these conditions here. I should like to emphasize instead that the constitutional theory of civil disobedience rests solely upon a conception of justice. Even the features of publicity and nonviolence are explained on this basis. And the same is true of the account of conscientious refusal, although it requires a further elaboration of the contract doctrine. At no point has a reference been made to other than political principles; religious or pacifist conceptions are not essential. While those engaging in civil disobedience have often been moved by convictions of this kind, there is no necessary connection between them and civil disobedience. For this form of political action can be understood as a way of addressing the sense of justice of the community, an invocation of the recognized principles of co-operation among equals. Being an appeal to the moral basis of civic life, it is a political and not a religious act. It relies upon common sense principles of justice that men can require one another to follow and not upon the affirmations of religious faith and love which they cannot demand that everyone accept. It do not mean, of course, that nonpolitical conceptions have no validity. They may, in fact, confirm our judgment and support our acting in ways known on other grounds to be just. Nevertheless, it is not these principles but the principles of justice, the fundamental terms of social co-operation between free and equal persons, that underlie the constitution. Civil disobedience as defined does not require a sectarian foundation but is derived from the public conception of justice that characterizes a democratic society. So understood a conception of civil disobedience is part of the theory of free government.

One distinction between medieval and modern constitutionalism is that in the former the supremacy of law was not secured by established institutional controls. The check to the ruler who in his judgments and edicts opposed the sense of justice of the community was limited for the most part to the right of resistance by the whole society, or any part. Even this right seems not to have been interpreted as a corporate act; an unjust king was simply put aside.[14] Thus the Middle Ages lacked the basic ideas of modern constitutional government, the idea of the sovereign people who have final authority and the institutionalizing of this authority by means of elections and parliaments, and other constitutional forms. Now in much the same way that the modern conception of constitutional government builds upon the medieval, the theory of civil disobedience supplements the purely legal conception of constitutional democracy. It attempts to formulate the grounds upon which legitimate democratic authority may be dissented from in ways that, while admittedly contrary to law, nevertheless express a fidelity to law and appeal to the fundamental political principles of a democratic regime. Thus to the legal forms of constitutionalism one may adjoin certain modes of illegal protest that do not violate the aims of a democratic constitution in view of the principles by which such dissent is guided. I have tried to show how these principles can be accounted for by the contract doctrine.

Some may object to this theory of civil disobedience that it is unrealistic. It presupposes that the majority has a sense of justice, and one might reply that moral sentiments are not significant political force. What moves men are various interests, the desires for power, prestige, wealth, and the like. Although they are clever at producing moral arguments to support their claims, between one situation and another their opinions do not fit into a coherent conception of justice. Rather their views at any given time are occasional pieces calculated to advance certain interests. Unquestionably there is much truth in this contention, and in some societies it is more true than in others. But the essential question is the relative strength of the tendencies that oppose the sense of justice and whether the latter is ever strong enough so that it can be invoked to some significant effect.

A few comments may make the account presented more plausible. First of all, I have assumed throughout that we have to do with a nearly just society. This implies that there exists a constitutional regime and a publicly recognized conception of justice. Of course, in any particular situation certain individuals and groups may be tempted to violate its principles but the collective sentiment in their behalf has considerable strength when properly addressed. These principles are affirmed as the necessary terms of co-operation between free and equal persons. If those who perpetrate injustice can be clearly identified and isolated from the larger community, the convictions of the greater part of society may be of sufficient weight. Or if the contending

---

[14] See J. H. Franklin, ed., *Constitutionalism and Resistance in the Sixteenth Century* (New York, Pegasus, 1969), in the introduction, pp. 11–15.

parties are roughly equal, the sentiment of justice of those not engaged can be the deciding factor. In any case, should circumstances of this kind not obtain, the wisdom of civil disobedience is highly problematic. For unless one can appeal to the sense of justice of the larger society, the majority may simply be aroused to more repressive measures if the calculation of advantages points in this direction. Courts should take into account the civilly disobedient nature of the protester's act, and the fact that it is justifiable (or may seem so) by the political principles underlying the constitution, and on these grounds reduce and in some cases suspend the legal sanction.[15] Yet quite the opposite may happen when the necessary background is lacking. We have to recognize then that justifiable civil disobedience is normally a reasonable and effective form of dissent only in a society regulated to some considerable degree by a sense of justice.

There may be some misapprehension about the manner in which the sense of justice is said to work. One may think that this sentiment expresses itself in sincere professions of principle and in actions requiring a considerable degree of self-sacrifice. But this supposition asks too much. A community's sense of justice is more likely to be revealed in the fact that the majority cannot bring itself to take the steps necessary to suppress the minority and to punish acts of civil disobedience as the law allows. Ruthless tactics that might be contemplated in other societies are not entertained as real alternatives. Thus the sense of justice affects, in ways we are often unaware of, our interpretation of political life, our perception of the possible courses of action, our will to resist the justified protests of others, and so on. In spite of its superior power, the majority may abandon its position and acquiesce in the proposals of the dissenters; its desire to give justice weakens its capacity to defend its unjust advantages. The sentiment of justice will be seen as a more vital political force once the subtle forms in which it exerts its influence are recognized, and in particular its role in rendering certain social positions indefensible.

In these remarks I have assumed that in a nearly just society there is a public acceptance of the same principles of justice. Fortunately this assumption is stronger than necessary. There can, in fact, be considerable differences in citizens' conceptions of justice provided that these conceptions lead to similar political judgments. And this is possible, since different premises can yield the same conclusion. In this case there exists what we may refer to as overlapping rather than strict consensus. In general, the overlapping of professed conceptions of justice suffices for civil disobedience to be a reasonable and prudent form of political dissent. Of course, this overlapping need

---

[15] For a general discussion, see Ronald Dworkin, 'On Not Persecuting Civil Disobedience', *The New York Review of Books*, 6 June, 1968.

not be perfect; it is enough that a condition of reciprocity is satisfied. Both sides must believe that however much their conceptions of justice differ, their views support the same judgment in the situation at hand, and would do so even should their respective positions be interchanged. Eventually, though, there comes a point beyond which the requisite agreement in judgment breaks down and society splits into more or less distinct parts that hold diverse opinions on fundamental political questions. In this case of strictly partitioned consensus, the basis for civil disobedience no longer obtains. For example, suppose those who do not believe in toleration, and who would not tolerate others had they the power, wish to protest their lesser liberty by appealing to the sense of justice of the majority which holds the principle of equal liberty. While those who accept this principle should, as we have seen, tolerate the intolerant as far as the safety of free institutions permits, they are likely to resent being reminded of this duty by the intolerant who would, if positions were switched, establish their own dominion. The majority is bound to feel that their allegiance to equal liberty is being exploited by others for unjust ends. This situation illustrates once again the fact that a common sense of justice is a great collective asset which requires the co-operation of many to maintain. The intolerant can be viewed as free-riders, as persons who seek the advantages of just institutions while not doing their share to uphold them. Although those who acknowledge the principles of justice should always be guided by them, in a fragmented society as well as in one moved by group egoisms, the conditions for civil disobedience do not exist. Still, it is not necessary to have strict consensus, for often a degree of overlapping consensus allows the reciprocity condition to be fulfilled.

There are, to be sure, definite risks in the resort to civil disobedience. One reason for constitutional forms and their judicial interpretation is to establish a public reading of the political conception of justice and an explanation of the application of its principles to social questions. Up to a certain point it is better that the law and its interpretation be settled than that it be settled rightly. Therefore it may be protested that the preceding account does not determine who is to say when circumstances are such as to justify civil disobedience. It invites anarchy by encouraging everyone to decide for himself, and to abandon the public rendering of political principles. The reply to this is that each person must indeed make his own decision. Even though men normally seek advice and counsel, and accept the injunctions of those in authority when these seem reasonable to them, they are always accountable for their deeds. We cannot divest ourselves of our responsibility and transfer the burden of blame to others. This is true on any theory of political duty and obligation that is compatible with the principles of a democratic constitution. The citizen is autonomous yet he is held responsible for what ne does. If we ordinarily think that we should comply with the law, this is because our political principles normally lead to this conclusion. Certainly in a state of near justice there is a presumption in favour of compliance in the absence of strong reasons to the contrary. The many free and reasoned decisions of individuals fit together into an orderly political regime.

But while each person must decide for himself whether the circumstances justify civil disobedience, it does not follow that one is to decide as one pleases. It is not by looking to our personal interests, or to our political allegiances narrowly construed, that we should make up our minds. To act autonomously and responsibly a citizen must look to the political principles that underlie and guide the interpretation of the constitution. He must try to assess how these principles should be applied in the existing circumstances. If he comes to the conclusion after due consideration that civil disobedience is justified and conducts himself accordingly, he acts conscientiously. And though he may be mistaken, he has not done as he pleased. The theory of political duty and obligation enables us to draw these distinctions.

There are parallels with the common understandings and conclusions reached in the sciences. Here, too, everyone is autonomous yet responsible. We are to assess theories and hypotheses in the light of the evidence by publicly recognized principles. It is true that there are authoritative works, but these sum up the consensus of many persons each deciding for himself. The absence of a final authority to decide, and so of an official interpretation that all must accept, does not lead to confusion, but is rather a condition of theoretical advance. Equals accepting and applying reasonable principles need have no established superior. To the question, who is to decide? The answer is: All are to decide, everyone taking counsel with himself, and with reasonableness, comity, and good fortune, it often works out well enough.

In a democratic society, then, it is recognized that each citizen is responsible for his interpretation of the principles of justice and for his conduct in the light of them. There can be no legal or socially approved rendering of these principles that we are always morally bound to accept, not even when it is given by a supreme court or legislature. Indeed each constitutional agency, the legislature, the executive, and the court, puts forward its interpretation of the constitution and the political ideals that inform it.[16] Although the court may have the last say in settling any particular case, it is not immune from powerful political influences that may force a revision of its reading of the constitution. The court presents its doctrine by reason and argument; its conception of the constitution must, if it is to endure, persuade the major part of the citizens of its soundness. The final court of appeal

[16] For a presentation of this view to which I am indebted, see A. M. Bickel, *The Least Dangerous Branch* (New York, Bobbs-Merrill, 1962), esp. Chs. V and VI.

is not the court, nor the executive, nor the legislature, but the electorate as a whole. The civilly disobedient appeal in a special way to this body. There is no danger of anarchy so long as there is a sufficient working agreement in citizens' conceptions of justice and the conditions for resorting to civil disobedience are respected. That men can achieve such an understanding and honour these limits when the basic political liberties are maintained is an assumption implicit in a democratic polity. There is no way to avoid entirely the danger of divisive strife, any more than one can rule out the possibility of profound scientific controversy. Yet if justified civil disobedience seems to threaten civic concord, the responsibility falls not upon those who protest but upon those whose abuse of authority and power justifies such opposition. For to employ the coercive apparatus of the state in order to maintain manifestly unjust institutions is itself a form of illegitimate force that men in due course have a right to resist.

VI

A DEFENCE OF ABORTION[1]

J. J. THOMSON

MOST opposition to abortion relies on the premise that the foetus is a human being, a person, from the moment of conception. The premise is argued for, but, as I think, not well. Take, for example, the most common argument. We are asked to notice that the development of a human being from conception through birth into childhood is continuous; then it is said that to draw a line, to choose a point in this development and say 'before this point the thing is not a person, after this point it is a person' is to make an arbitrary choice, a choice for which in the nature of things no good reason can be given. It is concluded that the foetus is, or anyway that we had better say it is, a person from the moment of conception. But this conclusion does not follow. Similar things might be said about the development of an acorn into an oak tree, and it does not follow that acorns are oak trees, or that we had better say they are. Arguments of this form are sometimes called 'slippery slope arguments'—the phrase is perhaps self-explanatory—and it is dismaying that opponents of abortion rely on them so heavily and uncritically.

I am inclined to agree, however, that the prospects for 'drawing a line' in the development of the foetus look dim. I am inclined to think also that we shall probably have to agree that the foetus has already become a human person well before birth. Indeed, it comes as a surprise when one first learns how early in its life it begins to acquire human characteristics. By the tenth week, for example, it already has a face, arms and legs, fingers and toes; it has internal organs, and brain activity is detectable.[2] On the other hand, I think that the premise is false, that the foetus is not a person from the moment of conception. A newly fertilized ovum, a newly implanted clump

---

From *Philosophy and Public Affairs*, vol. 1, no. 1 (Fall, 1971), 47–66. Reprinted by permission of Princeton University Press.

[1] I am much indebted to James Thomson for discussion, criticism, and many helpful suggestions.

[2] Daniel Callahan, *Abortion: Law, Choice and Morality* (New York, 1970), p. 373. This book gives a fascinating survey of the available information on abortion. The Jewish tradition is surveyed in David M. Feldman, *Birth Control in Jewish Law* (New York, 1968), Part 5, the Catholic tradition in John T. Noonan, Jr., 'An Almost Absolute Value in History', in *The Morality of Abortion*, ed. John T. Noonan, Jr. (Cambridge, Mass., 1970).

of cells, is no more a person than an acorn is an oak tree. But I shall not discuss any of this. For it seems to me to be of great interest to ask what happens if, for the sake of argument, we allow the premise. How, precisely, are we supposed to get from there to the conclusion that abortion is morally impermissible? Opponents of abortion commonly spend most of their time establishing that the foetus is a person, and hardly any time explaining the step from there to the impermissibility of abortion. Perhaps they think the step too simple and obvious to require much comment. Or perhaps instead they are simply being economical in argument. Many of those who defend abortion rely on the premise that the foetus is not a person, but only a bit of tissue that will become a person at birth; and why pay out more arguments than you have to? Whatever the explanation, I suggest that the step they take is neither easy nor obvious, that it calls for closer examination than it is commonly given, and that when we do give it this closer examination we shall feel inclined to reject it.

I propose, then, that we grant that the foetus is a person from the moment of conception. How does the argument go from here? Something like this, I take it. Every person has a right to life. So the foetus has a right to life. No doubt the mother has a right to decide what shall happen in and to her body; everyone would grant that. But surely a person's right to life is stronger and more stringent than the mother's right to decide what happens in and to her body, and so outweighs it. So the foetus may not be killed; an abortion may not be performed.

It sounds plausible. But now let me ask you to imagine this. You wake up in the morning and find yourself back to back in bed with an unconscious violinist. A famous unconscious violinist. He has been found to have a fatal kidney ailment, and the Society of Music Lovers has canvassed all the available medical records and found that you alone have the right blood type to help. They have therefore kidnapped you, and last night the violinist's circulatory system was plugged into yours, so that your kidneys can be used to extract poisons from his blood as well as your own. The director of the hospital now tells you, 'Look, we're sorry the Society of Music Lovers did this to you—we would never have permitted it if we had known. But still, they did it, and the violinist now is plugged into you. To unplug you would be to kill him. But never mind, it's only for nine months. By then he will have recovered from his ailment, and can safely be unplugged from you.' Is it morally incumbent on you to accede to this situation? No doubt it would be very nice of you if you did, a great kindness. But do you *have* to accede to it? What if it were not nine months, but nine years? Or longer still? What if the director of the hospital says, 'Tough luck, I agree, but you've now got to stay in bed, with the violinist plugged into you, for the rest of

your life. Because remember this. All persons have a right to life, and violinists are persons. Granted you have a right to decide what happens in and
to your body, but a person's right to life outweighs your right to decide what
happens in and to your body. So you cannot ever be unplugged from him.'
I imagine you would regard this as outrageous, which suggests that something really is wrong with that plausible-sounding argument I mentioned
a moment ago.

In this case, of course, you were kidnapped; you didn't volunteer for the
operation that plugged the violinist into your kidneys. Can those who
oppose abortion on the ground I mentioned make an exception for a pregnancy due to rape? Certainly. They can say that persons have a right to
life only if they didn't come into existence because of rape; or they can say
that all persons have a right to life, but that some have less of a right to
life than others, in particular, that those who came into existence because
of rape have less. But these statements have a rather unpleasant sound.
Surely the question of whether you have a right to life at all, or how much
of it you have, shouldn't turn on the question of whether or not you are
the product of a rape. And in fact the people who oppose abortion on the
ground I mentioned do not make this distinction, and hence do not make
an exception in case of rape.

Nor do they make an exception for a case in which the mother has to
spend the nine months of her pregnancy in bed. They would agree that would
be a great pity, and hard on the mother; but all the same, all persons have
a right to life, the foetus is a person, and so on. I suspect, in fact, that they
would not make an exception for a case in which, miraculously enough, the
pregnancy went on for nine years, or even the rest of the mother's life.

Some won't even make an exception for a case in which continuation of
the pregnancy is likely to shorten the mother's life; they regard abortion
as impermissible even to save the mother's life. Such cases are nowadays
very rare, and many opponents of abortion do not accept this extreme view.
All the same, it is a good place to begin: a number of points of interest come
out in respect to it.

1. Let us call the view that abortion is impermissible even to save the
mother's life 'the extreme view'. I want to suggest first that it does not issue
from the argument I mentioned earlier without the addition of some fairly
powerful premises. Suppose a woman has become pregnant, and now learns
that she has a cardiac condition such that she will die if she carries the baby
to term. What may be done for her? The foetus, being a person, has a right
to life, but as the mother is a person too, so has she a right to life. Presumably
they have an equal right to life. How is it supposed to come out that an
abortion may not be performed? If mother and child have an equal right

to life, shouldn't we perhaps flip a coin? Or should we add to the mother's right to life her right to decide what happens in and to her body, which everybody seems to be ready to grant—the sum of her rights now outweighing the foetus's right to life?

The most familiar argument here is the following. We are told that performing the abortion would be directly killing[3] the child, whereas doing nothing would not be killing the mother, but only letting her die. Moreover, in killing the child, one would be killing an innocent person, for the child has committed no crime, and is not aiming at his mother's death. And then there are a variety of ways in which this might be continued. (1) But as directly killing an innocent person is always and absolutely impermissible, an abortion may not be performed. Or, (2) as directly killing an innocent person is murder, and murder is always and absolutely impermissible, an abortion may not be performed.[4] Or, (3) as one's duty to refrain from directly killing an innocent person is more stringent than one's duty to keep a person from dying, an abortion may not be performed. Or, (4) if one's only options are directly killing an innocent person or letting a person die, one must prefer letting the person die, and thus an abortion may not be performed.[5]

Some people seem to have thought that these are not further premises which must be added if the conclusion is to be reached, but that they follow from the very fact that an innocent person has a right to life.[6] But this seems to me to be a mistake, and perhaps the simplest way to show this is to bring out that while we must certainly grant that innocent persons have a right to life, the theses in (1) through (4) are all false. Take (2), for example. If directly killing an innocent person is murder, and thus is impermissible, then the mother's directly killing the innocent person inside her is murder, and

---

[3] The term 'direct' in the arguments I refer to is a technical one. Roughly, what is meant by 'direct killing' is either killing as an end in itself, or killing as a means to some end, for example, the end of saving someone's life. See n. 6, below, for an example of its use.

[4] Cf. *Encyclical Letter of Pope Pius XI on Christian Marriage*, St. Paul Editions (Boston, n.d.), p. 32: 'however much we may pity the mother whose health and even life is gravely imperiled in the performance of the duty allotted to her by nature, nevertheless what could ever be a sufficient reason for excusing in any way the direct murder of the innocent? This is precisely what we are dealing with here'. Noonan (*The Morality of Abortion*, p. 43) reads this as follows: 'What cause can ever avail to excuse in any way the direct killing of the innocent? For it is a question of that.'

[5] The thesis in (4) is in an interesting way weaker than those in (1), (2), and (3): they rule out abortion even in cases in which both mother *and* child will die if the abortion is not performed. By contrast, one who held the view expressed in (4) could consistently say that one needn't prefer letting two persons die to killing one.

[6] Cf. the following passage from Pius XII, *Address to the Italian Catholic Society of Midwives*: 'The baby in the maternal breast has the right to life immediately from God.—Hence there is no man, no human authority, no science, no medical, eugenic, social, economic or moral "indication" which can establish or grant a valid juridical ground for a direct deliberate disposition of an innocent human life, that is a disposition which looks to its destruction either as an end or as a means to another end perhaps in itself not illicit.—The baby, still not born, is a man in the same degree and for the same reason as the mother' (quoted in Noonan, *The Morality of Abortion*, p. 45).

thus is impermissible. But it cannot seriously be thought to be murder if the mother performs an abortion on herself to save her life. It cannot seriously be said that she *must* refrain, that she *must* sit passively by and wait for her death. Let us look again at the case of you and the violinist. There you are, in bed with the violinist, and the director of the hospital says to you, 'It's all most distressing, and I deeply sympathize, but you see this is putting an additional strain on your kidneys, and you'll be dead within the month. But you *have* to stay where you are all the same. Because unplugging you would be directly killing an innocent violinist, and that's murder, and that's impermissible.' If anything in the world is true, it is that you do not commit murder, you do not do what is impermissible, if you reach around to your back and unplug yourself from that violinist to save your life.

The main focus of attention in writings on abortion has been on what a third party may or may not do in answer to a request from a woman for an abortion. This is in a way understandable. Things being as they are, there isn't much a woman can safely do to abort herself. So the question asked is what a third party may do, and what the mother may do, if it is mentioned at all, is deduced, almost as an afterthought, from what it is concluded that third parties may do. But it seems to me that to treat the matter in this way is to refuse to grant to the mother that very status of person which is so firmly insisted on for the foetus. For we cannot simply read off what a person may do from what a third party may do. Suppose you find yourself trapped in a tiny house with a growing child. I mean a very tiny house, and a rapidly growing child—you are already up against the wall of the house and in a few minutes you'll be crushed to death. The child on the other hand won't be crushed to death; if nothing is done to stop him from growing he'll be hurt, but in the end he'll simply burst open the house and walk out a free man. Now I could well understand it if a bystander were to say, 'There's nothing we can do for you. We cannot choose between your life and his, we cannot be the ones to decide who is to live, we cannot intervene.' But it cannot be concluded that you too can do nothing, that you cannot attack it to save your life. However innocent the child may be, you do not have to wait passively while it crushes you to death. Perhaps a pregnant woman is vaguely felt to have the status of house, to which we don't allow the right of self-defence. But if the woman houses the child, it should be remembered that she is a person who houses it.

I should perhaps stop to say explicitly that I am not claiming that people have a right to do anything whatever to save their lives. I think, rather, that there are drastic limits to the right of self-defence. If someone threatens you with death unless you torture someone else to death, I think you have not the right, even to save your life, to do so. But the case under consideration here is very different. In our case there are only two people involved, one whose life is threatened, and one who threatens it. Both are innocent: the one who is threatened is not threatened because of any fault, the one who threatens does not threaten because of any fault. For this reason we may feel that we bystanders cannot intervene. But the person threatened can.

In sum, a woman surely can defend her life against the threat to it posed by the unborn child, even if doing so involves its death. And this shows not merely that the theses in (1) through (4) are false; it shows also that the extreme view of abortion is false, and so we need not canvass any other possible ways of arriving at it from the argument I mentioned at the outset.

2. The extreme view could of course be weakened to say that while abortion is permissible to save the mother's life, it may not be performed by a third party, but only by the mother herself. But this cannot be right either. For what we have to keep in mind is that the mother and the unborn child are not like two tenants in a small house which has, by an unfortunate mistake, been rented to both: the mother *owns* the house. The fact that she does adds to the offensiveness of deducing that the mother can do nothing from the supposition that third parties can do nothing. But it does more than this: it casts a bright light on the supposition that third parties can do nothing. Certainly it lets us see that a third party who says 'I cannot choose between you' is fooling himself if he thinks this is impartiality. If Jones has found and fastened on a certain coat, which he needs to keep him from freezing, but which Smith also needs to keep him from freezing, then it is not impartiality that says 'I cannot choose between you' when Smith owns the coat. Women have said again and again 'This body is *my* body!' and they have reason to feel angry, reason to feel that it has been like shouting into the wind. Smith, after all, is hardly likely to bless us if we say to him, 'Of course it's your coat, anybody would grant that it is. But no one may choose between you and Jones who is to have it.'

We should really ask what it is that says 'no one may choose' in the face of the fact that the body that houses the child is the mother's body. It may be simply a failure to appreciate this fact. But it may be something more interesting, namely the sense that one has a right to refuse to lay hands on people, even where it would be just and fair to do so, even where justice seems to require that somebody do so. Thus justice might call for somebody to get Smith's coat back from Jones, and yet you have a right to refuse to be the one to lay hands on Jones, a right to refuse to do physical violence to him. This, I think, must be granted. But then what should be said is not 'no one may choose', but only, '*I* cannot choose', and indeed not even this, but '*I* will not *act*', leaving it open that somebody else can or should, and in particular that anyone in a position of authority, with the job of securing people's rights, both can and should. So this is no difficulty. I have not been arguing that any given third party must accede to the mother's request that he perform an abortion to save her life, but only that he may.

I suppose that in some views of human life the mother's body is only on loan to her, the loan not being one which gives her any prior claim to it. One who held this view might well think it impartiality to say 'I cannot choose'. But I shall simply ignore this possibility. My own view is that if a human being has any just, prior claim to anything at all, he has a just, prior claim to his own body. And perhaps this needn't be argued for here anyway, since, as I mentioned, the arguments against abortion we are looking at do grant that the woman has a right to decide what happens in and to her body.

But although they do grant it, I have tried to show that they do not take seriously what is done in granting it. I suggest the same thing will reappear even more clearly when we turn away from cases in which the mother's life is at stake, and attend, as I propose we now do, to the vastly more common cases in which a woman wants an abortion for some less weighty reason than preserving her own life.

3. Where the mother's life is not at stake, the argument I mentioned at the outset seems to have a much stronger pull. 'Everyone has a right to life, so the unborn person has a right to life.' And isn't the child's right to life weightier than anything other than the mother's own right to life, which she might put forward as ground for an abortion?

This argument treats the right to life as if it were unproblematic. It is not, and this seems to me to be precisely the source of the mistake.

For we should now, at long last, ask what it comes to, to have a right to life. In some views having a right to life includes having a right to be given at least the bare minimum one needs for continued life. But suppose that what in fact is the bare minimum a man needs for continued life is something he has no right at all to be given? If I am sick unto death, and the only thing that will save my life is the touch of Henry Fonda's cool hand on my fevered brow, then all the same, I have no right to be given the touch of Henry Fonda's cool hand on my fevered brow. It would be frightfully nice of him to fly in from the West Coast to provide it. It would be less nice, though no doubt well meant, if my friends flew out to the West Coast and carried Henry Fonda back with them. But I have no right at all against anybody that he should do this for me. Or again, to return to the story I told earlier, the fact that for continued life that violinist needs the continued use of your kidneys does not establish that he has a right to be given the continued use of your kidneys. He certainly has no right against you that you should give him continued use of your kidneys. For nobody has any right to use your kidneys unless you give him such a right; and nobody has the right against you that you shall give him this right—if you do allow him to go on using your kidneys, this is a kindness on your part, and not something he can claim from you as his due. Nor has he any right against anybody else that *they* should give him continued use of your kidneys. Certainly he had no right against the Society of Music Lovers that they should plug him into you in the first place. And if you now start to unplug yourself, having learned that you will otherwise have to spend nine years in bed with him, there is nobody in the world who must try to prevent you, in order to see to it that he is given something he has a right to be given.

Some people are rather stricter about the right to life. In their view, it does not include the right to be given anything, but amounts to, and only to, the right not to be killed by anybody. But here a related difficulty arises. If everybody is to refrain from killing that violinist, then everybody must refrain from doing a great many different sorts of things. Everybody must refrain from slitting his throat, everybody must refrain from shooting him—and everybody must refrain from unplugging you from him. But does he have a right against everybody that they shall refrain from unplugging you from him? To refrain from doing this is to allow him to continue to use your kidneys. It could be argued that he has a right against us that we should allow him to continue to use your kidneys. That is, while he had no right against us that we should give him the use of your kidneys, it might be argued that he anyway has a right against us that we shall not now intervene and deprive him of the use of your kidneys. I shall come back to third-party interventions later. But certainly the violinist has no right against you that *you* shall allow him to continue to use your kidneys. As I said, if you do allow him to use them, it is a kindness on your part, and not something you owe him.

The difficulty I point to here is not peculiar to the right to life. It reappears in connection with all the other natural rights; and it is something which an adequate account of rights must deal with. For present purposes it is enough just to draw attention to it. But I would stress that I am not arguing that people do not have a right to life—quite to the contrary, it seems to me that the primary control we must place on the acceptability of an account of rights is that it should turn out in that account to be a truth that all persons have a right to life. I am arguing only that having a right to life does not guarantee having either a right to be given the use of or a right to be allowed continued use of another person's body—even if one needs it for life itself. So the right to life will not serve the opponents of abortion in the very simple and clear way in which they seem to have thought it would.

4. There is another way to bring out the difficulty. In the most ordinary

sort of case, to deprive someone of what he has a right to is to treat him
unjustly. Suppose a boy and his small brother are jointly given a box of
chocolates for Christmas. If the older boy takes the box and refuses to give
his brother any of the chocolates, he is unjust to him, for the brother has
been given a right to half of them. But suppose that, having learned that
otherwise it means nine years in bed with that violinist, you unplug yourself
from him. You surely are not being unjust to him, for you gave him no right
to use your kidneys, and no one else can have given him any such right.
But we have to notice that in unplugging yourself, you are killing him; and
violinists, like everybody else, have a right to life, and thus in the view we
were considering just now, the right not to be killed. So here you do what
he supposedly has a right you shall not do, but you do not act unjustly to
him in doing it.

The emendation which may be made at this point is this: the right to life
consists not in the right not to be killed, but rather in the right not to be
killed unjustly. This runs a risk of circularity, but never mind: it would enable
us to square the fact that the violinist has a right to life with the fact that
you do not act unjustly toward him in unplugging yourself, thereby killing
him. For if you do not kill him unjustly, you do not violate his right of life,
and so it is no wonder you do him no injustice.

But if this emendation is accepted, the gap in the argument against abortion stares us plainly in the face: it is by no means enough to show that
the foetus is a person, and to remind us that all persons have a right to life—
we need to be shown also that killing the foetus violates its right to life,
i.e., that abortion is unjust killing. And is it?

I suppose we may take it as a datum that in a case of pregnancy due to
rape the mother has not given the unborn person a right to the use of her
body for food and shelter. Indeed, in what pregnancy could it be supposed
that the mother has given the unborn person such a right? It is not as if
there were unborn persons drifting about the world, to whom a woman who
wants a child says 'I invite you in.'

But it might be argued that there are other ways one can have acquired
a right to the use of another person's body than by having been invited to
use it by that person. Suppose a woman voluntarily indulges in intercourse,
knowing of the chance it will issue in pregnancy, and then she does become
pregnant; is she not in part responsible for the presence, in fact the very
existence, of the unborn person inside her? No doubt she did not invite it
in. But doesn't her partial responsibility for its being there itself give it a
right to the use of her body?[7] If so, then her aborting it would be more

[7] The need for a discussion of this argument was brought home to me by members of the Society
for Ethical and Legal Philosophy, to whom this paper was originally presented.

like the boy's taking away the chocolates, and less like your unplugging your-self from the violinist—doing so would be depriving it of what it does have a right to, and thus would be doing it an injustice.

And then, too, it might be asked whether or not she can kill it even to save her own life: If she voluntarily called it into existence, how can she now kill it, even in self-defence?

The first thing to be said about this is that it is something new. Opponents of abortion have been so concerned to make out the independence of the foetus, in order to establish that it has a right to life, just as its mother does, that they have tended to overlook the possible support they might gain from making out that the foetus is *dependent* on the mother, in order to establish that she has a special kind of responsibility for it, a responsibility that gives it rights against her which are not possessed by any independent person—such as an ailing violinist who is a stranger to her.

On the other hand, this argument would give the unborn person a right to its mother's body only if her pregnancy resulted from a voluntary act, undertaken in full knowledge of the chance a pregnancy might result from it. It would leave out entirely the unborn person whose existence is due to rape. Pending the availability of some further argument, then, we would be left with the conclusion that unborn persons whose existence is due to rape have no right to the use of their mothers' bodies, and thus that aborting them is not depriving them of anything they have a right to and hence is not unjust killing.

And we should also notice that it is not at all plain that this argument really does go even as far as it purports to. For there are cases and cases, and the details make a difference. If the room is stuffy, and I therefore open a window to air it, and a burglar climbs in, it would be absurd to say, 'Ah, now he can stay, she's given him a right to the use of her house—for she is partially responsible for his presence there, having voluntarily done what enabled him to get in, in full knowledge that there are such things as burglars, and that burglars burgle.' It would be still more absurd to say this if I had had bars installed outside my windows, precisely to prevent burglars from getting in, and a burglar got in only because of a defect in the bars. It remains equally absurd if we imagine it is not a burglar who climbs in, but an innocent person who blunders or falls in. Again, suppose it were like this: people-seeds drift about in the air like pollen, and if you open your windows, one may drift in and take root in your carpets or upholstery. You don't want children, so you fix up your windows with fine mesh screens, the very best you can buy. As can happen, however, and on very, very rare occasions does happen, one of the screens is defective; and a seed drifts in and takes root. Does the person-plant who now develops have a right to the use of your house? Surely not—despite the fact that you voluntarily opened your windows, you knowingly kept carpets and upholstered furniture, and you knew that screens were sometimes defective. Someone may argue that you are responsible for its rooting, that it does have a right to your house, because after all you *could* have lived your life with bare floors and furniture, or with sealed windows and doors. But this won't do—for by the same token anyone can avoid a pregnancy due to rape by having a hysterectomy, or anyway by never leaving home without a (reliable!) army.

[handwritten margin note: impossible avoid pregnancy due to rape]

It seems to me that the argument we are looking at can establish at most that there are *some* cases in which the unborn person has a right to the use of its mother's body, and therefore *some* cases in which abortion is unjust killing. There is room for much discussion and argument as to precisely which, if any. But I think we should side-step this issue and leave it open, for at any rate the argument certainly does not establish that all abortion is unjust killing.

5. There is room for yet another argument here, however. We surely must all grant that there may be cases in which it would be morally indecent to detach a person from your body at the cost of his life. Suppose you learn that what the violinist needs is not nine years of your life, but only one hour: all you need do to save his life is to spend one hour in that bed with him. Suppose also that letting him use your kidneys for that one hour would not affect your health in the slightest. Admittedly you were kidnapped. Admittedly you did not give anyone permission to plug him into you. Nevertheless it seems to me plain you *ought* to allow him to use your kidneys for that hour—it would be indecent to refuse.

Again, suppose pregnancy lasted only an hour, and constituted no threat to life or health. And suppose that a woman becomes pregnant as a result of rape. Admittedly she did not voluntarily do anything to bring about the existence of a child. Admittedly she did nothing at all which would give the unborn person a right to the use of her body. All the same it might well be said, as in the newly emended violinist story, that she *ought* to allow it to remain for that hour—that it would be indecent in her to refuse.

Now some people are inclined to use the term 'right' in such a way that it follows from the fact that you ought to allow a person to use your body for the hour he needs, that he has a right to use your body for the hour he needs, even though he has not been given that right by any person or act. They may say that it follows also that if you refuse, you act unjustly toward him. This use of the term is perhaps so common that it cannot be called wrong; nevertheless it seems to me to be an unfortunate loosening of what we would do better to keep a tight rein on. Suppose that box of chocolates I mentioned earlier had not been given to both boys jointly, but was given only to the older boy. There he sits, stolidly eating his way through the box, his small brother watching enviously. Here we are likely to say 'You ought not to be so mean. You ought to give your brother some of those chocolates.' My own view is that it just does not follow from the truth of this that the brother has any right to any of the chocolates. If the boy refuses to give his brother any, he is greedy, stingy, callous—but not unjust. I suppose that the people I have in mind will say it does follow that the brother has a right to some of the chocolates, and thus that the boy does act unjustly if he refuses to give his brother any. But the effect of saying this is to obscure what we should keep distinct, namely the difference between the boy's refusal in this case and the boy's refusal in the earlier case, in which the box was given to both boys jointly, and in which the small brother thus had what was from any point of view clear title to half.

A further objection to so using the term 'right' that from the fact that A ought to do a thing for B, it follows that B has a right against A that A do it for him, is that it is going to make the question of whether or not a man has a right to a thing turn on how easy it is to provide him with it; and this seems not merely unfortunate, but morally unacceptable. Take the case of Henry Fonda again. I said earlier that I had no right to the touch of his cool hand on my fevered brow, even though I needed it to save my life. I said it would be frightfully nice of him to fly in from the West Coast to provide me with it, but that I had no right against him that he should do so. But suppose he isn't on the West Coast. Suppose he has only to walk across the room, place a hand briefly on my brow—and lo, my life is saved. Then surely he ought to do it, it would be indecent to refuse. Is it to be said 'Ah, well, it follows that in this case she has a right to the touch of his hand on her brow, and so it would be an injustice in him to refuse'? So that I have a right to it when it is easy for him to provide it, though no right when it's hard? It's rather a shocking idea that anyone's rights should fade away and disappear as it gets harder and harder to accord them to him.

So my own view is that even though you ought to let the violinist use your kidneys for the one hour he needs, we should not conclude that he has a right to do so—we should say that if you refuse, you are, like the boy who owns all the chocolates and will give none away, self-centred and callous, indecent in fact, but not unjust. And similarly, that even supposing a case in which a woman pregnant due to rape ought to allow the unborn person use her body for the hour he needs, we should not conclude that he has a right to do so; we should conclude that she is self-centred, callous, indecent, but not unjust, if she refuses. The complaints are no less grave; they are just different. However, there is no need to insist on this point. If anyone does wish to deduce 'he has a right' from 'you ought', then all the same he must surely grant that there are cases in which it is not morally required of you that you allow that violinist to use your kidneys, and in which he does not have a right to use them, and in which you do not do him an injustice if you refuse. And so also for mother and unborn child. Except in such cases as the unborn person has a right to demand it—and we were leaving open the possibility that there may be such cases—nobody is morally *required* to make large sacrifices, of health, of all other interests and concerns, of all other duties and commitments, for nine years, or even for nine months, in order to keep another person alive.

6. We have in fact to distinguish between two kinds of Samaritan: the Good Samaritan and what we might call the Minimally Decent Samaritan. The story of the Good Samaritan, you will remember, goes like this:

> A certain man went down from Jerusalem to Jericho, and fell among thieves, which stripped him of his raiment, and wounded him, and departed, leaving him half dead.
> And by chance there came down a certain priest that way; and when he saw him, he passed by on the other side.
> And likewise a Levite, when he was at the place, came and looked on him, and passed by on the other side.
> But a certain Samaritan, as he journeyed, came where he was; and when he saw him he had compassion on him.
> And went to him, and bound up his wounds, pouring in oil and wine, and set him on his own beast, and brought him to an inn, and took care of him.
> And on the morrow, when he departed, he took out two pence, and gave them to the host, and said unto him, 'Take care of him; and whatsoever thou spendest more, when I come again, I will repay thee.'

(Luke 10:30–5)

The Good Samaritan went out of his way, at some cost to himself, to help one in need of it. We are not told what the options were, that is, whether or not the priest and the Levite could have helped by doing less than the Good Samaritan did, but assuming they could have, then the fact they did nothing at all shows they were not even Minimally Decent Samaritans, not because they were not Samaritans, but because they were not even minimally decent.

These things are a matter of degree, of course, but there is a difference, and it comes out perhaps most clearly in the story of Kitty Genovese, who, as you will remember, was murdered while thirty-eight people watched or listened, and did nothing at all to help her. A Good Samaritan would have rushed out to give direct assistance against the murderer. Or perhaps we had better allow that it would have been a Splendid Samaritan who did this, on the ground that it would have involved a risk of death for himself. But the thirty-eight not only did not do this, they did not even trouble to pick up a phone to call the police. Minimally Decent Samaritanism would call for doing at least that, and their not having done it was monstrous.

After telling the story of the Good Samaritan, Jesus said 'Go, and do thou likewise.' Perhaps he meant that we are morally required to act as the Good Samaritan did. Perhaps he was urging people to do more than is morally required of them. At all events it seems plain that it was not morally required of any of the thirty-eight that he rush out to give direct assistance at the risk of his own life, and that it is not morally required of anyone that he give long stretches of his life—nine years or nine months—to sustaining the life of a person who has no special right (we were leaving open the possibility of this) to demand it.

Indeed, with one rather striking class of exceptions, no one in any country in the world is *legally* required to do anywhere near as much as this for anyone else. The class of exceptions is obvious. My main concern here is not the state of the law in respect to abortion, but it is worth drawing attention to the fact that in none of the United States is any man compelled by law to be even a Minimally Decent Samaritan to any person; there is no law under which charges could be brought against the thirty-eight who stood by while Kitty Genovese died. By contrast, in most states in this country women are compelled by law to be not merely Minimally Decent Samaritans, but Good Samaritans to unborn persons inside them. This doesn't by itself settle anything one way or the other, because it may well be argued that there should be laws in this country—as there are in many European countries—compelling at least Minimally Decent Samaritanism.[8] But it does show that there is a gross injustice in the existing state of the law. And it shows also that the groups currently working against liberalization of abortion laws, in fact working toward having it declared unconstitutional for a state to permit abortion, had better start working for the adoption of Good Samaritan laws generally, or earn the charge that they are acting in bad faith.

I should think, myself, that Minimally Decent Samaritan laws would be one thing, Good Samaritan laws quite another, and in fact highly improper. But we are not here concerned with the law. What we should ask is not whether anybody should be compelled by law to be a Good Samaritan, but whether we must accede to a situation in which somebody is being compelled—by nature, perhaps—to be a Good Samaritan. We have, in other words, to look now at third-party interventions. I have been arguing that no person is morally required to make large sacrifices to sustain the life of another who has no right to demand them, and this even where the sacrifices

---

[8] For a discussion of the difficulties involved, and a survey of the European experience with such laws, see *The Good Samaritan and the Law*, ed. James M. Ratcliffe (New York, 1966).

do not include life itself; we are not morally required to be Good Samaritans or anyway Very Good Samaritans to one another. But what if a man cannot extricate himself from such a situation? What if he appeals to us to extricate him? It seems to me plain that there are cases in which we can, cases in which a Good Samaritan would extricate him. There you are, you were kidnapped, and nine years in bed with that violinist lie ahead of you. You have your own life to lead. You are sorry, but you simply cannot see giving up so much of your life to the sustaining of his. You cannot extricate yourself, and ask us to do so. I should have thought that—in light of his having no right to the use of your body—it was obvious that we do not have to accede to your being forced to give up so much. We can do what you ask. There is no injustice to the violinist in our doing so.

7. Following the lead of the opponents of abortion, I have throughout been speaking of the foetus merely as a person, and what I have been asking is whether or not the argument we began with, which proceeds only from the foetus's being a person, really does establish its conclusion. I have argued that it does not.

But of course there are arguments and arguments, and it may be said that I have simply fastened on the wrong one. It may be said that what is important is not merely the fact that the foetus is a person, but that it is a person for whom the woman has a special kind of responsibility issuing from the fact that she is its mother. And it might be argued that all my analogies are therefore irrelevant—for you do not have that special kind of responsibility for that violinist, Henry Fonda does not have that special kind of responsibility for me. And our attention might be drawn to the fact that men and women both *are* compelled by law to provide support for their children.

I have in effect dealt (briefly) with this argument in section 4 above; but a (still briefer) recapitulation now may be in order. Surely we do not have any such 'special responsibility' for a person unless we have assumed it, explicitly or implicitly. If a set of parents do not try to prevent pregnancy, do not obtain an abortion, and then at the time of birth of the child do not put it out for adoption, but rather take it home with them, then they have assumed responsibility for it, they have given it rights, and they cannot *now* withdraw support from it at the cost of its life because they now find it difficult to go on providing for it. But if they have taken all reasonable precautions against having a child, they do not simply by virtue of their biological relationship to the child who comes into existence have a special responsibility for it. They may wish to assume responsibility for it, or they may not wish to. And I am suggesting that if assuming responsibility for it would require large sacrifices, then they may refuse. A Good Samaritan would not refuse—or anyway, a Splendid Samaritan, if the sacrifices that had to be made were enormous. But then so would a Good Samaritan assume responsibility for that violinist; so would Henry Fonda, if he is a Good Samaritan, fly in from the West Coast and assume responsibility for me.

8. My argument will be found unsatisfactory on two counts by many of those who want to regard abortion as morally permissible. First, while I do argue that abortion is not impermissible, I do not argue that it is always permissible. There may well be cases in which carrying the child to term requires only Minimally Decent Samaritanism of the mother, and this is a standard we must not fall below. I am inclined to think it a merit of my account precisely that it does *not* give a general yes or a general no. It allows for and supports our sense that, for example, a sick and desperately frightened fourteen-year-old schoolgirl, pregnant due to rape, may *of course* choose abortion, and that any law which rules this out is an insane law. And it also allows for and supports our sense that in other cases resort to abortion is even positively indecent. It would be indecent in the woman to request an abortion, and indecent in a doctor to perform it, if she is in her seventh month, and wants the abortion just to avoid the nuisance of postponing a trip abroad. The very fact that the arguments I have been drawing attention to treat all cases of abortion, or even all cases of abortion in which the mother's life is not at stake, as morally on a par ought to have made them suspect at the outset.

Secondly, while I am arguing for the permissibility of abortion in some cases, I am not arguing for the right to secure the death of the unborn child. It is easy to confuse these two things in that up to a certain point in the life of the foetus it is not able to survive outside the mother's body; hence removing it from her body guarantees its death. But they are importantly different. I have argued that you are not morally required to spend nine months in bed, sustaining the life of that violinist; but to say this is by no means to say that if, when you unplug yourself, there is a miracle and he survives, you then have a right to turn round and slit his throat. You may detach yourself even if this costs him his life; you have no right to be guaranteed his death, by some other means, if unplugging yourself does not kill him. There are some people who will feel dissatisfied by this feature of my argument. A woman may be utterly devastated by the thought of a child, a bit of herself, put out for adoption and never seen or heard of again. She may therefore want not merely that the child be detached from her, but more, that it die. Some opponents of abortion are inclined to regard this as beneath contempt—thereby showing insensitivity to what is surely a powerful source of despair. All the same, I agree that the desire for the child's death is not one which anybody may gratify, should it turn out to be possible to detach the child alive.

At this place, however, it should be remembered that we have only been pretending throughout that the foetus is a human being from the moment of conception. A very early abortion is surely not the killing of a person, and so is not dealt with by anything I have said here.

VII

THE RIGHTS AND WRONGS OF ABOR-TION: A REPLY TO JUDITH THOMSON

J. FINNIS

FORTUNATELY, none of the arguments for and against abortion *need* be expressed in terms of 'rights'. As we shall see, Judith Thomson virtually admits as much in her 'A Defence of Abortion'.[1] But since she has chosen to conduct her case by playing off a 'right to life' against a 'right to decide what happens in and to one's body', I shall begin by showing how this way of arguing about the rights and wrongs of abortion needlessly complicates and confuses the issue. It is convenient and appropriate to speak of 'rights' for purposes and in contexts which I shall try to identify; it is most inconvenient and inappropriate when one is debating the moral permissibility of types of action—types such as 'abortions performed without the desire to kill', which is the type of action Thomson wishes to defend as morally permissible under most circumstances. So in section I of this essay I shall show how her specification and moral characterization of this type of action are logically independent of her discussion of 'rights'. Then in section II I shall outline some principles of moral characterization and of moral permissibility, principles capable of explaining some of the moral condemnations which Thomson expresses but which remain all too vulnerable and obscure in her paper. In section III I shall show how the elaboration of those principles warrants those condemnations of abortion which Thomson thinks mistaken as well as many of those attributions of human rights which she so much takes for granted. In section IV I briefly state the reason (misstated by Thomson and also by Wertheimer[2]) why the foetus from conception has human rights, i.e. should be given the same consideration as other human beings.

From *Philosophy and Public Affairs*, vol. 2, no. 2 (winter 1973), 117–45. Reprinted by permission of Princeton University Press. Professor Thomson has written a further reply to Dr. Finnis: 'Rights and Deaths', *Philosophy and Public Affairs*, vol. 2, no. 2 (winter 1973), 146–59.
    [1] *Philosophy and Public Affairs*, vol. 1, no. 1 (Fall 1971), 47–66. Otherwise unidentified page references in the text are to this article.
    [2] Roger Wertheimer, 'Understanding the Abortion Argument', *Philosophy and Public Affairs*, vol. 1, no. 1 (Fall 1971), pp. 67–95.

I

Thomson's reflections on rights develop in three stages. (A) She indicates a knot of problems about what rights are rights to; she dwells particularly on the problem 'what it comes to, to have a right to life' (p. 118). (B) She indicates, rather less clearly, a knot of problems about the source of rights; in particular she suggests that, over a wide range (left unspecified by her) of types of right, a person has a right only to what he has 'title' to by reason of some gift, concession, grant or undertaking to him by another person. (C) She cuts both these knots by admitting (but all too quietly) that her whole argument about abortion concerns simply what is 'morally required' or 'morally permissible'; that what is in question is really the scope and source of the mother's responsibility (and only derivatively, by entailment, the scope and source of the unborn child's rights). I shall now examine these three stages a little more closely, and then (D) indicate why I think it useful to have done so.

(A) How do we specify the content of a right? What is a right a right to? Thomson mentions at least nine different rights which a person might rightly or wrongly be said to have.[3] Of these nine, seven have the same logical structure;[4] viz., in each instance, the alleged right is a right with respect to P's action (performance, omission) as an action which may affect Q. In some of these seven instances,[5] the right with respect to P's action is P's right (which Hohfeld[6] called a privilege and Hohfeldians call a liberty). In the other instances,[7] the right with respect to P's action is Q's right (which Hohfeldians call a 'claim-right'). But in all these seven instances there is what

---

[3] Rights which Thomson is willing to allow that a person has:

R1. a right to life (p. 115);
R2. a right to decide what happens in and to one's body (p. 115) (to be equated, apparently, with a just prior claim to one's own body, p. 117);
R3. a right to defend oneself (i.e. to self-defence, p. 116);
R4. a right to refuse to lay hands on other people (even when it would be just and fair to do so, p. 117)—more precisely, a right not to lay hands on other people.

Rights which she thinks it would be coherent but mistaken to claim that a person has or in any event always has:

R5. a right to demand that someone else give one assistance (p. 125)—more precisely, a right to be given assistance by ... ;
R6. a right to be given whatever one needs for continued life (p. 118);
R7. a right to the use of (or to be given, or to be allowed to continue, the use of) someone else's body (or house) (p. 119);
R8. a right not to be killed by anybody (p. 119);
R9. a right to slit another's throat (an instance, apparently, of a 'right to be guaranteed his death') (p. 127);
[4] Namely, R3 through R9 in the list of note 3 above.
[5] Namely, R3, R4, and, in one of their senses, R7 and R9.
[6] W. H. Hohfeld, *Fundamental Legal Conceptions* (New Haven, 1923).
[7] Namely, R5, R6, R8, and, in another of their senses, R7 and R9.

I shall call a 'Hohfeldian right': to assert a Hohfeldian right is to assert a three-term relation between two persons and the action of one of those persons in so far as that action concerns the other person.

The other two rights mentioned by Thomson have a different logical structure.[8] In both these instances, the alleged right is a right with respect to a thing (one's 'own body', or the state of affairs referred to as one's 'life'). Here the relation is two-term: between one person and some thing or state of affairs. Rights in this sense cannot be completely analysed in terms of some unique combination of Hohfeldian rights.[9] P's right to a thing (land, body, life) can and normally should be secured by granting or attributing Hohfeldian rights to him or to others; but just which combination of such Hohfeldian rights will properly or best secure his single right to the thing in question will vary according to time, place, person, and circumstance. And since moral judgments centrally concern *actions*, it is this specification of Hohfeldian rights that we need for moral purposes, rather than invocations of rights to things.

Since Thomson concentrates on the problematic character of the 'right to life', I shall illustrate what I have just said by reference to the 'right to one's own body', which she should (but seems, in practice, not to) regard as equally problematic. Now her two explicit versions of this right are: one's 'just, prior claim to his own body', and one's 'right to decide what happens in and to one's body'. But both versions need much specification[10] before they can warrant moral judgments about particular sorts of action. For example, the 'right to decide' may be *either* (i) a right (Hohfeldian liberty) to do things to or with one's own body (e.g. to remove those kidney plugs, or that baby, from it—but what else? anything? do I have the moral liberty to decide not to raise my hand to the telephone to save Kitty Genovese from her murderers?); *or* (ii) a right (Hohfeldian claim-right) that other people shall not (at least without one's permission) do things to or with one's own body (e.g. draw sustenance from, or inhabit, it—but what else? any-

---

[8] Namely, R1 and R2.

[9] This proposition is elaborated in a juridical context by A. M. Honore, 'Rights of Exclusion and Immunities against Divesting', *University of Tulane Law Review*, vol. 34 (1960), p. 453.

[10] Insufficient specification causes needless problems, besides those mentioned in the text. For example, against 'so using the term "right" that from the fact that A ought to do a thing for B, it follows that B has a right against A that A do it for him', Thomson objects that any such use of the term 'right' is 'going to make the question of whether or not a man has a right to a thing turn on how easy it is to provide him with it' (pp. xxx–xx); and she adds that it's 'rather a shocking idea that anybody's rights should fade away and disappear as it gets harder and harder to accord them to him' (p. xxx). So she says she has no 'right' to the touch of Henry Fonda's cool hand, *because*, although he ought to cross the room to touch her brow (and thus save her life), he is not morally obliged to cross America to do so. But this objection rests merely on inadequate specification of the right as against Henry Fonda. For if we say that she has a right that Henry Fonda should cross-the-room-to-touch-her-fevered-brow, and that she has no right that he should cross-America-to-touch-her-fevered-brow, then we can (if we like!) continue to deduce rights from duties.

thing?); *or* (iii) some combination of these forms of right with each other or with other forms of right such as (a) the right (Hohfeldian power) to change another person's right (liberty) to use one's body by making a grant of or permitting such use (*any* such use?), or (b) the right (Hohfeldian immunity) not to have one's right (claim-right) to be free from others' use of one's body diminished or affected by purported grants or permissions by third parties. And as soon as we thus identify these possible sorts of right, available to give concrete moral content to the 'right to one's body', it becomes obvious that the actions which the right entitles, disentitles, or requires one to perform (or entitles, disentitles, or requires others to perform) *vary* according to the identity and circumstances of the two parties to each available and relevant Hohfeldian right. And this, though she didn't recognize it, is the reason why Thomson found the 'right to life' problematic, too.

(B) I suspect it was her concentration on non-Hohfeldian rights ('title' to things like chocolates or bodies) that led Thomson to make the curious suggestion which appears and reappears, though with a very uncertain role, in her paper. I mean, her suggestion that we should speak of 'rights' only in respect of what a man has 'title' to (usually, if not necessarily, by reason of gift, concession, or grant to him).

This suggestion,[11] quite apart from the dubious centrality it accords to ownership and property in the spectrum of rights, causes needless confusion in the presentation of Thomson's defence of abortion. For if the term 'right' were to be kept on the 'tight rein' which she suggests (p. 122), then (a) the Popes and others whose appeal to 'the right to life' she is questioning would deprive her paper of its starting-point and indeed its pivot by simply rephrasing their appeal so as to eliminate all reference to rights (for, as I show in the next section, they are not alleging that the impropriety of abortion follows from any grant, gift, or concession of 'rights' to the unborn child); and (b) Thomson would likewise have to rephrase claims she herself makes, such as that innocent persons certainly have a right to life, that mothers have the right to abort themselves to save their lives, that P has a right not to

---

[11] It is perhaps worth pointing out that, even if we restrict our attention to the rights involved in gifts, concessions, grants, contracts, trusts, and the like, Thomson's proposed reining-in of the term 'right' will be rather inconvenient. Does only the donee have the 'rights'? Suppose that uncle U gives a box of chocolates to nephew N1, with instructions to share it with nephew N2, and asks father F to see that this sharing is done. Then we want to be able to say that U has a right that N1 and N2 shall each get their share, that N1 shall give N2 that share, that F shall see to it that this is done, and so on; and that N1 has the right to his share, the right not to be interfered with by F or N2 or anyone else in eating his share, and so on; and that N2 has a similar set of rights; and that F has the right to take steps to enforce a fair distribution, the right not to be interfered with in taking those steps, and so on. Since disputes may arise about any one of these relations between the various persons and their actions and the chocolates thereby affected, it is convenient to have the term 'right' on a loose rein, to let it ride round the circle of relations, picking up the action in dispute and fitting the competing claims about 'the right thing to do' into intelligible and typical three-term relationships. Yet some of the rights involved in the gift of the chocolates, for example U's rights, are not acquired by any grant to the right-holder.

be tortured to death by Q even if R is threatening to kill Q unless Q does so, and so on. But if such rephrasing is possible (as indeed it is), then it is obvious that suggestions about the proper or best way to use the term 'a right' are irrelevant to the substantive moral defence or critique of abortion.

But this terminological suggestion is linked closely with Thomson's substantive thesis that we do not have any 'special [sc. Good Samaritan or Splendid Samaritan] responsibility' for the life or well-being of others 'unless we have assumed it, explicitly or implicitly' (p. 126). It is this (or some such) thesis about *responsibility* on which Thomson's whole argument, in the end, rests.

(C) Thomson's explicit recognition that her defence of abortion *need* not have turned on the assertion or denial of rights comes rather late in her paper, when she says that there is 'no need to insist on' her suggested reined-in use of the term 'right':

If anyone does wish to deduce 'he has a right' from 'you ought', then all the same he must surely grant that there are cases in which it is not morally required of you that you allow that violinist to use your kidneys....[12] And so also for mother and unborn child. Except in such cases as the unborn person has a right to demand it ... nobody is morally *required* to make large sacrifices ... in order to keep another person alive (pp. 123–4).

In short, the dispute is about what is 'morally required' (i.e. about what one 'must' and, for that matter, 'may' or 'can' [not] do: see p. 118; that is to say, about the rights and wrongs of abortion. True, on page 125 there is still that 'right to demand large sacrifices' cluttering up the margins of the picture. But when we come to the last pages of her paper (pp. 126–8) even that has been set aside, and the real question is identified as not whether the child has a 'right to demand large sacrifices' of its mother, but whether the mother has a 'special responsibility' to or for the child (since, if she has, then she may be morally required to make large sacrifices for it and *therefore* we will be able to assert, by a convenient locution, the child's 'right to [demand] those sacrifices').

(D) So in the end most of the argument about rights was a red herring. I have bothered to track down this false trail, not merely to identify some very common sorts and sources of equivocation (more will come to light

---

[12] The sentence continues: 'and in which he does not have a right to use them, and in which you do not do him an injustice if you refuse'. But these are merely remnants of the 'rhetoric' in which she has cast her argument. Notice, incidentally, that her suggestion that 'justice' and 'injustice' should be restricted to respect for and violation of rights in her reined-in sense is of no importance since she grants that actions not in her sense unjust may be self-centred, callous, and indecent, and that these vices are 'no less grave'.

in the next two sections), but also to show how Thomson's decision to conduct her defence in terms of 'rights' makes it peculiarly easy to miss a most important weak point in her defence. This weak point is the connection or relation between one's 'special responsibilities' and one's ordinary (not special) responsibilities; and one is enabled to miss it easily if one thinks (a) that the whole problem is essentially one of rights, (b) that rights typically or even essentially depend on grant, concession, assumption, etc., (c) that special responsibilities likewise depend on grants, concessions, assumptions, etc., and (d) that therefore the whole moral problem here concerns one's *special* responsibilities. Such a train of thought is indeed an enthymeme, if not a downright fallacy; but that is not surprising, since I am commenting here not on an argument offered by Thomson but on a likely effect of her 'rhetoric'.

What Thomson, then, fails to attend to adequately is the claim (one of the claims implicit, I think, in the papal and conservative rhetoric of rights) that the mother's duty not to abort herself is *not* an incident of any special responsibility which she assumed or undertook for the child, but is a straightforward incident of an ordinary duty everyone owes to his neighbour. Thomson indeed acknowledges that such ordinary nonassumed duties exist and are as morally weighty as duties of justice in her reined-in sense of 'justice'; but I cannot discern the principles on which she bases, and (confidently) delimits the range of, these duties.[13]

She speaks, for instance, about 'the drastic limits to the right of self-defence': 'If someone threatens you with death unless you torture someone else to death, I think you have not the right, even to save your life, to do so' (p. 116). Yet she also says: 'If anything in the world is true, it is that you do not ... do what is impermissible, if you reach around to your back and unplug yourself from that violinist to save your life' (p. 116). So why, in the first case, has one the strict responsibility not to bring about the death demanded? Surely she is not suggesting that the pain ('torture') makes the difference, or that it *is* morally permissible to kill *painlessly* another person on the orders of a third party who threatens you with death for noncompliance? And, since she thinks that 'nobody is morally *required* to make large

---

[13] Perhaps this is the point at which to note how dubious is Thomson's assertion that 'in no state in this country is any man compelled by law to be even a Minimally Decent Samaritan to any person', and her insinuation that this is a manifestation of discrimination against women. This sounds so odd coming from a country in which a young man, not a young woman, is compelled by law to 'give up long stretches of his life' to defending his country at considerable 'risk of death for himself'. True, he is not doing this for 'a person who has no special right to demand it'; indeed, what makes active military service tough is that one is not risking one's life to save *anybody* in particular from any *particular* risk. And are we to say that young men have *assumed* a 'special responsibility' for defending other people? Wouldn't that be a gross fiction which only a lame moral theory could tempt us to indulge in? But it is just this sort of social contractarianism that Thomson is tempting us with.

sacrifices, of health, of all other interests and concerns, of all other duties and commitments, for nine years, or even for nine months, in order to keep another person alive' (p. 124), will she go on to say that it is permissible, when a third party threatens you with such 'large sacrifices' (though well short of your life), to *kill* (painlessly) another person, or two or ten other persons?

If Thomson balks at such suggestions, I think it must be because she does in the end rely on some version of the distinction, forced underground in her paper, between 'direct killing' and 'not keeping another person alive'.

The more one reflects on Thomson's argument, the more it seems to turn and trade on some version of this distinction. Of course she starts by rejecting the view that it is always wrong to directly kill, because that view would (she thinks) condemn one to a lifetime plugged into the violinist. But she proceeds, as we have noted, to reject at least one form of killing to save one's life, on grounds that seem to have nothing to do with consequences and everything to do with the formal context and thus structure of one's action (the sort of formal considerations that usually are wrapped up, as we shall see, in the word 'direct'). And indeed the whole movement of her argument in defence of abortion is to assimilate abortion to the range of Samaritan problems, on the basis that having an abortion is, or can be, justified as *merely* a way of *not rendering special assistance*. Again, the argument turns, not on a calculus of consequences, but on the formal characteristics of one's choice itself.

Well, why should this apparently *formal* aspect of one's choice determine one's precise responsibilities in a certain situation whatever the other circumstances and expected consequences or upshots? When we know *why*, on both sides of the debate about abortion, we draw and rely on these distinctions, then we will be better placed to consider (i) whether or not unplugging from the violinist is, after all, direct killing in the sense alleged to be relevant by Popes and others, and (ii) whether or not abortion is, after all, just like unplugging the captive philosopher from the moribund musician.

II

Like Thomson's moral language (setting off the 'permissible' against the 'impermissible'), the traditional rule about killing doubtless gets its peremptory sharpness primarily (historically speaking) from the injunction, respected as divine and revealed: 'Do not kill the innocent and just.'[14] But the handful of peremptory negative moral principles correspond to the handful of really basic aspects of human flourishing, which in turn correspond

[14] Exodus 23:7; cf. Exodus 20:13, Deuteronomy 5:17, Genesis 9:6, Jeremiah 7:6 and 22:3.

to the handful of really basic and controlling human needs and human incli-
nations. To be fully reasonable, one must remain *open* to every basic aspect
of human flourishing, to every basic form of human good. For is not each
irreducibly basic, and none merely means to end? Are not the basic goods
incommensurable? Of course it is reasonable to concentrate on realizing
those forms of good, in or for those particular communities and persons
(first of all oneself), which one's situation, talents, and opportunities most
fit one for. But concentration, specialization, particularization is one thing;
it is quite another thing, rationally and thus morally speaking, to make a
choice which cannot but be characterized as a choice *against* life (to kill),
against communicable knowledge of truth (to lie, where truth is at stake in
communication), *against* procreation, *against* friendship and the justice that
is bound up with friendship. Hence the strict negative precepts.[15]

The general sense of 'responsibility', 'duty', 'obligation', 'permissibility' is
not my concern here, but rather the *content* of our responsibilities, duties,
obligations, of the demands which human good makes on each of us. The
general demand is that we remain adequately open to, attentive to, respectful
of, and willing to pursue human good in so far as it can be realized and
respected in our choices and dispositions. Now most moral failings are not
by way of violation of strict negative precepts—i.e. are not straightforward
choices against basic values. Rather, they are forms of negligence, of *insufficient* regard for these basic goods, or for the derivative structures reasonably created to support the basic goods. And when someone is accused of
violating directly a basic good, he will usually plead that he was acting out
of a proper care and concern for the realization of that or another basic
value in the *consequences* of his chosen act though not in the act itself. For
example, an experimenter accused of killing children in order to conduct
medical tests will point out that these deaths are necessary to these tests,
and these tests to medical discoveries, and the discoveries to the saving of
many more lives—so that, in view of the foreseeable consequences of his
deed, he displays (he will argue) a fully adequate (indeed, the only adequate)
and reasonable regard for the value of human life.

But to appeal to consequences in this fashion is to set aside one criterion
of practical reasonableness and hence of morality—namely, that one remain
open to each basic value, and attentive to some basic value, in each of one's
chosen acts—in favour of quite another criterion—namely, that one choose
so to act as to bring about consequences involving a greater balance of good
over bad than could be expected to be brought about by doing any alterna-

---

[15] These remarks are filled out somewhat in my 'Natural Law and Unnatural Acts', *Heythrop
Journal* 11 (1970): 365. See also Germain Grisez, *Abortion: the Myths, the Realities and the Arguments* (New York 1970), Ch. 6. My argument owes much to this and other works by Grisez.

tive action open to one. Hare has observed that *'for practical purposes* there is no important difference' between most of the currently advocated theories in ethics; they all are 'utilitarian', a term he uses to embrace Brandt's ideal observer theory, Richards's (Rawls's?) rational contractor theory, specific rule-utilitarianism, universalistic act-utilitarianism and his own universal prescriptivism.[16] All justify and require, he argues, the adoption of 'the principles whose general inculcation will have, all in all, the best consequences'.[17] I offer no critique of this utilitarianism here; Thomson's paper is not, on its face, consequentialist. Suffice it to inquire how Hare and his fellow consequentialists know the future that to most of us is hidden. How do they know what unit of computation to select from among the incommensurable and irreducible basic aspects of human flourishing; what principle of distribution of goods to commend to an individual considering his own interests, those of his friends, his family, his enemies, his *patria* and those of all men present and future? How do they know how to define the 'situation' whose universal specification will appear in the principle whose adoption (singly? in conjunction with other principles?) 'will' have best consequences;[18] whether and how to weigh future and uncertain consequences against present and certain consequences? And how do they know that net good consequences would in fact be maximized (even if *per impossible* they were calculable) by general adoption of consequentialist principles of action along with consequentialist 'principles' to justify nonobservance of consequentialist 'principles' in hard cases'?[19] One cannot understand the Western moral tradition, with its peremptory negative (forbearance-requiring) principles (the positive principles being relevant in all, but peremptory in few, particular situations), unless one sees why that tradition rejected consequentialism as mere self-delusion—for Hare and his fellow consequentialists can provide no satisfactory answer to any of the foregoing lines of inquiry, and have no coherent rational account to give of any level of moral thought above that of the man who thinks how good it would be to act 'for the best'.[20] Expected total consequences of one's action do not provide a sufficient ground for making a choice that cannot but be regarded as *itself* a choice directly against a basic value (even that basic value which it is hoped will

[16] R. M. Hare, 'Rules of War and Moral Reasoning', *Philosophy and Public Affairs*, vol. 1, no. 2 (winter 1972), pp. 167, 168.

[17] Ibid., p. 174.

[18] Cf. H.-N. Castaneda, 'On the Problem of Formulating a Coherent Act-Utilitarianism', *Analysis* 32 (1972), p. 118; Harold M. Zellner, 'Utilitarianism and Derived Obligation', *Analysis* 32 (1972), p. 124.

[19] See D. H. Hodgson, *Consequences of Utilitarianism* (Oxford, 1967).

[20] Cf. Hare, op. cit., p. 174: 'The defect in most deontological theories . . . is that they have no coherent rational account to give of any level of moral thought above that of the man who knows some good simple moral principles and sticks to them. . . . [The] simple principles of the deontologist . . . are what we should be trying to inculcate into ourselves and our children if we want to stand the best chance . . . of doing what is for the best.'

be realized in the *consequences*)—for expected total consequences cannot be given an evaluation sufficiently reasonable and definitive to be the decisive measure of our response to the call of human values, while a choice directly against a basic good provides, one might say, its own definitive evaluation of itself.

I do not expect these isolated and fragmentary remarks to be in themselves persuasive. I do not deny that the traditional Western willingness, (in theory) to discount expected consequences wherever the action itself could not but be characterized as against a basic value, is or was supported by the belief that Providence would inevitably provide that 'all manner of things shall be well' (i.e. that the whole course of history would turn out to have been a fine thing, indisputably evil deeds and their consequences turning out to have been 'all to the good' like indisputably saintly deeds and their consequences). Indeed, the consequentialist moralist, who nourishes his moral imagination on scenarios in which by killing an innocent or two he saves scores, thousands, millions, or even the race itself, rather obviously is a post-Christian phenomenon—such an assumption of the role of Providence would have seemed absurd to the pre-Christian philosophers[21] known to Cicero and Augustine. I am content to suggest the theoretical and moral context in which the casuistry of 'direct' and 'indirect' develops, within the wider context of *types* of action to be considered 'impermissible' (I leave the term incompletely accounted for) because *inescapably* (i.e. whatever the hoped-for consequences) choices *against* a basic value of human living and doing. In short, one's responsibility for the realization of human good, one's fostering of or respect for human flourishing in future states of affairs at some greater or lesser remove from one's present action, does not override one's responsibility to respect each basic form of human good which comes directly in question in one's present action itself.

But how does one choose 'directly against' a basic form of good? When is it the case, for example, that one's choice, one's intentional act, 'cannot but be' characterized as 'inescapably' anti-life? Is abortion always (or ever) such a case? A way to tackle these questions can be illustrated by reference to three hard cases whose traditional 'solutions' contributed decisively to the traditional judgment about abortion. The relevance of these 'hard cases' and 'solutions' to the discussion with Thomson should be apparent in each case, but will become even more apparent in the next section.

(i) *Suicide.* Considered as a fully deliberate choice (which it doubtless only rather rarely is), suicide is a paradigm case of an action that is always wrong because it cannot but be characterized as a choice directly against

[21] Not to mention the Jewish moralists: see D. Daube, *Collaboration with Tyranny in Rabbinic Law* (Oxford, 1965).

a fundamental value, life. The characterization is significant, for what makes the killing of oneself attractive is usually, no doubt, the prospect of peace, relief, even a kind of freedom or personal integration, and sometimes is an admirable concern for others; but no amount of concentration on the allure of these positive values can disguise from a clear-headed practical reasoner that it is *by* and *in* killing himself that he intends or hopes to realize those goods. And the characterization is given sharpness and definition by the contrast with heroic self-sacrifices in battle or with willing martyrdom.[22] Where Durkheim treated martyrdom as a case of suicide,[23] anybody concerned with the intentional structure of actions (rather than with a simplistic analysis of movements with foreseen upshots) will grant that the martyr is not directly choosing death, either as end or as means. For, however certainly death may be expected to ensue from the martyr's choice not to accede to the tyrant's threats, still it will ensue through, and as the point of, *someone else's* deliberate act (the tyrant's or the executioner's), and thus the martyr's chosen act of defiance need not be interpreted as itself a choice against the good of life.

The case of suicide has a further significance. The judgments, the characterizations, and the distinctions made in respect of someone's choices involving his *own* death will be used in respect of choices involving the death of *others*. In other words, *rights* (such as the 'right to life') are not the fundamental rationale for the judgment that the killing of other (innocent) persons is impermissible. What is impermissible is an intention set against the value of human life where that value is directly at stake in any action by virtue of the intentional and causal structure of that action; and such an impermissible intention may concern my life or yours—and no one speaks of his 'right to life' as against himself, as something that would explain why *his* act of self-killing would be wrongful.

Indeed, I think the real justification for speaking of 'rights' is to make the point that, when it comes to characterizing intentional actions in terms of their openness to basic human values, those human values are, and are to be, realized in the lives and well-being of others as well as in the life and well-being of the actor. That is, the point of speaking of 'rights' is to stake out the relevant claims to equality and nondiscrimination (claims that are not to absolute equality, since *my* life and *my* well-being have some reasonable priority in the direction of *my* practical effort, if only because I am better placed to secure them). But the claims are to equality of *treatment*; so, rather than speak emptily of (say) a 'right to life', it would be better to speak of

---

[22] Note that I am not asserting (or denying) that self-sacrificial heroism and martyrdom are moral duties; I am explaining why they need not be regarded as moral faults.
[23] *Le Suicide* (Paris, 1897), p. 5. Cf. also Daube's remarks on Donne in 'The Linguistics of Suicide', *Philosophy and Public Affairs*, vol. 1, no. 4 (summer 1972), pp. 418ff.

(say, *inter alia*) a 'right not to be killed intentionally'—where the meaning and significance of 'intentional killing' can be illuminated by consideration of the right and wrong of killing oneself (i.e. of a situation where no 'rights' are in question and one is alone with the bare problem of the right relation between one's acts and the basic values that can be realized or spurned in human actions).

Finally, the case of suicide and its traditional solution remind us forcefully that traditional Western ethics simply does not accept that a person has 'a right to decide what shall happen in and to his body', a right which Thomson thinks, astonishingly (since she is talking of Pius XI and Pius XII), that 'everybody seems to be ready to grant'. Indeed, one might go so far as to say that traditional Western ethics holds that, because and to the extent that one does *not* have the 'right' to decide what shall happen in and to one's body, one *therefore* and to that extent does not have the right to decide what shall, by way of one's own acts, happen in and to anyone else's body. As I have already hinted, and shall elaborate later, this would be something of an oversimplification, since one's responsibility for one's own life, health, etc. is reasonably regarded as prior to one's concern for the life, health, etc. of others. But the oversimplification is worth risking in order to make the point that the traditional condemnation of abortion (as something one makes happen in and to a baby's body) *starts* by rejecting what Thomson thinks everyone will admit.

(ii) *D's killing an innocent V in order to escape death at the hands of P, who has ordered D to kill V.* This case has been traditionally treated on the same footing as cases such as D's killing V in order to save Q (or Q_1, Q_2 ... Q_n) from death (perhaps at the hands of P) or from disease (where D is a medical researcher); for all such cases cannot but be characterized as choices to act directly against human life. Of course, in each case, the reason for making the choice is to save life; but such saving of life will be effected, if at all, through the choices of other actors (e.g. P's choice not to kill D where D has killed V; or P's choice not to kill Q) or through quite distinct sequences of events (e.g. Q's being given life-saving drugs discovered by D).

Hence the traditional ethics affirms that 'there are drastic limits to the right of self-defence' in much the same terms as Thomson. 'If someone threatens you with death unless you torture someone else to death ... you have not the right, even to save your own life, to do so' (p. 116). And it was this very problem that occasioned the first ecclesiastical pronouncement on abortion in the modern era, denying that 'it is licit to procure abortion before animation of the foetus in order to prevent a girl, caught pregnant, being

THE RIGHTS AND WRONGS OF ABORTION 141

killed or dishonoured'.[24] The choice to abort here cannot but be characterized as a choice against life, since its intended good life- or reputation-
saving effects are merely expected consequences, occurring if at all through
the further acts of other persons, and thus are not what is being *done* in
and by the act of abortion itself. But I do not know how one could arrive
at any view of this second sort of hard case by juggling, as Thomson seems
to be willing to, with a 'right to life', a 'right to determine what happens
in and to your own body', a 'right of self-defence' and a 'right to refuse to
lay hands on other people'—all rights shared equally by D, V, P, and Q,
$Q_1, Q_2 \ldots$!

(iii) *Killing the mother to save the child.* This was the only aspect of abortion that Thomas Aquinas touched on, but he discussed it thrice.[25] For if
it is accepted that eternal death is worse than mere bodily death, shouldn't
one choose the lesser evil? So if the unborn child is likely to die unbaptized,
shouldn't one open up the mother, rip out the child and save-it-from-eternal-
death-by-baptizing-it? (If you find Aquinas's problem unreal, amend it—
consider instead the cases where the child's life seems so much more valuable,
whether to itself or to others, than the life of its sick or old or low-born
mother). No, says Aquinas. He evidently considers (for reasons I consider
in section III) that the project involves a direct choice against life and is
straightforwardly wrong, notwithstanding the good consequences.

So the traditional condemnation of therapeutic abortion flows not from
a prejudice against women or in favour of children but from a straightforward application of the solution in the one case to the other case, on
the basis that mother and child are *equally* persons in whom the value of
human life is to be realized (or the 'right to life' respected) and not directly
attacked.[26]

III

But now at last let us look at this 'traditional condemnation of abortion'
a little more closely than Thomson does. It is not a condemnation of the

[24] Decree of the Holy Office. 2 March 1679, error no 34; see Denzinger and Schönmetzer,
Enchiridion symbolorum definitionum et declarationum de rebus fidei et morum (Barcelona, 1967),
par. 2134; Grisez, *Abortion: the Myths, the Realities and the Arguments*, p. 174; John T. Noonan,
Jr., 'An Almost Absolute Value in History', in *The Morality of Abortion*, ed. John T. Noonan,
Jr. (Cambridge, Mass., 1970), p. 34.

[25] See *Summa Theologiae* III, q. 68, art. II; in *4 Sententiarum* d. 6, q. 1, a. 1, q. 1, ad. 4; d. 23,
q. 2, a. 2, 1. q. 1, ad 1 & 2; Grisez, op. cit., p. 154; Noonan, op. cit., p. 24.

[26] Pius XII's remark, quoted by Thomson, that 'the baby in the maternal breast has the right
to life immediately from God' has its principal point, not (*pace* Thomson, p. 51) in the assertion
of a premise from which one could deduce the wrongfulness of direct killing, but in the assertion
that *if* anybody—e.g. the mother—has the right not to be directly killed, *then* the baby has the
same right, since as Pius XII goes on immediately 'the baby, still not born, is a man in the same
degree and for the same reason as the mother'.

administration of medications to a pregnant mother whose life is threatened by, say, a high fever (whether brought on by pregnancy or not), in an effort to reduce the fever, even if it is known that such medications have the side effect of inducing miscarriage. It is not a condemnation of the removal of the malignantly cancerous womb of a pregnant woman, even if it is known that the foetus within is not of viable age and so will die. It is quite doubtful whether it is a condemnation of an operation to put back in its place the displaced womb of a pregnant woman whose life is threatened by the displacement, even though the operation necessitates the draining off of the amniotic fluids necessary to the survival of the foetus.[27]

But why are these operations not condemned? As Foot has remarked, the distinction drawn between these and other death-dealing operations 'has evoked particularly bitter reactions on the part of non-Catholics. If you are permitted to bring about the death of the child, what does it matter how it is done?'[28] Still, she goes some way to answering her own question; she is not content to let the matter rest where Hart had left it, when he said:

Perhaps the most perplexing feature of these cases is that the overriding aim in all of them is the same good result, namely ... to save the mother's life. The differences between the cases are differences of causal structure leading up to the applicability of different verbal distinctions. There seems to be no relevant moral difference between them on any theory of morality ... [to attribute moral relevance to distinctions drawn in this way] in cases where the ultimate purpose is the same can only be explained as the result of a legalistic conception of morality as if it were conceived in the form of a law in rigid form prohibiting all intentional killing as distinct from knowingly causing death.[29]

Foot recognizes that attention to 'overriding aim' and 'ultimate purpose' is not enough if we are to keep clear of moral horrors such as saving life by killing innocent hostages, etc. As a general though not exclusive and not (it seems) at-all-costs principle, she proposes that one has a duty to refrain from doing injury to innocent people and that this duty is stricter than one's duty to aid others; this enables her to see that 'we might find' the traditional conclusion correct, that we must not crush the unborn child's skull in order to save the mother (in a case where the child could be saved if one let the mother die): 'for in general we do not think that we can kill one innocent person to rescue another'.[30] But what is it to 'do injury to' innocent people?

[27] The three cases mentioned in this paragraph are discussed in a standard and conservative Roman Catholic textbook: Marcellino Zalba, *Theologiae Moralis Compendium* (Madrid, 1958), i. 885.
[28] Philippa Foot, 'The Problem of Abortion and the Doctrine of Double Effect', *The Oxford Review*, vol. 5 (1967), p. 6.
[29] H. L. A. Hart, 'Intention and Punishment', *The Oxford Review*, vol. 4 (1967), p. 13; reprinted in Hart, *Punishment and Responsibility* (Oxford, 1968), pp. 124–5.
[30] Foot, op. cit., p. 15.

She does not think it an injury to blow a man to pieces, or kill and eat him, in order to save others trapped with him in a cave, *if he is certain to die soon anyway*.[31] So I suppose that, after all, she *would* be willing (however reluctantly) to justify the killing by D of hostages V, V_1, V_2, whenever the blackmailer P threatened to kill *them too*, along with Q, Q_1, Q_2, unless D killed them himself. One wonders whether this is not an unwarranted though plausible concession to consequentialism.

In any event, Foot was aware, not only that the 'doctrine of the double effect' 'should be taken seriously in spite of the fact that it sounds rather odd',[32] but also of what Thomson has not recorded in her brief footnote (p. 115, n. 3) on the technical meaning given to the term 'direct' by moralists using the 'doctrine' to analyse the relation between choices and basic values, namely that the 'doctrine' requires more than that a certain bad effect or aspect (say, someone's being killed) of one's deed be not intended either as end or as means. If one is to establish that one's death-dealing deed need not be characterized as directly or intentionally against the good of human life, the 'doctrine' requires further that the good effect or aspect, which *is* intended, should be proportionate (say, saving someone's life), i.e. sufficiently good and important relative to the bad effect or aspect: otherwise (we may add, in our own words) one's choice, although not directly and intentionally to kill, will reasonably be counted as a choice inadequately open to the value of life.[33] And this consideration alone might well suffice to rule out abortions performed in order simply to remove the unwanted foetus from the body of women who conceived as a result of forcible rape, even if one were to explicate the phrase 'intended directly as end or as means' in such a way that the abortion did not amount to a directly intended killing (e.g. because the mother desired only the removal, not the death of the foetus, and would have been willing to have the foetus reared in an artificial womb had one been available).[34]

Well, how *should* one explicate these central requirements of the 'doctrine' of double effect? When *should* one say that the expected bad effect or aspect of an action is not intended either as end or as means and hence does not determine the moral character of the act as a choice not to respect one of

---

[31] Ibid., p. 14.

[32] Ibid., p. 8.

[33] Ibid., p. 7. This is the fourth of the four usual conditions for the application of the 'Doctrine of Double Effect'; see e.g. Grisez, op. cit., p. 329. G.E.M. Anscombe, 'War and Murder', in *Nuclear Weapons and Christian Conscience*, ed. W. Stein, (London, 1961), p. 57, formulates the 'principle of double effect', in relation to the situation where 'someone innocent will die unless I do a wicked thing', thus: 'you are no murderer if a man's death was neither your aim nor your chosen means, *and if you had to act in the way that led to it or else do something absolutely forbidden*' (emphasis added).

[34] Grisez argues thus, op. cit., p. 343; also in 'Toward a Consistent Natural-Law Ethics of Killing', *American Journal of Jurisprudence*, vol. 15 (1970), p. 95.

the basic human values? Since it is in any case impossible to undertake a full discussion of this question here, let me narrow the issue down to the more difficult and controverted problem of 'means'. Clearly enough, D intends the death of V *as a means* when he kills him in order to conform to the orders of the blackmailer P (with the object of thereby saving the lives of Q *et al.*), since the good effect of D's act will follow only by virtue of *another* human act (here P's). But Grisez (no consequentialist!) argues that the bad effects or aspects of some *natural* process or chain of causation need not be regarded as intended as means to the good effects or aspects of that process even if the good effects or aspects *depend* on them in the causal sense (and provided that those good effects could not have been attained in some other way by that agent in those circumstances).[35] So he would, I think, say that Thomson could rightly unplug herself from the violinist (at least where the hook-up endangered her life) even if 'unplugging' could only be effected by chopping the violinist in pieces. He treats the life-saving abortion operation in the same way, holding that there is no direct choice against life involved in chopping up the foetus if what is intended as end is to save the life of the mother and what is intended as means is no more than the removal of the foetus and the consequential relief to the mother's body.[36] As a suasive, he points again to the fact that *if* an artificial womb or restorative operation were available for the aborted foetus, a right-thinking mother and doctor in such a case would wish to make these available to the foetus; this shows, he says, that a right-thinking mother and doctor, even where such facilities are *not* in fact available, need not be regarded as intending the death of the foetus they kill.[37] For my part, I think Grisez's reliance on such counter-factual hypotheses to specify the morally relevant meaning or intention of human acts is excessive, for it removes morally relevant 'intention' too far from common-sense intention, tends to unravel the traditional and common-sense moral judgments on suicide (someone would say: 'It's not death I'm choosing, only a long space of peace and quiet, after which I'd willingly be revived, if that were possible'!), and likewise disturbs our judgments on murder and in particular on the difference between administering (death-hastening) drugs to relieve pain and administering drugs to relieve-pain-by-killing.

In any event, the version of traditional nonconsequentialist ethics which has gained explicit ecclesiastical approval in the Roman church these last

[35] Ibid., p. 333 and pp. 89–90 respectively.
[36] Ibid., p. 341 and p. 94 respectively.
[37] Ibid., p. 341 and p. 95 respectively. I agree with Grisez that the fact that, if an artificial womb were available, many women would *not* transfer their aborted offspring to it shows that those women are directly and wrongfully intending the *death* of their offspring. I suspect Judith Thomson would agree.

ninety years treats the matter differently; it treats a bad or unwanted aspect or effect of act A_1 as an *intended* aspect of A_1, not only when the good effect (unlike the bad) follows only by virtue of another human act A_2, but also *sometimes* when both the good effect and the bad effect are parts of one natural causal process requiring no further human act to achieve its effect. *Sometimes*, but not always; so when?

A variety of factors are appealed to explicitly or relied on implicitly in making a judgment that the bad effect is to count as intended-as-a-means; Bennett would call the set of factors a 'jumble',[38] but they are even more various than he has noted. It will be convenient to set them out while at the same time observing their bearing on the two cases centrally in dispute, the craniotomy to save a mother's life and that notable scenario in which 'you reach around to your back and unplug yourself from that violinist to save your life'.

(1) Would the chosen action have been chosen if the victim had not been present? If it would, this is ground for saying that the bad aspects of the action, viz. its death-dealing effects on the victim (child or violinist), are not being intended or chosen either as end or means, but are genuinely incidental side effects that do not necessarily determine the character of one's action as (not) respectful of human life. This was the principal reason the ecclesiastical moralists had for regarding as permissible the operation to remove the cancerous womb of the pregnant woman.[39] And the 'bitter' reaction which Foot cites and endorses—'If you are permitted to bring about the death of the child, what does it matter how it is done?'—seems, here, to miss the point. For what is in question, here, is not a mere matter of technique, of different ways of doing something. Rather it is a matter of the very reason one has for acting in the way one does, and such reasons can be constitutive of the act as an intentional performance. One has no reason even to want to be rid of the foetus within the womb, let alone to want to kill it; and so one's act, though certain, causally, to kill, is not, intentionally, a choice against life.

But of course, *this* factor does not serve to distinguish a craniotomy from unplugging that violinist; in both situations, the oppressive presence of the victim is what makes one minded to do the act in question.

(2) Is the person making the choice the one whose life is threatened by

[38] Jonathan Bennett, ' "Whatever the Consequences",' *Analysis*, vol. 26 (1966), p. 92 n. 1.
[39] See the debate between A. Gemelli and P Vermeersch, summarized in *Ephemerides Theologicae Lovaniensis*, ii (1934), 525–61; see also Noonan, op. cit., p. 49; Zalba, *Theologiae Moralis Compendium*, i. 885.

the presence of the victim? Thomson rightly sees that this is a relevant question, and Thomas Aquinas makes it the pivot of his discussion of self-defen-
sive killing (the discussion from which the 'doctrine' of double effect, as a
theoretically elaborated way of analysing intention, can be said to have
arisen). He says:

Although it is not permissible to intend to kill someone else in order to defend oneself
(since it is not right to do the act 'killing a human being', except [in some cases of
unjust aggression] by public authority and for the general welfare), still it is not
morally necessary to omit to do what is strictly appropriate to securing one's own
life simply in order to avoid killing another, for to make provision for one's own life
is more strictly one's moral concern than to make provision for the life of another
person.[40]

As Thomson has suggested, a bystander, confronted with a situation in which
one innocent person's presence is endangering the life of another innocent
person, is in a different position; to choose to intervene, in order to kill one
person to save the other, involves a choice to make himself a master of life
and death, a judge of who lives and who dies; and (we may say) this context
of his choice prevents him from saying, reasonably, what the man defending
himself can say: 'I am not choosing to kill; I am just doing what—as a single
act and not simply by virtue of remote consequences or of someone else's
subsequent act—is strictly needful to protect my own life, by forcefully
removing what is threatening it.' Now the traditional condemnation of abortion[41] concerns the bystander's situation: a bystander cannot but be choosing to kill if (a) he rips open the mother, in a way foreseeably fatal to her,
in order to save the child from the threatening enveloping presence of the
mother (say, because the placenta has come adrift and the viable child is
trapped and doomed unless it can be rescued, or because the mother's blood
is poisoning the child, in a situation in which the bystander would prefer
to save the child, either because he wants to save it from eternal damnation,
or because the child is of royal blood and the mother low born, or because
the mother is in any case sick, or old, or useless, or 'has had her turn', while
the child has a whole rich life before it); or if (b) he cuts up or drowns the
child in order to save the mother from the child's threatening presence.
'Things being as they are, there isn't much a woman can safely do to abort
herself', as Thomson says (p. 116)—at least, not without the help of bystanders, who by helping (directly) would be making the same choice as if

---

[40] *Summa Theologiae* II-II, q. 64, art. 7: 'Nec est necessarium ad salutem ut homo actum mode-
ratae tuteiae practermittat ad evitandum occisionem alterius; quia plus tenetur homo vitae suae
providere quam vitae alienae. Sed quia occidere hominem non licet nisi publica auctoritate propter
bonum commune, ut ex supra dictis patet [art. 3], illicitum est quod homo intendat occidere
hominem ut seipsum defendat.'
[41] Ibid., arts. 2 and 3.

they did it themselves. But the unplugging of the violinist is done by the very person defending herself. Thomson admits that this gives quite a different flavour to the situation, but she thinks that the difference is not decisive, since bystanders have a decisive reason to intervene in favour of the *mother* threatened by her child's presence. And she finds this reason in the fact that the mother *owns* her body, just as the person plugged in to the violinist owns his own kidneys and is entitled to their unencumbered use. Well, this too has always been accounted a factor in these problems, as we can see by turning to the following question.

(3) Does the chosen action involve not merely a denial of aid and succour to someone but an actual intervention that amounts to an assault on the body of that person? Bennett wanted to deny all relevance to any such question,[42] but Foot[43] and Thomson have rightly seen that in the ticklish matter of respecting human life in the persons of others, and of characterizing choices with a view to assessing their respect for life, it *can* matter that one is directly injuring and not merely failing to maintain a life-preserving level of assistance to another. Sometimes, as here, it is the causal structure of one's activity that involves one willy-nilly in a choice for or against a basic value. The connection between one's activity and the destruction of life may be so close and direct that intentions and considerations which would give a different dominant character to mere nonpreservation of life are incapable of affecting the dominant character of a straightforward taking of life. This surely is the reason why Thomson goes about and about to represent a choice to have an abortion as a choice *not* to provide assistance or facilities, *not* to be a Good or at any rate a Splendid Samaritan; and why, too, she carefully describes the violinist affair so as to minimize the degree of intervention against the violinist's body, and to maximize the analogy with simply refusing an invitation to volunteer one's kidneys for his welfare (like Henry Fonda's declining to cross America to save Judith Thomson's life). 'If anything in the world is true, it is that you do not commit murder, you do not do what is impermissible, if you reach around to your back and unplug yourself from that violinist to save your life'. Quite so. It might nevertheless be useful to test one's moral reactions a little further: suppose, not simply that 'unplugging' required a *bystander's* intervention, but also that (for medical reasons, poison in the bloodstream, shock, etc.) unplugging could not safely be performed unless and until the violinist had first been dead for six hours and had moreover been killed outright, say by drowning or decapitation (though not necessarily while conscious). Could one then be *so* confident, as a bystander, that it was right to kill the violinist in order to save the philo-

[42] Bennett, op. cit.
[43] Foot, op. cit., pp. 11–13.

sopher? But I put forward this revised version principally to illustrate *another* reason for thinking that, within the traditional casuistry, the violinist-unplugging in Thomson's version is *not* the 'direct killing' which she claims it is, and which she *must* claim it is if she is to make out her case for rejecting the traditional principle about direct killing.

Let us now look back to the traditional rule about abortion. If the mother needs medical treatment to save her life, she gets it, subject to one proviso, even if the treatment is certain to kill the unborn child—for after all, her body is *her* body, as 'women have said again and again' (and they have been heard by the traditional casuists!). And the proviso? That the medical treatment not be *via* a straightforward assault on or intervention against the child's body. For after all *the child's body is the child's body, not the woman's.* The traditional casuists have admitted the claims made on behalf of one 'body' up to the very limit where those claims become *mere* (*understandable*) *bias, mere* (*understandable*) *self-interested* refusal to listen to the *very same* claim ('This body is *my* body') when it is made by or on behalf of another person.[44] Of course, a traditional casuist would display an utter want of feeling if he didn't most profoundly sympathise with women in the desperate circumstances under discussion. But it is vexing to find a philosophical Judith Thomson, in a cool hour, unable to see when an argument cuts both ways, and unaware that the casuists have seen the point before her and have, unlike her, allowed the argument to cut both ways impartially. The child, like his mother, has a 'just prior claim to his own body', and abortion involves laying hands on, manipulating, that body. And here we have perhaps the decisive reason why abortion cannot be assimilated to the range of Samaritan problems and why Thomson's location of it within that range is a mere (ingenious) novelty.

(4) But is the action against someone who had a duty not to be doing what he is doing, or not to be present where he is present? There seems no doubt that the 'innocence' of the victim whose life is taken makes a difference to the characterizing of an action as open to and respectful of the good of human life, and as an intentional killing. Just how and why it makes a difference is difficult to unravel; I shall not attempt an unravelling here. We all, for whatever reason, recognize the difference and Thomson has expressly allowed its relevance (p. 115).

But her way of speaking of 'rights' has a final unfortunate effect at this point. We can grant, and have granted, that the unborn child has no Hohfeldian *claim-right* to be allowed to stay within the mother's body under all

---

[44] Not, of course, that they have used Thomson's curious talk of 'owning' one's own body with its distracting and legalistic connotations and its dualistic reduction of subjects of justice to objects.

circumstances; the mother is not under a strict duty to allow it to stay under all circumstances. In *that* sense, the child 'has no right to be there'. But Thomson discusses also the case of the burglar in the house; and he, too, has 'no right to be there', even when she opens the window! But beware of the equivocation! The burglar not merely has no claim-right to be allowed to enter or stay; he also has a strict duty *not* to enter or stay, i.e. he has no Hohfeldian *liberty*—and it is *this* that is uppermost in our minds when we think that he 'has no right to be there': it is actually unjust for him to be there. Similarly with Jones who takes Smith's coat, leaving Smith freezing. And similarly with the violinist. He and his agents had a strict duty not to make the hook-up to Judith Thomson or her gentle reader. Of course, the violinist himself may have been unconscious and so not himself at fault; but the whole affair is a gross injustice to the person whose kidneys are made free with, and the injustice to that person is not measured simply by the degree of moral fault of one of the parties to the injustice. Our whole view of the violinist's situation is coloured by this burglarious and persisting wrongfulness of his presence plugged into his victim.

But can any of this reasonably be said or thought of the unborn child? True, the child had no *claim-right* to be allowed to come into being within the mother. But it was not in breach of any *duty* in coming into being nor in remaining present within the mother; Thomson gives no arguments at all in favour of the view that the child is in breach of duty in being present (though her counter examples show that she is often tacitly assuming this). (Indeed, if we are going to use the wretched analogy of owning houses, I fail to see why the unborn child should not with justice say of the body around it: 'That is my house. No one *granted* me property rights in it, but equally no one *granted* my mother any property rights in it.' The fact is that both persons *share* in the use of this body, both by the same sort of title, viz., that this is the way they happened to come into being. But it would be better to drop this ill-fitting talk of 'ownership' and 'property rights' altogether.) So though the unborn child 'had no right to be there' (in the sense that it never had a claim-right to be allowed to *begin* to be there), in another straightforward and more important sense it *did* 'have a right to be there' (in the sense that it was not in breach of duty in being or continuing to be there). All this is, I think, clear and clearly different from the violinist's case. Perhaps forcible rape is a special case; but even then it seems fanciful to say that the child is or could be in any way at fault, as the violinist is at fault or would be but for the adventitious circumstance that he was unconscious at the time.

Still, I don't want to be dogmatic about the justice or injustice, innocence or fault, involved in a rape conception. (I have already remarked that the impermissibility of abortion in any such case, where the mother's life is not in danger, does not depend necessarily on showing that the act is a choice directly to kill.) It is enough that I have shown how in three admittedly important respects the violinist case differs from the therapeutic abortion performed to save the life of the mother. As presented by Thomson, the violinist's case involves (i) no bystander, (ii) no intervention against or assault upon the body of the violinist, and (iii) an indisputable injustice to the agent in question. Each of these three factors is absent from the abortion cases in dispute. Each has been treated as relevant by the traditional casuists whose condemnations Thomson was seeking to contest when she plugged us into the violinist.

When all is said and done, however, I haven't rigorously answered my own question. When should one say that the expected bad effect or aspect of an act is not intended even as a means and hence does not determine the moral character of the act as a choice not to respect one of the basic human values? I have done no more than list some factors. I have not discussed how one decides which combinations of these factors suffice to answer the question one way rather than the other. I have not discussed the man on the plank, or the man off the plank; or the woman who leaves her baby behind as she flees from the lion, or the other woman who feeds *her* baby to the lion in order to make good her own escape; or the 'innocent' child who threatens to shoot a man dead, or the man who shoots that child to save himself;[45] or the starving explorer who kills himself to provide food for his fellows, or the other explorer who wanders away from the party so as not to hold them up or diminish their rations. The cases are many, various, instructive. Too generalized or rule-governed an application of the notion of 'double effect' would offend against the Aristotelian, common-law, Wittgensteinian wisdom that here 'we do not know how to draw the boundaries of the concept'—of intention, of respect for the good of life, and of action as distinct from consequences—'except for a special purpose'.[46] But I think that those whom Aristotle bluntly calls wise can come to clear judgments on most of the abortion problems, judgments that will not coincide with Thomson's.

IV

I have been assuming that the unborn child is, from conception, a person and hence is not to be discriminated against on account of age, appearance,

---

[45] This case is (too casually) used in Brody, 'Thomson on Abortion', *Philosophy and Public Affairs*, vol. 1, no. 3 (spring 1972), p. 335.

[46] Cf. Wittgenstein, *Philosophical Investigations* (Oxford, 1953), sec. 69.

or other such factors in so far as such factors are reasonably considered irrelevant where respect for basic human values is in question. Thomson argues
against this assumption, but not, as I think, well. She thinks (like Wertheimer,[47] mutatis mutandis) that the argument in favour of treating a newly
conceived child as a person is merely a 'slippery slope' argument (p. 112),
rather like (I suppose) saying that one should call all men bearded because
there is no line one can confidently draw between beard and clean shaven-
ness. More precisely, she thinks that a newly conceived child is like an acorn,
which after all is not an oak! It is discouraging to see her relying so heavily
and uncritically on this hoary muddle. An acorn can remain for years in
a stable state, simply but completely an acorn. Plant it and from it will sprout
an oak sapling, a new, dynamic biological system that has nothing much
in common with an acorn save that it came from an acorn and is capable
of generating new acorns. Suppose an acorn is formed in September 1971,
picked up on 1 February 1972, and stored under good conditions for three
years, then planted in January 1975; it sprouts on 1 March 1975 and fifty
years later is a fully mature oak tree. Now suppose I ask: When did that
oak begin to grow? Will anyone say September 1971 or February 1972?
Will anyone look for the date on which it was first noticed in the garden?
Surely not. If we know it sprouted from the acorn on 1 March 1975, that
is enough (though a biologist could be a trifle more exact about 'sprouting');
that is when *the oak* began. *A fortiori* with the conception of a child, which
is no *mere* germination of a seed. Two cells, each with only twenty-three
chromosomes, unite and more or less immediately fuse to become a new
cell with forty-six chromosomes providing a unique genetic constitution (not
the father's, not the mother's, and not a mere juxtaposition of the parents')
which thenceforth throughout its life, however long, will substantially determine the new individual's makeup.[48] This new cell is the first stage in a
dynamic integrated system that has nothing much in common with the individual male and female sex cells, save that it sprang from a pair of them
and will in time produce new sets of them. To say that *this* is when a person's
life began is not to work backwards from maturity, sophistically asking at
each point 'How can one draw the line *here*?' Rather it is to point to a perfectly clear-cut beginning to which each one of us can look back and in looking back see how, in a vividly intelligible sense, 'in my beginning is my end'.
Judith Thomson thinks she began to 'acquire human characteristics' 'by the
tenth week' (when fingers, toes, etc. became visible). I cannot think why she
overlooks the most radically and distinctively human characteristic of all—
the fact that she was conceived of human parents. And then there is Henry

[47] 'Understanding the Abortion Argument.'
[48] See Grisez, op. cit., Ch. 1 and pp. 273–87, with literature there cited.

Fonda. From the time of his conception, though not before, one could say, looking at his unique personal genetic constitution, not only that 'by the tenth week' Henry Fonda would have fingers, but also that in his fortieth year he would have a cool hand. That is why there seems no rhyme or reason in waiting 'ten weeks' until his fingers and so on actually become visible before declaring that he *now* has the human rights which Judith Thomson rightly but incompletely recognizes.

VIII

A THEORY OF FREEDOM OF EXPRESSION

T. SCANLON[1]

> Persecution for the expression of opinions seems to me perfectly logical. If you have no doubt of your premises or your power and want a certain result with all your heart you naturally express your wishes in law and sweep away all opposition. To allow opposition by speech seems to indicate that you think the speech impotent, as when a man says that he has squared the circle, or that you do not care wholeheartedly for the result, or that you doubt either your power or your premises. But . . .
>
> —Oliver Wendell Holmes[2]

I

THE doctrine of freedom of expression is generally thought to single out a class of 'protected acts' which it holds to be immune from restrictions to which other acts are subject. In particular, on any very strong version of the doctrine there will be cases where protected acts are held to be immune from restriction despite the fact that they have as consequences harms which would normally be sufficient to justify the imposition of legal sanctions. It is the existence of such cases which makes freedom of expression a significant doctrine and which makes it appear, from a certain point of view, an irrational one. This feeling of irrationality is vividly portrayed by Justice Holmes in the passage quoted.

To answer this charge of irrationality is the main task of a philosophical defence of freedom of expression. Such an answer requires, first, a clear

From *Philosophy and Public Affairs*, vol. 1, no. 2 (winter 1972), 204–26. Reprinted by permission of Princeton University Press.

[1] This paper is derived from one presented to the Society for Ethical and Legal Philosophy, and I am grateful to the members of that group, as well as to a number of other audiences willing and unwilling, for many helpful comments and criticisms.
[2] Dissenting in *Abrams* v. *United States*, 250 U.S. 616 (1919).

account of what the class of protected acts is, and then an explanation of the nature and grounds of its privilege. The most common defence of the doctrine of freedom of expression is a consequentialist one. This may take the form of arguing with respect to a certain class of acts, e.g., acts of speech, that the good consequences of allowing such acts to go unrestricted outweigh the bad. Alternatively, the boundaries of the class of protected acts may themselves be *defined* by balancing good consequences against bad, the question of whether a certain species of acts belongs to the privileged genus being decided in many if not all cases just by asking whether its inclusion would, on the whole, lead to more good consequences than bad. This seems to be the form of argument in a number of notable court cases, and at least some element of balancing seems to be involved in almost every landmark First Amendment decision.[3] Thus one thing which an adequate philosophical account of freedom of expression should do is to make clear in what way the definition of the class of protected acts and the justification for their privilege depend upon a balancing of competing goals or interests and to what extent they rest instead on rights or other absolute, i.e. nonconsequentialist, principles. In particular, one would like to know to what extent a defender of freedom of expression must rest his case on the claim that the long-term benefits of free discussion will outweigh certain obvious and possibly severe short-run costs, and to what extent this calculation of long-term advantage depends upon placing a high value on knowledge and intellectual pursuits as opposed to other values.

A further question that an adequate account of freedom of expression should answer is this: To what extent does the doctrine rest on natural moral principles and to what extent is it an artificial creation of particular political institutions? An account of freedom of expression might show the doctrine to be artificial in the sense I have in mind if, for example, it identified the class of protected acts simply as those acts recognized as legitimate forms of political activity under a certain constitution *and* gave as the defence of their privilege merely a defence of that constitution as reasonable, just, and binding on those to whom it applied. A slightly different 'artificial' account of freedom of expression is given by Meiklejohn,[4] who finds the basis for the privileged status of acts of expression in the fact that the right to perform such acts is necessary if the citizens of a democratic state are to perform their duties as self-governing citizens. On his view it appears that citizens

---

[3] The balancing involved in such decisions is not always strictly a matter of maximizing good consequences, since what is 'balanced' often includes personal rights as well as individual and social goods. The problems involved in 'balancing' rights in this way are forcefully presented by Ronald Dworkin in 'Taking Rights Seriously', *New York Review of Books*, 17 December 1970, pp. 23–31.

[4] Alexander Meiklejohn, *Political Freedom* (2nd edn., New York, 1965). See esp. p. 79.

not expected to 'govern themselves' would lack (at least one kind of) right to freedom of expression. In contrast to either of these views, Mill's famous argument offers a defence of 'the liberty of thought and discussion' which relies only on general moral grounds and is independent of the features of any particular laws or institutions. It seems clear to me that our (or at least my) intuitions about freedom of expression involve both natural and artificial elements. An adequate account of the subject should make clear whether these two kinds of intuitions represent rival views of freedom of expression or whether they are compatible or complementary.

Although I will not consider each of these questions about freedom of expression in turn, I hope by the end of this discussion to have presented a theory which gives answers to all of them. I begin with an oblique attack on the first.

II

The only class of acts I have mentioned so far is the class 'acts of expression', which I mean to include any act that is intended by its agent to communicate to one or more persons some proposition or attitude. This is an extremely broad class. In addition to many acts of speech and publication it includes displays of symbols, failures to display them, demonstrations, many musical performances, and some bombings, assassinations, and self-immolations. In order for any act to be classified as an act of expression it is sufficient that it be linked with some proposition or attitude which it is intended to convey.

Typically, the acts of expression with which a theory of 'free speech' is concerned are addressed to a large (if not the widest possible) audience, and express propositions or attitudes thought to have a certain generality of interest. This accounts, I think, for our reluctance to regard as an act of expression in the relevant sense the communication between the average bank robber and the teller he confronts. This reluctance is diminished somewhat if the note the robber hands the teller contains, in addition to the usual threat, some political justification for his act and an exhortation to others to follow his example. What this addition does is to broaden the projected audience and increase the generality of the message's interest. The relevance of these features is certainly something which an adequate theory of freedom of expression should explain, but it will be simpler at present not to make them part of the definition of the class of acts of expression.

Almost everyone would agree, I think, that the acts which are protected by a doctrine of freedom of expression will all be acts of expression in the sense I have defined. However, since acts of expression can be both violent

and arbitrarily destructive, it seems unlikely that anyone would maintain
that as a class they were immune from legal restrictions. Thus the class of
protected acts must be some proper subset of this class. It is sometimes held
that the relevant subclass consists of those acts of expression which are instances of 'speech' as opposed to 'action'. But those who put forward such
a view have generally wanted to include within the class of protected acts
some which are not speech in any normal sense of the word (for instance,
mime and certain forms of printed communication) and to exclude from it
some which clearly are speech in the normal sense (talking in libraries, falsely
shouting 'fire' in crowded theatres etc). Thus if acts of speech are the relevant
subclass of acts of expression, then 'speech' is here functioning as a term
of art which needs to be defined. To construct a theory following these traditional lines we might proceed to work out a technical correlate to the distinction between speech and action which seemed to fit our clearest intuitions about which acts do and which do not qualify for protection.[5]

To proceed in this way seems to me, however, to be a serious mistake.
It seems clear that the intuitions we appeal to in deciding whether a given
restriction infringes freedom of expression are not intuitions about which
things are properly called speech as opposed to action, even in some refined
sense of 'speech'. The feeling that we must look for a definition of this kind
has its roots, I think, in the view that since any adequate doctrine of freedom
of expression must extend to some acts a privilege not enjoyed by all, such
a doctrine must have its theoretical basis in some difference between the
protected acts and others, i.e., in some definition of the protected class. But
this is clearly wrong. It could be, and I think is, the case that the theoretical
bases of the doctrine of freedom of expression are multiple and diverse, and
while the net effect of these elements taken together is to extend to some
acts a certain privileged status, there is no theoretically interesting (and certainly no simple and intuitive) definition of the class of acts which enjoys
this privilege. Rather than trying at the outset to carve out the privileged
subset of acts of expression, then, I propose to consider the class as a whole
and to look for ways in which the charge of irrationality brought against
the doctrine of freedom of expression might be answered without reference
to a single class of privileged acts.

As I mentioned at the start, this charge arises from the fact that under
any nontrivial form of the doctrine there will be cases in which acts of expression are held to be immune from legal restriction despite the fact that they
give rise to undoubted harms which would in other cases be sufficient to
justify such restriction. (The 'legal restriction' involved here may take the

---

[5] This task is carried out by Thomas Emerson in *Toward a General Theory of the First
Amendment* (New York, 1966). See esp. pp. 60–2.

form either of the imposition of criminal sanctions or of the general recognition by the courts of the right of persons affected by the acts to recover through civil suits for damages.) Now it is not in general sufficient justification for a legal restriction on a certain class of acts to show that certain harms will be prevented if this restriction is enforced. It might happen that the costs of enforcing the restriction outweigh the benefits to be gained, or that the enforcement of the restriction infringes some right either directly (e.g. a right to the unimpeded performance of exactly those acts to which the restriction applies) or indirectly (e.g. a right which under prevailing circumstances can be secured by many only through acts to which the restriction applies). Alternatively, it may be that while certain harms could be prevented by placing legal restrictions on a class of acts, those to whom the restriction would apply are not responsible for those harms and hence cannot be restricted in order to prevent them.

Most defences of freedom of expression have rested upon arguments of the first two of these three forms. In arguments of both these forms factors which taken in isolation might have been sufficient to justify restrictions on a given class of acts are held in certain cases to be overridden by other considerations. As will become clear later, I think that appeals both to rights and to the balancing of competing goals are essential components of a complete theory of freedom of expression. But I want to begin by considering arguments which, like disclaimers of responsibility, have the effect of showing that what might at first seem to be reasons for restricting a class of acts cannot be taken as such reasons at all.

My main reason for beginning in this way is this: it is easier to say what the classic violations of freedom of expression have in common than it is to define the class of acts which is protected by that doctrine. What distinguishes these violations from innocent regulation of expression is not the character of the acts they interfere with but rather what they hope to achieve—for instance, the halting of the spread of heretical notions. This suggests that an important component of our intuitions about freedom of expression has to do not with the illegitimacy of certain restrictions but with the illegitimacy of certain justifications for restrictions. Very crudely, the intuition seems to be something like this: those justifications are illegitimate which appeal to the fact that it would be a bad thing if the view communicated by certain acts of expression were to become generally believed; justifications which are legitimate, though they may sometimes be overridden, are those that appeal to features of acts of expression (time, place, loudness) other than the views they communicate.

As a principle of freedom of expression this is obviously unsatisfactory as it stands. For one thing, it rests on a rather unclear notion of 'the view communicated' by an act of expression; for another, it seems too restrictive, since, for example, it appears to rule out any justification for laws against defamation. In order to improve upon this crude formulation, I want to consider a number of different ways in which acts of expression can bring about harms, concentrating on cases where these harms clearly can be counted as reasons for restricting the acts that give rise to them. I will then try to formulate the principle in a way which accommodates these cases. I emphasize at the outset that I am not maintaining in any of these cases that the harms in question are always sufficient justification for restrictions on expression, but only that they can always be taken into account.

1. Like other acts, acts of expression can bring about injury or damage as a direct physical consequence. This is obviously true of the more bizarre forms of expression mentioned above, but no less true of more pedestrian forms: the sound of my voice can break glass, wake the sleeping, trigger an avalanche, or keep you from paying attention to something else you would rather hear. It seems clear that when harms brought about in this way are intended by the person performing an act of expression, or when he is reckless or negligent with respect to their occurrence, then no infringement of freedom of expression is involved in considering them as possible grounds for criminal penalty or civil action.

2. It is typical of the harms just considered that their production is in general quite independent of the view which the given act of expression is intended to communicate. This is not generally true of a second class of harms, an example of which is provided by the common-law notion of assault. In at least one of the recognized senses of the term, an assault (as distinct from a battery) is committed when one person intentionally places another in apprehension of imminent bodily harm. Since assault in this sense involves an element of successful communication, instances of assault may necessarily involve expression. But assaults and related acts can also be part of larger acts of expression, as for example when a guerrilla theatre production takes the form of a mock bank robbery which starts off looking like the real thing, or when a bomb scare is used to gain attention for a political cause. Assault is sometimes treated as inchoate battery, but it can also be viewed as a separate offence which consists in actually bringing about a specific kind of harm. Under this analysis, assault is only one of a large class of possible crimes which consist in the production in others of harmful or unpleasant states of mind, such as fear, shock, and perhaps certain kinds of offence. One may have doubts as to whether most of these harms are serious enough to be recognized by the law or whether standards of proof could be established for dealing with them in court. In principle, however,

there seems to be no alternative to including them among the possible justifications for restrictions on expression.

3. Another way in which an act of expression can harm a person is by causing others to form an adverse opinion of him or by making him an object of public ridicule. Obvious examples of this are defamation and interference with the right to a fair trial.

4. As Justice Holmes said, 'The most stringent protection of free speech would not protect a man in falsely shouting fire in a theatre and causing a panic.'[6]

5. One person may through an act of expression contribute to the production of a harmful act by someone else, and at least in some cases the harmful consequences of the latter act may justify making the former a crime as well. This seems to many people to be the case when the act of expression is the issuance of an order or the making of a threat or when it is a signal or other communication between confederates.

6. Suppose some misanthropic inventor were to discover a simple method whereby anyone could make nerve gas in his kitchen out of gasoline, table salt, and urine. It seems just as clear to me that he could be prohibited by law from passing out his recipe on handbills or broadcasting it on television as that he could be prohibited from passing out free samples of his product in aerosol cans or putting it on sale at Abercrombie & Fitch. In either case his action would bring about a drastic decrease in the general level of personal safety by radically increasing the capacity of most citizens to inflict harm on each other. The fact that he does this in one case through an act of expression and in the other through some other form of action seems to me not to matter.

It might happen, however, that a comparable decrease in the general level of personal safety could be just as reliably predicted to result from the distribution of a particularly effective piece of political propaganda which would undermine the authority of the government, or from the publication of a theological tract which would lead to a schism and a bloody civil war. In these cases the matter seems to me to be entirely different, and the harmful consequence seems clearly not to be a justification for restricting the acts of expression.

What I conclude from this is that the distinction between expression and other forms of action is less important than the distinction between expression which moves others to act by pointing out what they take to be good reasons for action and expression which gives rise to action by others in other ways, e.g., by providing them with the means to do what they wanted

---

[6] In *Schenck* v. *United States*, 249 U.S. 47 (1919).

to do anyway. This conclusion is supported, I think, by our normal views about legal responsibility.

If I were to say to you, an adult in full possession of your faculties, 'What you ought to do is rob a bank', and you were subsequently to act on this advice, I could not be held legally responsible for your act, nor could my act legitimately be made a separate crime. This remains true if I supplement my advice with a battery of arguments about why banks should be robbed or even about why a certain bank in particular should be robbed and why you in particular are entitled to rob it. It might become false—what I did might legitimately be made a crime—if certain further conditions held: for example, if you were a child, or so weak-minded as to be legally incompetent, and I knew this or ought to have known it; or if you were my subordinate in some organization and what I said to you was not advice but an order, backed by the discipline of the group; or if I went on to make further contributions to your act, such as aiding you in preparations or providing you with tools or giving you crucial information about the bank.

The explanation for these differences seems to me to be this. A person who acts on reasons he has acquired from another's act of expression acts on what *he* has come to believe and has judged to be a sufficient basis for action. The contribution to the genesis of his action made by the act of expression is, so to speak, superseded by the agent's own judgment. This is not true of the contribution made by an accomplice, or by a person who knowingly provides the agent with tools (the key to the bank) or with technical information (the combination of the safe) which he uses to achieve his ends. Nor would it be true of my contribution to your act if, instead of providing you with reasons for thinking bank robbery a good thing, I issued orders or commands backed by threats, thus changing your circumstances so as to *make* it a (comparatively) good thing for you to do.

It is a difficult matter to say exactly when legal liability arises in these cases, and I am not here offering any positive thesis about what constitutes being an accessory, inciting, conspiring, etc. I am interested only in maintaining the negative thesis that whatever these crimes involve, it has to be something more than merely the communication of persuasive reasons for action (or perhaps some special circumstances, such as diminished capacity of the person persuaded).

I will now state the principle of freedom of expression which was promised at the beginning of this section. The principle, which seems to me to be a natural extension of the thesis Mill defends in Chapter II of *On Liberty*, and which I will therefore call the Millian Principle, is the following:

There are certain harms which, although they would not occur but for certain acts of expression, nonetheless cannot be taken as part of a justification for legal restrictions on these acts. These harms are: (a) harms to certain individuals which consist in their coming to have false beliefs as a result of those acts of expression; (b) harmful consequences of acts performed as a result of those acts of expression, where the connection between the acts of expression and the subsequent harmful acts consists merely in the fact that the act of expression led the agents to believe (or increased their tendency to believe) these acts to be worth performing.

I hope it is obvious that this principle is compatible with the examples of acceptable reasons for restricting expression presented in 1 through 6 above. (One case in which this may not be obvious, that of the man who falsely shouts 'fire', will be discussed more fully below.) The preceding discussion, which appealed in part to intuitions about legal responsibility, was intended to make plausible the distinction on which the second part of the Millian Principle rests and, in general, to suggest how the principle could be reconciled with cases of the sort included in 5 and 6. But the principle itself goes beyond questions of responsibility. In order for a class of harms to provide a justification for restricting a person's act it is not necessary that he fulfil conditions for being legally responsible for any of the individual acts which actually produce those harms. In the nerve-gas case, for example, to claim that distribution of the recipe may be prevented one need not claim that a person who distributed it could be held legally responsible (even as an accessory) for any of the particular murders the gas is used to commit. Consequently, to explain why this case differs from sedition it would not be sufficient to claim that providing means involves responsibility while providing reasons does not.

I would like to believe that the general observance of the Millian Principle by governments would, in the long run, have more good consequences than bad. But my defence of the principle does not rest on this optimistic outlook. I will argue in the next section that the Millian Principle, as a general principle about how governmental restrictions on the liberty of citizens may be justified, is a consequence of the view, coming down to us from Kant and others, that a legitimate government is one whose authority citizens can recognize while still regarding themselves as equal, autonomous, rational agents. Thus, while it is not a principle about legal responsibility, the Millian Principle has its origins in a certain view of human agency from which many of our ideas about responsibility also derive.

Taken by itself, the Millian Principle obviously does not constitute an adequate theory of freedom of expression. Much more needs to be said about when the kinds of harmful consequences which the principle allows us to consider can be taken to be sufficient justification for restrictions on expression. Nonetheless, it seems to me fair to call the Millian Principle the basic principle of freedom of expression. This is so, first, because a successful defence of the principle would provide us with an answer to the charge of irrationality by explaining why certain of the most obvious consequences of acts of expression cannot be appealed to as a justification for legal restrictions against them. Second, the Millian Principle is the only plausible principle of freedom of expression I can think of which applies to expression in general and makes no appeal to special rights (e.g., political rights) or to the value to be attached to expression in some particular domain (e.g., artistic expression or the discussion of scientific ideas). It thus specifies what is special about acts of expression as opposed to other acts and constitutes in this sense the usable residue of the distinction between speech and action.

I will have more to say in section IV about how the Millian Principle is to be supplemented to obtain a full account of freedom of expression. Before that, however, I want to consider in more detail how the principle can be justified.

III

As I have already mentioned, I will defend the Millian Principle by showing it to be a consequence of the view that the powers of a state are limited to those that citizens could recognize while still regarding themselves as equal, autonomous, rational agents. Since the sense of autonomy to which I will appeal is extremely weak, this seems to me to constitute a strong defence of the Millian Principle as an exceptionless restriction on governmental authority. I will consider briefly in section V, however, whether there are situations in which the principle should be suspended.

To regard himself as autonomous in the sense I have in mind a person must see himself as sovereign in deciding what to believe and in weighing competing reasons for action. He must apply to these tasks his own canons of rationality, and must recognize the need to defend his beliefs and decisions in accordance with these canons. This does not mean, of course, that he must be perfectly rational, even by his own standard of rationality, or that his standard of rationality must be exactly ours. Obviously the content of this notion of autonomy will vary according to the range of variation we are willing to allow in canons of rational decision. If just anything counts as such a canon then the requirements I have mentioned will become mere tautologies: an autonomous man believes what he believes and decides to do what he decides to do. I am sure I could not describe a set of limits on what can count as canons of rationality which would secure general agreement, and I will not try, since I am sure that the area of agreement on this question extends far beyond anything which will be relevant to the applications of the notion of autonomy that I intend to make. For present purposes what will be important is this. An autonomous person cannot accept without independent consideration the judgment of others as to what he should believe or what he should do. He may rely on the judgment of others, but when he does so he must be prepared to advance independent reasons for thinking their judgment likely to be correct, and to weigh the evidential value of their opinion against contrary evidence.

The requirements of autonomy as I have so far described them are extremely weak. They are much weaker than the requirements Kant draws from essentially the same notion,[7] in that being autonomous in my sense (like being free in Hobbes's) is quite consistent with being subject to coercion with respect to one's actions. A coercer merely changes the considerations which militate for or against a certain course of action; weighing these conflicting considerations is still up to you.

An autonomous man may, if he believes the appropriate arguments, believe that the state has a distinctive right to command him. That is, he may believe that (within certain limits, perhaps) the fact that the law requires a certain action provides him with a very strong reason for performing that action, a reason which is quite independent of the consequences, for him or others, of his performing it or refraining. How strong this reason is—what, if anything, could override it—will depend on his view of the arguments for obedience to law. What is essential to the person's remaining autonomous is that in any given case his mere recognition that a certain action is required by law does not settle the question of whether he will do it. That question is settled only by his own decision, which may take into account his current assessment of the general case for obedience and the exceptions it admits, consideration of his other duties and obligations, and his estimate of the consequences of obedience and disobedience in this particular case.[8]

Thus, while it is not obviously inconsistent with being autonomous to recognize a special obligation to obey the commands of the state, there are limits on the *kind* of obligation which autonomous citizens could recognize. In particular, they could not regard themselves as being under an 'obligation' to believe the decrees of the state to be correct, nor could they concede to

---

[7] Kant's notion of autonomy goes beyond the one I employ in that for him there are special requirements regarding the reasons which an autonomous being can act on. (See the second and third sections of *Foundations of the Metaphysics of Morals*.) While his notion of autonomy is stronger than mine, Kant does not draw from it the same limitations on the authority of states (see *Metaphysical Elements of Justice*, sections 46–9).

[8] I am not certain whether I am here agreeing or disagreeing with Robert Paul Wolff (*In Defense of Anarchism*, New York, 1970). At any rate I would not call what I am maintaining anarchism. The limitation on state power I have in mind is that described by John Rawls in the closing paragraphs of 'The Justification of Civil Disobedience', in *Civil Disobedience: Theory and Practice*, ed. Hugo Bedau (New York, 1969).

the state the right to have its decrees obeyed without deliberation. The Millian Principle can be seen as a refinement of these limitations.

The apparent irrationality of the doctrine of freedom of expression derives from its apparent conflict with the principle that it is the prerogative of a state—indeed, part of its duty to its citizens—to decide when the threat of certain harms is great enough to warrant legal action, and when it is, to make laws adequate to meet this threat. (Thus Holmes's famous reference to 'substantive evils that Congress has a right to prevent.'[9]) Obviously this principle is not acceptable in the crude form in which I have just stated it; no one thinks that Congress can do *anything* it judges to be required to save us from 'substantive evils'. The Millian Principle specifies two ways in which this prerogative must be limited if the state is to be acceptable to autonomous subjects. The argument for the first part of the principle is as follows.

The harm of coming to have false beliefs is not one that an autonomous man could allow the state to protect him against through restrictions on expression. For a law to provide such protection it would have to be in effect and deterring potential misleaders while the potentially misled remained susceptible to persuasion by them. In order to be protected by such a law a person would thus have to concede to the state the right to decide that certain views were false and, once it had so decided, to prevent him from hearing them advocated even if he might wish to. The conflict between doing this and remaining autonomous would be direct if a person who authorized the state to protect him in this way necessarily also bound himself to accept the state's judgment about which views were false. The matter is not quite this simple, however, since it is conceivable that a person might authorize the state to act for him in this way while still reserving to himself the prerogative of deciding, on the basis of the arguments and evidence left available to him, where the truth was to be found. But such a person would be 'deciding for himself' only in an empty sense, since in any case where the state exercised its prerogative he would be 'deciding' on the basis of evidence preselected to include only that which supported one conclusion. While he would not be under an obligation to accept the state's judgment as correct, he would have conceded to the state the right to deprive him of grounds for making an independent judgment.

The argument for the second half of the Millian Principle is parallel to this one. What must be argued against is the view that the state, once it has declared certain conduct to be illegal, may when necessary move to prevent that conduct by outlawing its advocacy. The conflict between this thesis and the autonomy of citizens is, just as in the previous case, slightly oblique. Conceding to the state the right to use this means to secure com-

[9] In *Schenck* v. *United States*.

pliance with its laws does not immediately involve conceding to it the right to require citizens to believe that what the law says ought not to be done ought not to be done. None the less, it is a concession that autonomous citizens could not make, since it gives the state the right to deprive citizens of the grounds for arriving at an independent judgment as to whether the law should be obeyed.

These arguments both depend on the thesis that to defend a certain belief as reasonable a person must be prepared to defend the grounds of his belief as not obviously skewed or otherwise suspect. There is a clear parallel between this thesis and Mill's famous argument that if we are interested in having truth prevail we should allow all available arguments to be heard.[10] But the present argument does not depend, as Mill's may appear to, on an empirical claim that the truth is in fact more likely to win out if free discussion is allowed. Nor does it depend on the perhaps more plausible claim that, given the nature of people and governments, to concede to governments the power in question would be an outstandingly poor strategy for bringing about a situation in which true opinions prevail.

It is quite conceivable that a person who recognized in himself a fatal weakness for certain kinds of bad arguments might conclude that everyone would be better off if he were to rely entirely on the judgment of his friends in certain crucial matters. Acting on this conclusion, he might enter into an agreement, subject to periodic review by him, empowering them to shield him from any sources of information likely to divert him from their counsel on the matters in question. Such an agreement is not obviously irrational, nor, if it is entered into voluntarily, for a limited time, and on the basis of the person's own knowledge of himself and those he proposes to trust, does it appear to be inconsistent with his autonomy. The same would be true if the proposed trustees were in fact the authorities of the state. But the question we have been considering is quite different: Could an autonomous individual regard the state as having, not as part of a special voluntary agreement with him but as part of its normal powers *qua* state, the power to put such an arrangement into effect without his consent whenever *it* (i.e., the legislative authority) judged that to be advisable? The answer to this question seems to me to be quite clearly no.

Someone might object to this answer on the following grounds. I have allowed for the possibility that an autonomous man might accept a general argument to the effect that the fact that the state commands a certain thing is in and of itself a reason why that thing should be done. Why couldn't he also accept a similar argument to the effect that the state *qua* state is in the best position to decide when certain counsel is best ignored?

[10] In Ch. II of *On Liberty*.

I have already argued that the parallel suggested here between the state's right to command action and a right to restrict expression does not hold. But there is a further problem with this objection. What saves temporary, voluntary arrangements of the kind considered above from being obvious violations of autonomy is the fact that they can be based on a firsthand estimation of the relative reliability of the trustee's judgment and that of the 'patient'. Thus the person whose information is restricted by such an arrangement has what he judges to be good grounds for thinking the evidence he does receive to be a sound basis for judgment. A principle which provided a corresponding basis for relying on the state *qua* state would have to be extremely general, applying to all states of a certain kind, regardless of who occupied positions of authority in them, and to all citizens of such states. Such a principle would have to be one which admitted variation in individual cases and rested its claim on what worked out best 'in the long run'. Even if some generalization of this kind were true, it seems to me altogether implausible to suppose that it could be rational to rely on such a general principle when detailed knowledge of the individuals involved in a particular case suggested a contrary conclusion.

A more limited case for allowing states the power in question might rest not on particular virtues of governments but on the recognized fact that under certain circumstances individuals are quite incapable of acting rationally. Something like this may seem to apply in the case of the man who falsely shouts 'fire' in a crowded theatre. Here a restriction on expression is justified by the fact that such acts would lead others (give them reason) to perform harmful actions. Part of what makes the restriction acceptable is the idea that the persons in the theatre who react to the shout are under conditions that diminish their capacity for rational deliberation. This case strikes us as a trivial one. What makes it trivial is, first, the fact that only in a very far-fetched sense is a person who is prevented from hearing the false shout under such circumstances prevented from making up his own mind about some question. Second, the diminished capacity attributed to those in the theatre is extremely brief, and applies equally to anyone under the relevant conditions. Third, the harm to be prevented by the restriction is not subject to any doubt or controversy, even by those who are temporarily 'deluded'. In view of all these facts, the restriction is undoubtedly one which would receive unanimous consent if that were asked.[11]

This is not true, however, of most of the other exceptions to the Millian Principle that might be justified by appeal to 'diminished rationality'. It is

---

[11] This test is developed as a criterion for justifiable paternalism by Gerald Dworkin in his essay 'Paternalism', in *Morality and the Law*, ed. Richard Wasserstrom (Belmont, Calif., 1971).

doubtful, for example, whether any of the three conditions I have mentioned would apply to a case in which political debate was to be suspended during a period of turmoil and impending revolution. I cannot see how nontrivial cases of this kind could be made compatible with autonomy.

The arguments I have given may sound like familiar arguments against paternalism, but the issue involved is not simply that. First, a restriction on expression justified on grounds contrary to the Millian Principle is not necessarily paternalistic, since those who are to be protected by such a restriction may be other than those (the speaker and his audience) whose liberty is restricted. When such a restriction is paternalistic, however, it represents a particularly strong form of paternalism, and the arguments I have given are arguments against paternalism only in this strong form. It is quite consistent with a person's autonomy, in the limited sense I have employed, for the law to restrict his freedom of action 'for his own good', for instance by requiring him to wear a helmet while riding his motorcycle. The conflict arises only if compliance with this law is then promoted by forbidding, for example, expression of the view that wearing a helmet isn't worth it, or is only for sissies.

It is important to see that the argument for the Millian Principle rests on a limitation of the authority of states to command their subjects rather than on a right of individuals. For one thing, this explains why this particular principle of freedom of expression applies to governments rather than to individuals, who do not have such authority to begin with. There are surely cases in which individuals have the right not to have their acts of expression interfered with by other individuals, but these rights presumably flow from a general right to be free from arbitrary interference, together with considerations which make certain kinds of expression particularly important forms of activity.

If the argument for the Millian Principle were thought to rest on a right, 'the right of citizens to make up their own minds', then that argument might be thought to proceed as follows. Persons who see themselves as autonomous see themselves as having a right to make up their own minds, hence also a right to whatever is necessary for them to do this; what is wrong with violations of the Millian Principle is that they infringe this right.

A right of this kind would certainly support a healthy doctrine of freedom of expression, but it is not required for one. The argument given above was much more limited. Its aim was to establish that the authority of governments to restrict the liberty of citizens in order to prevent certain harms does not include authority to prevent these harms by controlling people's sources of information to ensure that they will maintain certain beliefs. It is a long step from this conclusion to a right which is violated whenever someone is deprived of information necessary for him to make an informed decision on some matter that concerns him.

There are clearly cases in which individuals have a right to the information necessary to make informed choices and can claim this right against the government. This is true in the case of political decisions, for example, when the right flows from a certain conception of the relation between a democratic government and its citizens. Even where there is no such right, the provision of information and other conditions for the exercise of autonomy is an important task for states to pursue. But these matters take us beyond the Millian Principle.

IV

The Millian Principle is obviously incapable of accounting for all of the cases that strike us as infringements of freedom of expression. On the basis of this principle alone we could raise no objection against a government that banned all parades or demonstrations (they interfere with traffic), outlawed posters and handbills (too messy), banned public meetings of more than ten people (likely to be unruly), and restricted newspaper publication to one page per week (to save trees). Yet such policies surely strike us as intolerable. That they so strike us is a reflection of our belief that free expression is a good which ranks above the maintenance of absolute peace and quiet, clean streets, smoothly flowing traffic, and rock-bottom taxes.

Thus there is a part of our intuitive view of freedom of expression which rests upon a balancing of competing goods. By contrast with the Millian Principle, which provides a single defence for all kinds of expression, here it does not seem to be a matter of the value to be placed on expression (in general) as opposed to other goods. The case seems to be different for, say, artistic expression than for the discussion of scientific matters, and different still for expression of political views.

Within certain limits, it seems clear that the value to be placed on having various kinds of expression flourish is something which should be subject to popular will in the society in question. The limits I have in mind here are, first, those imposed by considerations of distributive justice. Access to means of expression for whatever purposes one may have in mind is a good which can be fairly or unfairly distributed among the members of a society, and many cases which strike us as violations of freedom of expression are in fact instances of distributive injustice. This would be true of a case where, in an economically inegalitarian society, access to the principal means of expression was controlled by the government and auctioned off by it to the highest bidders, as is essentially the case with broadcasting licences in the

United States today. The same might be said of a parade ordinance which allowed the town council to forbid parades by unpopular groups because they were too expensive to police.

But to call either of these cases instances of unjust distribution tells only part of the story. Access to means of expression is in many cases a necessary condition for participation in the political process of the country, and therefore something to which citizens have an independent right. At the very least the recognition of such rights will require governments to ensure that means of expression are readily available through which individuals and small groups can make their views on political issues known, and to ensure that the principal means of expression in the society do not fall under the control of any particular segment of the community. But exactly what rights of access to means of expression follow in this way from political rights will depend to some extent on the political institutions in question. Political participation may take different forms under different institutions, even under equally just institutions.

The theory of freedom of expression which I am offering, then, consists of at least four distinguishable elements. It is based upon the Millian Principle, which is absolute but serves only to rule out certain justifications for legal restrictions on acts of expression. Within the limits set by this principle the whole range of governmental policies affecting opportunities for expression, whether by restriction, positive intervention, or failure to intervene, are subject to justification and criticism on a number of diverse grounds. First, on grounds of whether they reflect an appropriate balancing of the value of certain kinds of expression relative to other social goods; second, whether they ensure equitable distribution of access to means of expression throughout the society; and third, whether they are compatible with the recognition of certain special rights, particularly political rights.

This mixed theory is somewhat cumbersome, but the various parts seem to me both mutually irreducible and essential if we are to account for the full range of cases which seem intuitively to constitute violations of 'free speech'.

V

The failure of the Millian Principle to allow certain kinds of exceptions may seem to many the most implausible feature of the theory I have offered. In addition to the possibility mentioned earlier, that exceptions should be allowed in cases of diminished rationality, there may seem to be an obvious case for allowing deviations from the principle in time of war or other grave emergency.

It should be noticed that because the Millian Principle is much narrower than, say, a blanket protection of 'speech', the theory I have offered can already accommodate some of the restrictions on expression which wartime conditions may be thought to justify. The Millian Principle allows one, even in normal times, to consider whether the publication of certain information might present serious hazards to public safety by giving people the capacity to inflict certain harms. It seems likely that risks of this kind which are worth taking in time of peace in order to allow full discussion of, say, certain scientific questions, might be intolerable in wartime.

But the kind of emergency powers that governments feel entitled to invoke often go beyond this and include, for example, the power to cut off political debate when such debate threatens to divide the country or otherwise to undermine its capacity to meet a present threat. The obvious justification for such powers is clearly disallowed by the Millian Principle, and the theory I have offered provides for no exceptions of this kind.

It is hard for me at the present moment to conceive of a case in which I would think the invocation of such powers by a government right. I am willing to admit that there might be such cases, but even if there are I do not think that they should be seen as 'exceptions' to be incorporated within the Millian Principle.

That principle, it will be recalled, does not rest on a right of citizens but rather expresses a limitation on the authority governments can be supposed to have. The authority in question here is that provided by a particular kind of political theory, one which has its starting point in the question: How could citizens recognize a right of governments to command them while still regarding themselves as equal, autonomous, rational agents? The theory is normally thought to yield the answer that this is possible if, but only if, that right is limited in certain ways, and if certain other conditions, supposed to ensure citizen control over government, are fulfilled. I have argued that one of the necessary limitations is expressed by the Millian Principle. If I am right, then the claim of a government to rule by virtue of this particular kind of authority is undermined, I think completely, if it undertakes to control its citizens in the ways that the Millian Principle is intended to exclude.

This does not mean, however, that it could not in an extreme case be right for certain people, who normally exercised the kind of authority held to be legitimate by democratic political theory, to take measures which this authority does not justify. These actions would have to be justified on some other ground (e.g. utilitarian), and the claim of their agents to be obeyed would not be that of a legitimate government in the usual (democratic) sense. None the less most citizens might, under the circumstances, have good reason to obey.

There are a number of different justifications for the exercise of coercive authority. In a situation of extreme peril to a group, those in the group who are in a position to avert disaster by exercising a certain kind of control over the others may be justified in using force to do so, and there may be good reason for their commands to be obeyed. But this kind of authority differs both in justification and extent from that which, if democratic political theory is correct, a legitimate democratic government enjoys. What I am suggesting is that if there are situations in which a general suspension of civil liberties is justified—and, I repeat, it is not clear to me that there are such—these situations constitute a shift from one kind of authority to another. The people involved will probably continue to wear the same hats, but this does not mean that they still rule with the same title.

It should not be thought that I am here giving governments licence to kick over the traces of constitutional rule whenever this is required by the 'national interest'. It would take a situation of near catastrophe to justify a move of the kind I have described, and if governments know what they are doing it would take such a situation to make a move of this sort inviting. For a great deal is given up in such a move, including any notion that the commands of government have a claim to be obeyed which goes beyond the relative advantages of obedience and disobedience.

When the situation is grave and the price of disorder enormous, such utili-tarian considerations may give the government's commands very real bind-ing force. But continuing rule on this basis would be acceptable only for a society in permanent crisis or for a group of people who, because they could see each other only as obedient servants or as threatening foes, could not be ruled on any other.

NOTES ON THE CONTRIBUTORS

H. L. A. HART is Principal of Brasenose College, Oxford and until 1968 was Professor of Jurisprudence at Oxford. Among his publications are *Causation in the Law* (with A. M. Honore, 1959), *The Concept of Law* (1961), and *The Morality of the Criminal Law* (1965).

RONALD DWORKIN, editor of this volume, is Professor of Jurisprudence at Oxford, and was formerly Professor of Law at Yale Law School. He has published many articles in legal and philosophical periodicals, and is author of *Taking Rights Seriously* (1976).

LORD DEVLIN was a Lord Justice of Appeal from 1960, a Lord of Appeal in Ordinary until 1964, and has held with distinction many public appointments. Among his writings are *Trial by Jury* (1956) and *The Enforcement of Morals* (1965).

JOHN RAWLS is Professor of Philosophy at Harvard. His widely discussed work *A Theory of Justice* was published in 1972.

JUDITH JARVIS THOMSON is Professor of Philosophy at Massachusetts Institute of Technology. She is the editor, with G. Dworkin, of *Ethics* (1969).

JOHN FINNIS is a Fellow of University College, Oxford, and Reader in Commonwealth and American Law. He has published a number of articles on moral and legal philosophy.

THOMAS SCANLON is a Professor of Philosophy at Princeton.

BIBLIOGRAPHY

ESSAY I. POSITIVISM AND THE MORALITY OF LAW

FULLER, L. L., 'Positivism and Fidelity to Law—A Reply to Professor Hart', *Harvard Law Review* 71 (1958), 630–72.

HART, H. L. A., *The Concept of Law*, Oxford, Clarendon Press, 1961, Chs. VIII and IX.

ROSS, A., 'Validity and the Conflict Between Legal Positivism and Natural Law', *Revista Juridica de Buenos Aires* 4 (1961), 46–92.

FULLER, L. L., *The Morality of Law*, New Haven and London, Yale University Press, 1964; revised edn., 1969.

HART, H. L. A., Review of Fuller's *The Morality of Law*, *Harvard Law Review* 78 (1965), 1281–96.

DWORKIN, R., 'Philosophy, Morality and Law—Observations Prompted by Professor Fuller's Novel Claim', *University of Pennsylvania Law Review* 113 (1965), 668–90.

DWORKIN, R., 'The Elusive Morality of Law'; COHEN, M., 'Law, Morality and Purpose'; FULLER, L. L., 'A Reply to Professors Cohen and Dworkin', *Villanova Law Review* 10 (1965), 631–9; 640–54; 655–66.

SUMMERS, R. S., 'Professor Fuller on Morality and Law', *The Journal of Legal Education* 18 (1966), 1–27; rpr. in Summers, R. S., ed., *More Essays in Legal Philosophy*, Oxford, Basil Blackwell, 1971, 101–30.

D'ENTREVES. A. P., *Natural Law*, 2nd edn., London, Hutchinson, 1970.

LYONS, D., 'The Internal Morality of Law', *Proceedings of the Aristotelian Society* 71 (1970–1), 105–19.

NICHOLSON, P. P., 'The Internal Morality of Law: Fuller and his Critics', *Ethics* 84 (1974), 307–26.

MULLOCK, P., 'The Inner Morality of Law', *Ethics* 84 (1974), 327–31.

RAZ, J., *Practical Reason and Norms*, London, Hutchinson, 1975, 162–70.

ESSAY II. LEGAL RULES AND THE UNITY OF LEGAL SYSTEMS

DWORKIN, R., 'Judicial Discretion', *The Journal of Philosophy* 60 (1963), 624–38.

MACCALLUM, G. C., 'Dworkin on Judicial Discretion', *The Journal of Philosophy* 60 (1963), 638–41.

CHRISTIE, G. C., 'The Model of Principles', *Duke Law Journal* [1968], 649–69.

HUGHES, G. H., 'Rules, Policy and Decision Making', *Yale Law Journal* 77 (1968), 411–39.

RAZ, J., *The Concept of a Legal System*, Oxford, Clarendon Press, 1970, Ch. 8.

TAPPER, C., 'A Note on Principles', *The Modern Law Review* 34 (1971), 628–34.

174

SARTORIUS, R., 'Social Policy and Judicial Legislation', *American Philosophical Quarterly* 8 (1971), 151–60.

RAZ, J., 'The Identity of Legal Systems', *California Law Review* 59 (1971), 795–815.

CARRIO, G. E., trans., O'Connell, M. I., *Legal Principles and Legal Positivism*, Buenos Aires, 1971.

RAZ, J., 'Legal Principles and the Limits of Law', *Yale Law Journal* 81 (1972), 795–815.

DWORKIN, R., 'Social Rules and Legal Theory', *Yale Law Journal* 81 (1972), 855–890.

BELL, R. S., 'Understanding the Model of Rules: Towards a Reconciliation of Dworkin and Positivism', *Yale Law Journal* 81 (1972), 912–48.

KEARNS, T. R., 'Rules, Principles and the Law', *American Journal of Jurisprudence* 18 (1973), 114–35.

RAZ, J., *Practical Reason and Norms*, London, Hutchinson, 1975, Ch. 4.

DWORKIN, R., 'Hard Cases', *Harvard Law Review* 88 (1975), 1057–1109.

ESSAYS III AND IV. THE LEGAL ENFORCEMENT OF MORALITY

MILL, J. S., *On Liberty*, London, 1859; republished in Mill ed. Warnock, M., *Utilitarianism*, London; Collins, 1962, 126–250.

STEPHEN, J. F., *Liberty, Equality, Fraternity*, 2nd edn., London, 1874; republished, ed. White, R. J., Cambridge, Cambridge University Press, 1967.

WOLLHEIM, R., 'Crime, Sin and Mr. Justice Devlin', *Encounter* 13 (1959) 34–40; repr. in Hanson, D. W., and Fowler, R. B., eds., *Obligation and Dissent: An Introduction to Politics*, Boston, Little, Brown, 1971, 102–10.

ROSTOW, E., 'The Enforcement of Morals', *Cambridge Law Journal* [1960], 174–198.

HART, H. L. A., 'The Use and Abuse of the Criminal Law', *The Oxford Lawyer* 4 (1961), 7–12; repr. in *The Lawyer* 8 (1965), 47–51.

HUGHES, G., 'Morals and the Criminal Law', *Yale Law Journal* 71 (1962), 662–683; repr. with revisions in Summers, R., ed., *Essays in Legal Philosophy*, Oxford, Basil Blackwell, 1968, 183–207.

HART, H. L. A., *Law, Liberty and Morality*, London, Oxford University Press, 1963.

DEVLIN, P., *The Enforcement of Morals*, London, Oxford University Press, 1965.

HART, H. L. A., *The Morality of the Criminal Law*, London, Oxford University Press, 1965, Lecture II.

DWORKIN, R., 'Lord Devlin and the Enforcement of Morality', *Yale Law Journal* 75 (1966), 986–1005; repr. in Wasserstrom, R., ed., *Morality and the Law*, Belmont, Calif., Wadsworth, 1971, 55–72.

HART, H. L. A., 'Social Solidarity and the Enforcement of Morality', *University of Chicago Law Review* 35 (1967), 1–13.

MITCHELL, B., *Law, Morality and Religion in a Secular Society*, London, Oxford University Press, 1967.

BROWN, D. G., 'Mill on Liberty and Morality', *The Philosophical Review* 81 (1972), 133–58.

SARTORIUS, R., 'The Enforcement of Morality', *Yale Law Journal* 81 (1972), 891–910.

CONWAY, D. A., 'Law, Liberty and Indecency', *Philosophy* 49 (1974), 135–47.

ESSAY V. CIVIL DISOBEDIENCE

BEDAU, H. A., 'On Civil Disobedience', *The Journal of Philosophy* 58 (1961), 653–665.

BROWN, S. M., 'Civil Disobedience', *The Journal of Philosophy* 58 (1961), 670–81.

WASSERSTROM, R. A., 'The Obligation to Obey the Law', *University of California at Los Angeles Law Review* 10 (1963), 780–807; repr. in Summers, R. S., ed., *Essays in Legal Philosophy*, Oxford, Basil Blackwell, 1970, 274–304.

HOOK, S., ed., *Law and Philosophy*, New York, New York University Press, 1964, Part I.

PITKIN, H., 'Obligation and Consent', *American Political Science Review* 59 (1965), 990–9, and 60 (1966), 39–52; repr. in Laslett, P., Runciman, W. B., and Skinner, Q., eds., *Philosophy, Politics and Society*, Fourth Series, Oxford, Basil Blackwell, 1972, 45–85.

MACFARLANE, L. J., 'Justifying Political Disobedience', *Ethics* 79 (1968), 24–55.

DWORKIN, R., 'Taking Rights Seriously', *The New York Review of Books*, 18 Dec. 1970; repr. in Simpson, A. W. B., ed., *Oxford Essays in Jurisprudence*, Second Series, Oxford, Clarendon Press, 1973, 202–27.

BEDAU, H. A., ed., *Civil Disobedience: Theory and Practice*, Indianapolis and New York, Pegasus, 1969.

HUGHES, G. C., 'Civil Disobedience and the Political Question Doctrine'; DWORKIN, R., 'A Theory of Civil Disobedience'; CLARK, T. C., 'Philosophy, Law and Civil Disobedience' in Kiefer, H. E., and Munitz, M. K., eds., *Ethics and Social Justice*, Albany, State University of New York Press, 1970, 207–224; 225–39; 240–51.

PENNOCK, J. R., and CHAPMAN, J. W., eds., *Nomos XII: Political and Legal Obligation*, New York, Atherton Press, 1970.

The Monist 54, no. 4 (1970): *Legal Obligation and Civil Disobedience*.

MACFARLANE, L. J., *Political Disobedience*, London, Macmillan, 1971.

COHEN, C., *Civil Disobedience: Conscience, Tactics and the Law*, New York and London, Columbia University Press, 1971.

COHEN, M., 'Liberalism and Disobedience', *Philosophy and Public Affairs* 1 (1971–1972), 283–314.

FRAZIER, C., 'Between Obedience and Revolution', *Philosophy and Public Affairs* 1 (1971–2), 315–34

SMITH, M. B. E., 'Is There a *Prima Facie* Obligation to Obey the Law?', *Yale Law Journal* 82 (1973), 950–76.

FLATHMAN, R. E., *Political Obligation*, London, Croom Held, 1973.

SINGER, P., *Democracy and Disobedience*, Oxford, Clarendon Press, 1973.

FEINBERG, J., 'Duty and Obligation in the Non-Ideal World', *The Journal of Philosophy* 70 (1973), 263–75.

ESSAYS VI AND VII. ABORTION

WILLIAMS, G., *The Sanctity of Life and the Criminal Law*, London, Faber & Faber, 1958, Ch. 6.

FOOT, P., 'The Problem of Abortion and the Doctrine of Double Effect', *The Oxford Review* 5 (1967), 5–15.

NOONAN, J. T., 'Abortion and the Catholic Church: A Summary History', *Natural Law Forum* 12 (1967), 85–131.

NOONAN, J. T., *The Morality of Abortion*, Cambridge, Mass., Harvard University Press, 1970.

CALLAHAN, D., *Abortion: Law, Choice and Morality*, New York, Collier-Macmillan, 1970.

BRODY, B. A., 'Abortion and the Law', *The Journal of Philosophy* 68 (1971), 357–369.

HART, H. L. A., 'Abortion Law Reform: The English Experience', *Melbourne University Law Review* 8 (1971–2), 388–411.

WERTHEIMER, R., 'Understanding the Abortion Argument', *Philosophy and Public Affairs* 1 (1971–2), 67–95.

BRODY, B., 'Thomson on Abortion', *Philosophy and Public Affairs* 1 (1971–2), 335–340.

BRANDT, R. B., 'The Morality of Abortion', *The Monist* 56 (1972), 503–26.

TOOLEY, M., 'Abortion and Infanticide', *Philosophy and Public Affairs* 2 (1972–1973), 37–65.

THOMSON, J. J., 'Rights and Deaths', *Philosophy and Public Affairs* 2 (1972–3), 146–59.

WARREN, M. A., 'On the Moral and Legal Status of Abortion', *The Monist* 57 (1973), 43–61.

DEVINE, P. E., 'The Doctrine of Double Effect', *The American Journal of Jurisprudence* 19 (1974), 44–60.

HUGHES, G. C., 'Who is a Victim?' *Dalhousie Law Journal* 1 (1974), 425–40.

HARE, R. M., 'Abortion and the Golden Rule', *Philosophy and Public Affairs* 4 (1974–1975), 201–22.

ESSAY VIII. FREEDOM OF EXPRESSION

MILL, J. S., *On Liberty*, cited in section on Essays III and IV above, Ch. 2.

STEPHEN, J. F., *Liberty, Equality, Fraternity*, cited in section on Essays III and IV above. Ch. 2.

CHAFEE, Z., *Free Speech in the United States*, Cambridge, Mass., Harvard University Press, 1942.

MCCLOSKEY, H. J., 'Liberty of Expression: its Grounds and Limits (I)', *Inquiry* 13 (1970), 219–37.

MONRO, D. H., 'Liberty of Expression: its Grounds and Limits (II)', *Inquiry* 13 (1970), 238–53.

MARSHALL, G., *Constitutional Theory*, Oxford, Clarendon Press, 1971, Ch. VIII.

RICHARDS, D. A. J., 'Free Speech and Obscenity Law: Towards a Moral Theory of the First Amendment', *University of Pennsylvania Law Review* 123 (1974), 45–91.

FEINBERG, J., 'Limits to the Free Expression of Opinion', in Feinberg, J., and Gross, H., eds., *Philosophy of Law*, Encino and Belmont, Calif., Dickenson, 1975, 135–51.

INDEX OF NAMES

(not including authors mentioned only in the Bibliography)